STUDIES IN FRENCH LANGUAGE
LITERATURE AND HISTORY

GENERAL EDITORS
on behalf of the Faculty of Arts of
the University of Birmingham
FRASER MACKENZIE
R. C. KNIGHT
J. M. MILNER

STUDIES
IN FRENCH LANGUAGE
LITERATURE AND HISTORY

PRESENTED TO

R. L. GRÆME RITCHIE

CAMBRIDGE
AT THE UNIVERSITY PRESS
1949

CAMBRIDGE
UNIVERSITY PRESS

University Printing House, Cambridge CB2 8BS, United Kingdom

Cambridge University Press is part of the University of Cambridge.

It furthers the University's mission by disseminating knowledge in the pursuit of
education, learning and research at the highest international levels of excellence.

www.cambridge.org
Information on this title: www.cambridge.org/9781107544765

© Cambridge University Press 1949

This publication is in copyright. Subject to statutory exception
and to the provisions of relevant collective licensing agreements,
no reproduction of any part may take place without the written
permission of Cambridge University Press.

First published 1949
First paperback edition 2015

A catalogue record for this publication is available from the British Library

ISBN 978-1-107-54476-5 Paperback

Cambridge University Press has no responsibility for the persistence or accuracy of
URLs for external or third-party internet websites referred to in this publication,
and does not guarantee that any content on such websites is, or will remain, accurate
or appropriate.

TO

R. L. GRÆME RITCHIE

WHO HAS CONTRIBUTED SO MUCH
TO THE ADVANCEMENT OF FRENCH STUDIES AND
THE ESTABLISHMENT OF MODERN LANGUAGE TEACHING
IN BRITISH UNIVERSITIES

CONTENTS

CONTENTS

CONTENTS

FOREWORD

BY

JANE JOHNSTON MILNE

Formerly Senior Lecturer in French in the
University of Birmingham

IN the summer of 1946 Robert L. Græme Ritchie reached the limit of his tenure of the Chair of French Language and Literature in the University of Birmingham, which he had held with distinction for twenty-six years. His many friends among scholars of this and other Universities have chosen to bid him farewell by the publication of a volume of studies in his honour, thus to show their admiration for the scholarship of the Master, and their gratitude for the outstanding service he has given to the cause of French, and of France.

From the country rectory of his boyhood on Donside he passed through the Grammar School, and the University, of Aberdeen. Both have a high tradition of teaching, where Latin and Greek have pride of place, and the foundations of nice scholarship are well and truly laid. There he learned that the benefit of a classical education lies in the superiority of the spirit in which ancient authors are taught, rather than in any superiority in the ancient texts themselves. A classical scholar he first became, and the study of French Language and Literature, which he has made his life-work, is based on the solid rock of a severe discipline in language, aimed always at the choice of the exact word. *Esprit de justesse*, Pascal named it. As a Carnegie Research Scholar, and afterwards Fellow, he went to France and to Paris, and five years lived there endowed him with that other gift to *les âmes bien nées*—that *esprit de finesse* which has graced all that he has printed and all that he has said. His advent in 1910 as Lecturer in the Department of French in the University of Edinburgh, fortified with a Paris Doctorate and a published thesis solving many a *joli problème* in the syntax of the conjunction 'Que', amazed Scottish students not yet acquainted with a sound method or a competent University teacher, and they took him to their hearts. The 'little doctor', or the 'wee mester', brought a new song. During the ten years of his work in Edinburgh, and in Glasgow, where he also kept the University French Department going through the difficulties of the 1914–18 war, his renown went forth, and the good cause was furthered far and wide in the land by those who had been his students. In 1919 he was appointed to the Chair of French in the University of Birmingham.

But a Chair in a vigorous civic University promises the scholar no academic seclusion. Instead, it seems to require of him sacrifices he would fain avoid—of time and thought to be given to the affairs of the University state, to educational occasions, to endless deliberations in committee. So it happened to Professor Ritchie. He was soon caught in the toils. His opinion and experience became of value beyond the limits of Birmingham, and presently he seemed to serve the country as a general consultant in matters French. Yet he had always time to be approachable and encouraging to his own students. He served a term also, albeit unwilling, as Dean of his Faculty. Honours came to him from other Universities and particularly from France. He was 'dix fois docteur'.

But with Professor Ritchie first things come first, and the first for him is scholarship. His accumulated learning came to fruition in the publication of Barbour's *Buik of Alexander*, edited with the French originals, *Li Fuerres de Gadres* and *Les Vœux du Paon*, in four volumes, 1921–9. This majestic piece of research belongs to a field of study which he has long cherished for further exploration—the French element in Middle Scots, and, more generally, the study of French influences at work in mediæval Scotland. On this theme may we hope to be given one day yet more. Literary theories and judgments, however, must repose upon true understanding of the written word, and Professor Ritchie assigned himself the task of providing Manuals of French Composition and Translation for the serious student of French, as well as the edition of a series of selections from French authors for the ordinary reader. Let no one think that these were done without trouble. Whilst literary researches win easy praise in academic circles, the production of these humble, yet necessary, 'tools' demands a serious effort, and Professor Ritchie admits that they 'took considerable doing'. But the Manuals have proved their worth long since.

The scholar is not always so fortunate as to possess, with a taste for serious learning, a light-hearted spirit with which to adorn it.

Professor Ritchie is happy in that wit and humour, irony and a never-failing sense of the ludicrous, are his in abundance. These temper the severest of his utterances and judgments, and enliven the monotony of academic routine, while they delight his colleagues. And indeed that *esprit français* which has graced his native *perfervidum Scotorum ingenium*, and has perfected his scholarship, has also endeared him to the whole University. In him she found her first Public Orator, and once a year at Degree Congregations his diverting assessments of the merits of famous men seated before him awaiting an Honorary Degree delighted those who heard him.

From University College, Exeter, which has now claimed him, Professor Ritchie will, we hope, continue to give forth the fruits of his learning in his own inimitable style. This testimony of admiration and friendship is presented in affectionate remembrance of his days in Birmingham.

SELECTED PUBLICATIONS

OF

R. L. G. RITCHIE

Recherches sur la syntaxe de la conjonction 'Que' dans l'ancien français, depuis les origines de la langue jusqu'au commencement du XIIIe siècle, etc. Pp. xxviii + 197, Paris, 1907. 8°.

The Buik of Alexander or the Buik of the most notable and valiant conquerour Alexander the Grit by John Barbour Archdeacon of Aberdeen, edited . . . together with the French originals (*Li Fuerres de Gadres* and *Les Vœux du Paon*) in 4 volumes. Printed for the Scottish Text Society, Edinburgh and London, by W. Blackwood and Sons, 1921–9. 8°. (Scottish Text Society publications, N.S., nos. 12, 17, 21, 25.)

[Editor of] *France: A companion to French studies.* (Methuen's companions to modern studies.) Pp. x + 514. London, 1937. 8°.

Honoris Causa: being speeches made in the University of Birmingham, 1934–45. Birmingham, the University, 1946.

IN PERIODICALS AND OTHER PUBLICATIONS

(With C. R. Borland.) 'Fragments d'une traduction française en vers de la *Chronique en prose* de Guillaume le Breton.' *Romania,* XLII (1913), 1–22.

'Early instances of words for the *N.E.D.*' *Notes and Queries,* 11th ser., IX, 387; X, 127–8 (1914).

'The teaching of modern languages.' In A. W. Bain, *The Modern Teacher,* London, 1921.

'On translating from French.' *The French Quarterly,* IV (1922), 37–48.

'Some recent French translations.' *The French Quarterly,* VIII (1926), 103–16.

'Le "Père Hoop" de Diderot.' In *A Miscellany of Studies in Romance Languages and Literatures, presented to Leon E. Kastner,* Cambridge, 1932.

'Early instances of French loan-words in Scots and English.' *Englische Studien,* Leipzig, LXII (1928–9), 41–58.

'Early instances of French loan-words in Scots and English' [second series]. In *Studies in French language and mediaeval literature presented to Professor Mildred K. Pope,* Manchester, 1939.

SELECTED PUBLICATIONS

REVIEWS

Le origini di 'Salammbô', by L. F. Benedetto. Flaubert and Maupassant: a literary relationship, by A. R. Riddell. *M.L.R.*, XVI (1921), 94–5.

Sainte-Beuve's critical theory and practice, by L. Macclintock. *M.L.R.*, XVI (1921), 199.

French terminologies in the making, by H. J. Swann. *M.L.R.*, XVI (1921), 182–3.

Le dernier séjour de J.-J. Rousseau à Paris, by E. A. Foster. *M.L.R.*, XVII (1922), 439.

Le langage parisien au XIXe siècle, by L. Sainéan. *M.L.R.*, XVII (1922), 328.

France and England: their relations in the Middle Ages and now, by T. F. Tout. *M.L.R.*, XVII (1922), 314–15.

Harrap's Standard French and English Dictionary, edited by J. E. Mansion. Part I: French–English. *M.L.R.*, XXIX (1934), 355–7.

Études sur les mots français d'origine néerlandaise, by M. Valkhoff. *M.L.R.*, XXXV (1935), 390–2.

French the Third Classic: an Inaugural Lecture given at the University of Edinburgh on 10 October 1933, by John Orr. *M.L.R.*, XXX (1935), 102–4.

The Language of the Eighth Century Texts in Northern France, by M. A. Pei. *M.L.R.*, XXX (1935), 242–5.

The French Background of Middle Scots Literature, by Janet M. Smith. *Medium Ævum*, IV (1935), 44–7.

Einleitung in die Encyclopädie der französischen Aufklärung, by F. Schalk. *M.L.R.*, XXXII (1937), 631–3.

Harrap's Standard French and English Dictionary, edited by J. E. Mansion. Part II: English–French. *M.L.R.*, XXXV (1940), 550.

Les Adverbes en -*ment* compléments d'un verbe en français moderne: étude de classement, by H. Nillson-Ehle. *M.L.R.*, XXXVII (1942), 221–3.

Studies by members of the French Department of Yale University, edited by A. Feuillerat. *M.L.R.*, XXXVII (1942), 506–7.

The mediaeval French *Roman d'Alexandre*, vol. IV. *M.L.R.*, XLI (1945), 56–7.

SAINTE-BEUVE'S *TABLEAU DE LA POÉSIE FRANÇAISE AU XVIe SIÈCLE* AND CARY'S *EARLY FRENCH POETS*

IVOR D. O. ARNOLD

*Professor of French Language and Literature
in the University of Leeds*

IN 1827 Philarète Chasles, the future professor in the Collège de France, wrote of the courage needed to read the works of Ronsard, 'œuvres où le ridicule et la bizarrerie dominent', and although his rival for the Academy Prize of 1828, Saint-Marc Girardin, was inclined to a more lenient view, it is probable that Chasles represented the generality of informed opinion in France at the time. In July 1828 Sainte-Beuve, who had, during the previous year, published a series of articles on the sixteenth-century poets, ended the Introduction to his *Œuvres choisies de Ronsard* by inscribing his own name 'after those of Mesdemoiselles de Gournay and Scudéry, after Chapelain and Colletet', on the roll of the defenders of the unappreciated leader of the Pléiade; and he concluded with the fine sonnet which appeared later in the same year among the works of the regretted Joseph Delorme, and which runs:

> A toi, Ronsard, à toi, qu'un sort injurieux
> Depuis deux siècles livre aux mépris de l'histoire,
> J'élève de mes mains l'autel expiatoire
> Qui te purifiera d'un arrêt odieux.
>
> Non que j'espère encore au trône radieux
> D'où jadis tu régnais replacer ta mémoire.
> Tu ne peux de si bas remonter à la gloire;
> Vulcain impunément ne tomba point des dieux.
>
> Mais qu'un peu de pitié console enfin tes mânes;
> Que, déchiré longtemps par des rires profanes,
> Ton nom, d'abord fameux, recouvre un peu d'honneur;

K   I   I

Qu'on dise: Il osa trop, mais l'audace était belle;
Il lassa sans la vaincre une langue rebelle,
Et de moins grands depuis eurent plus de bonheur.

In the third, revised, edition of the *Tableau de la Poésie française au XVIe siècle* (1843), of which the study on Ronsard forms part, Sainte-Beuve felt able to say that Ronsard's reputation among the general public had reached the height which he had assigned to it, a height, as may be judged from the sonnet, not particularly vertiginous; and he added modestly that his study was a small thing, 'malgré la réputation outrée que quelques-uns ont daigné faire à ma tentative'. In the edition of Brunet's *Manuel*, however, which appeared from 1863 (s.v. *Ronsard* in the Supplement), the author speaks of Blanchemain's edition, which had just been published, as 'breaking the silence which had reigned since 1630 over the Prince of Poets', and adds insult to injury by remarking 'il fallait un poète . . . pour chercher à faire revivre cet illustre mort'; in 1851 the essays of Saint-Marc Girardin and Philarète Chasles also reached their second edition. However, it is not my intention to discuss here the delicate problems concerned with the resuscitation of Ronsard's reputation in France; I am content to accept the view of M. Henri Chamard, in his *Histoire de la Pléiade*, that the *Tableau de la Poésie française au XVIe siècle*, if it had no immediate effect, at all events prepared the future (vol. I, p. 40); to this cautious estimate one can scarcely take exception. But when M. Chamard expands Sainte-Beuve's rôle by implication to the European field, when his bibliographical study names Walter Pater as the first Englishman of note to interest himself in the poetry of the Renaissance in France, when he argues that Sainte-Beuve was the first in Europe to appreciate a forgotten school of poets, and in consequence that 'il est clair que ce sont les savants de la France qui ont mis en valeur les poètes de la France', it would not seem improper that attention should be called to precursors of the French critic in the European field. There is, for instance, Scipione Maffeï, who, nearly a century earlier, was earning the reproaches of l'Abbé Goujet by the 'louanges excessives qu'il a données à Ronsard . . . en plusieurs occasions'. But I wish to raise a small voice from this side of the Channel on behalf of Henry Francis Cary, whose studies on the

2

poets of the Pléïade were published before Sainte-Beuve had made his break with medicine, and begun his literary career.

Henry Francis Cary (1772–1844) is best known in England as the translator of Dante; it was under that title that Dr R. W. King wrote his biography in 1925 (*The translator of Dante: the life, works and friendships of Henry Francis Cary*). In 1820 the short-lived *London Magazine* published its first number, and Cary, who had at first been thought of as its editor, became a frequent contributor to its pages. In the summer of 1821, six years before Sainte-Beuve began the series of articles in the *Globe* which form the *Tableau de la Poésie française au XVIe siècle*, Cary spent ten weeks in Versailles, and here, in the Royal Library, he devoted himself to reading early editions of pre-Classical French poetry. The results of his study were a series of essays, portraits, rather in the manner which Sainte-Beuve was later to make his own, in which an author's writings, his life and his personality each play a part in the delineation. These essays appeared in the *London Magazine* between 1821 and 1824; they were published in one volume in 1843, and again (in abbreviated form) in 1923 (Campion Reprints).

Sidney Lee calls these studies 'discursive and slender'; they are indeed only brief sketches, together with quotations and translations into English verse; yet, taking them up to-day, after more than a century has passed, they read with a freshness and gaiety which suit well the spirit of the Renaissance, and in particular the youthful innovators of 1550. Nor is this unexpected from a critic of Cary's colossal reading and romantic spirit. As a student, he had taken part in the controversy which raged for months in the *Gentleman's Magazine*, and had expressed his preference for 'the wilderness of Dryden against the regular yet elegant parterres of Pope'. For many years he had fought a lonely battle for Dante in England, and his reading had ranged over a great part of European literature, and had given him an intimate knowledge of the characteristics of Pindar, Petrarch and Anacreon, all of whom he began to study while still a school-boy. He was a clergyman; and will confess to a dislike of Parny; but he will never think of blaming Salel or Ronsard, as l'abbé Goujet does, because their poems 'presque toutes roulent sur l'amour, et sont remplies d'expressions peu chastes et de sentimens trop passionnés' (XII, 5). Goujet is always amusing on

3

this subject, and I cannot resist quoting his final evaluation of Ronsard.

Ronsard [he says] eut encore un autre défaut qui lui fut plus nuisible que la vanité; on voit par beaucoup d'endroits de ses écrits que l'amour et la galanterie l'ont souvent occupé. Ces tendres sentimens, ces galanteries portées à l'excès, ces désespoirs métaphoriques, ces morts idéales, plaisoient beaucoup au siècle de Ronsard, et le poète croyoit, sans doute, que la postérité s'intéresseroit encore à ses *Amours*. Il s'est trompé. Personne ne les lit plus depuis longtems; et, si quelqu'un s'en rappelle encore le souvenir, ce n'est que pour plaindre l'Auteur d'avoir si mal usé de ses talens [xII, 211].

All that we know of Cary makes it certain that he would not be impressed by the assumption of the French, with whatever conviction it was held, and with whatever vigour sustained, that the seventeenth and the eighteenth centuries in France represented what might be called 'an all-time high' in world literature. He was prepared to judge the Pléïade on its merits, and, if necessary, to put the Classics in their place: witness his comment on Jodelle's tragedy of *Didon*: 'the speeches are long, and often tedious, but there is more of what we should call poetry in it than in the tragedies of Corneille and Racine.' Or quoting, from Salel, the line

Marguerite aux yeulx rians et verds

he goes on to say:

The laughing eye would be too bold an expression for a Frenchman now-a-days; and accordingly one of them, who met with it in translating Dante—

Ond'ella pronta e con occhi ridenti,

has translated it:

L'ombre me répondit d'un air satisfait.

Sainte-Beuve, on the other hand, romantic though he thought himself in 1828, is a good Frenchman. He measures his authors by the yard-stick of the *Grand Siècle*. Ronsard has talent but not genius; that term is reserved for the seventeenth and eighteenth centuries, and in France alone. With how many restrictive and apologetic phrases does Sainte-Beuve hedge about his 'rehabilitation' of the Pléïade! Cary will have none of this pandering to refined taste. He says of the French:

4

I do not know of any other people who have set up an exclusive standard of this sort. What would the Greeks of the age of Pericles have said to a literary censor that should have endeavoured to persuade them to throw aside the works of Homer and Hesiod because he could have pointed out to them in every page modes of expression that would not have passed muster in a coterie at Aspasia's? What reply should we make to a critic that would fain put us out of conceit with some of the finest things in Spenser and Shakespeare because they were cast in a mould utterly differing from that impressed on the language of our politer circles, though similar enough to the stamp of our country folks' talk? Let anyone take up Voltaire's commentary on the tragedies of Corneille and he will see to what a pitch this fastidiousness has been carried in the instance of a writer comparatively modern. . . . Our ignorance is a happy security from this danger.

This, I confess, seems to me an attitude which gives Cary some advantage, at all events for English readers, in his presentation of the French Renaissance writers. Marot reminds him now of Chaucer, now of Spenser, Salel of Lydgate, Bertaut of Cowley, and these comparisons do not oblige him constantly to depreciate the subjects of his study, as Sainte-Beuve, a classic at heart, and with his eye on the reading public in France, was forced to do.

It may be argued that Sainte-Beuve was doing something more than Cary, namely, re-writing the literary history of a period, and that this obliged him to relate everything to a high point to which literature was progressing with gradual steps. I am not inclined to give Sainte-Beuve the benefit of this argument. It is true that he makes much play with 1549, but whether the segregation of authors into sheep and goats on either side of a date is creditable to a critic, even in his youth, seems to me doubtful. In 1549, 'quelque chose finit et quelque chose commence'; and all poets who wrote before that date are mediaeval, Louise Labé and Maurice Scève, Salel and Héroët. 'Quelque différence qu'il y ait entre la *Parfaite Amye* d'Héroët et l'épigramme contre *magister Lourdis*, on y saisit toujours plus ou moins l'accent de Charles d'Orléans, ou de Villon, de Thibaut de Champagne ou du Roman de la Rose.' For Cary, nothing remarkable occurred in French literature in 1549; the *Deffense et Illustration* is merely 'a judicious and well-written treatise', in which 'the author betrays a want of reverence for his predecessors which has been amply retaliated by posterity of his own age'. To spend any time discussing the importance of this work as the manifesto of a school of poets would have been contrary to Cary's conception of his task, which was to present individuals, to stress differences, not similarities. In any case, if Sainte-Beuve was writing literary history, in what can it be said that he was an innovator? It seems to me almost sufficient to quote Sainte-Beuve's summary of his work, from the preface to the third edition, together with the introductory words of one of the prize-winners of 1828:

Quelque chose finit au XVIe siècle en poésie, et quelque chose commence ou tente de commencer. Je constate ce qui finit; j'épie et dénote avec intérêt et curiosité ce qui commence.

Pour la première fois, un point, ce me semble, a été bien posé et éclairci: le moment et le caractère de la tentative de la Pléïade, c'est à dire de notre première poésie classique avortée.

Elle débute sous et avec Henri II, et non auparavant; elle se prolonge plus qu'on n'avait cru. Des Portes et Bertaut, sous Henri III, s'y rattachent sans rompre. Les troubles de la Ligue préparent l'interruption, Malherbe vient et coupe court, aussi bien à Des Portes qu'à Ronsard. . . . Je n'ai voulu faire dans cet Essai qu'une sorte d'introduction à l'histoire de notre poésie classique proprement dite. . . . (Sainte-Beuve, May 1842.)

Saint-Marc Girardin, in his prize essay, said presumably the sort of thing that people were thinking in 1827, and this is what he wrote:

Il y a dans la poésie française au seizième siècle trois époques distinctes, et chaque époque a son école. Au commencement, l'école de Marot, héritier de Villon et de son genre d'esprit: cette école dure jusqu'au milieu du règne de Henri II. Alors naît une autre école, celle de Dubellay et de Ronsard, qui dure avec Desportes jusque sous Henri IV. Enfin Malherbe vint, qui, empruntant beaucoup à ses devanciers, rend à notre langue son tour et son génie original, c'est-à-dire quelque chose de clair et de précis, en même temps qu'il garde de Ronsard des habitudes de noblesse et de majesté, inconnues à notre langue avant le temps de François Ier.

It may then be that Sainte-Beuve's contribution to the history of French Renaissance literature was not as considerable as is sometimes thought; it may be that the important and permanent contribution he made to our understanding of the period lies in the studies of

individual writers of the time, and in this he was preceded by
Cary. It is not my purpose to do more than suggest this possibility;
it would be an interesting study to consider the reactions of these
representatives of France and England to Renaissance poetry at
length, but I will confine myself here to one striking agreement and
one sharp conflict of opinion.

The agreement relates to Marot's *Temple de Cupido*. Goujet
gives Marot fifty pages of his *Bibliothèque*, about the same alloca-
tion as to Ronsard, and he mentions the *Temple de Cupido* in two
lines (XI, 66). Neither Saint-Marc Girardin nor Philarète Chasles
thought it necessary to mention it at all, but Cary begins his portrait
with a detailed summary of 'this exquisite sketch, worthy of
Chaucer', and Sainte-Beuve was clearly equally attracted by the
poem, for he adopts the same procedure. The divergence is in the
estimate which the two authors make of Robert Garnier. Neither
Girardin nor Chasles mentions Garnier at all, but Cary gives him a
comparatively long chapter of qualified approval, in the course of
which he summarizes the plot of *Porcie* act by act, and one or two
others more briefly. When he reaches *Hippolyte*, the comparison
with Racine's *Phèdre* suggests itself and Cary wanders off on a little
iconoclastic détour, which begins like this:

It must be owned that there is something in all this more to our
English taste; in short, that it has more of character and of picturesque
effect than the opening of Racine's *Phèdre*, in which the tutor of Hippolytus is trying to extort from his pupil a confession of his being enamoured
of Aricia, which a little prudery alone restrains him from avowing.

> Il n'en faut pas douter, vous aimez, vous brûlez,
> Vous périssez d'un mal que vous dissimulez.
> La charmante Aricie a-t-elle su vous plaire?

> HIPPOLYTE
> Théramène, je pars, et vais chercher mon père,

and so on.

Is it possible that these sacrilegious words came to Sainte-
Beuve's ears in some way or another (perhaps through M. Corneille,
with whom Cary stayed at Versailles, or through the 'ingenious
French gentleman' mentioned by Cary as having recited a poem
by Bertaut to him)? One is tempted to believe something of the

sort on considering the roughness of the treatment which Sainte-Beuve accords to Garnier. He gives him two pages, one of which is a summary of *Porcie*, act by act, and in much the same words as Cary's; in the other he says that two things have been said by critics in Garnier's favour; first, that his language is finer than Jodelle's (as in Cary's article). But this, Sainte-Beuve continues, is in no way to the man's credit, for language is always improving by the nature of things and Garnier 'n'a fait que suivre les progrès naturels de la langue et obéir à une sorte de perfectibilité chronologique'. Secondly, Garnier is thought by historians of the French theatre to have made a first step from Jodelle towards the theatre of the seventeenth century. Sainte-Beuve concedes the step, but not its direction. 'L'on aurait pu faire beaucoup de pas semblables sans hâter d'un instant l'apparition du *Cid* ou d'*Andromaque*.'

I do not know whether there is any evidence that Sainte-Beuve was habitually sensitive to criticisms of French classical drama. Were it so, should not the melodrama of the letter of February 1830 be re-written, and also, indeed, the whole story of Sainte-Beuve's secession from the Romantics?

NOTE. I regret I have not been able to consult the article on Cary's *Early French Poets* by Sir Edmund Gosse, in the *Sunday Times* of 24 February 1924, which is mentioned by Mr King as being 'suggestive and stimulating'.

ON THE ORIGIN AND HISTORY OF
THREE FRENCH WORDS

BY

the late PAUL BARBIER

Professor of French Language and Literature in the University of Leeds

French *désobstruer*

A CURIOUS case is presented by the French *désobstruer* and possible relations with the Engl. verb *to disobstruct*, its normal equivalent. To the Engl. verb, the *O.E.D.* has devoted the following short article:

> Disobstruct, *v.* ? obs. [Dis- 6.] *Trans.* To free from obstruction; = Deobstruct.
>
> [1611 Florio: *Disopilare*, to open or unstop, to disobstruct.—1668 Power *Exp. Philos.*, I, 68: 'The optick nerve being... disobstructed and relaxed ...'—1738 A. Stuart, in *Phil. Trans.* XL, 8: 'Applications ... intended to ... discuss stagnating animal fluids, or disobstruct the vessels.']

And nothing more; if the verb is to be considered obsolete, it would seem to have been obsolescent since the middle of the eighteenth century; from it, further, not a single derivative, such as might be *disobstructive* or *disobstruction*, is quoted.

But, in addition to the verb *to disobstruct*, and having exactly the same meaning, English has another verb *to deobstruct*, which is not the normal morphological equivalent of French *désobstruer*, and no form *déobstruer* is known to have occurred in French at any time. The *O.E.D.* has found Engl. *to deobstruct* in 1647, 1653 and 1738; and of the derivatives: *deobstruent* as an adjective in 1718 and 1830, *deobstruent* as a substantive in a. 1691, 1697 and 1844; *deobstructing* as an adjective in one example of 1702; *deobstruction* in one example of 1664; *deobstructive* as an adjective in one example of 1782.

I now give the history of the verb *désobstruer*, in so far as I can put it together. The *D.G.*'s earliest example of this verb is of 1778

from Tissot's *Traité des nerfs*, IV, 360. The three earlier examples
I have found are all from translations of English books:

1734 Dover, *Legs d'un ancien médecin*, 85: 'Non seulement il [*i.e.*
le mercure] désobstruë les vaisseaux, mais encore il brise constamment
les pointes des acides . . .'

1747 *Essais et observations de médecine de la Soc. d'Édimbourg*,
VI, 118: 'Les parties volatiles et actives des mouches cantharides . . .
rétabliront la transpiration . . . en desobstruant les vaisseaux destinés
à cette évacuation . . .'

1760 J. Savary, translating D. Monro, *Essai sur l'hydropisie*, p. 178:
'Désobstruer l'entrée de la trompe dans la matrice par les bains chauds
et par les émétiques. . . .'

Mme d'Épinay jestingly uses *désobstruer* as a reflexive:

1773 Mme d'Épinay, *Lettre à Galiani*, in Galiani, *Correspondance* (ed.
1818), II, 187: 'Je vous annonce que je commence un peu à me désobstruer; mais c'est bien peu de chose encore. Je ne suis désenflée que
d'un oreiller. Il m'en fallait cinq pour dormir; à présent je me contente
de quatre.'

So far *désobstruer* is a medical term. In 1798 the word was inserted
in the *Dictionnaire de l'Académie*, firstly as a medical term, but also
with a new meaning:

Désobstruer, *v.a.* T. de médecine. Détruire une obstruction.
Désobstruer le foie, les entrailles. On dit familièrement et par extension:
'*Désobstruer une rue, un canal, un passage* de ce qui l'embarrasse.'

In 1835 the sixth edition of the *Dictionnaire de l'Académie* repeated
the article of 1798, but inverted the order of the two meanings,
and added, in reference to the medical use: 'Ce sens a vieilli.' The
medical sense 'to remove obstruction from parts of the human or
animal body' did not become obsolescent till the nineteenth century
and the extended meaning 'to remove obstructions from roads,
canals and so forth' is still quite current.

That the French *désobstruer* in its medical sense was common
in the eighteenth century is shown by the derivatives, two of which
were inserted in the *Dictionnaire de l'Académie*, one, *désobstructif*, in
1798, and the other, *désobstruant*, in 1835, both in the medical sense
of *apéritif*.

Of these derivatives I quote examples:

(1) *désobstruant.* adj.

1835 *Dict. de l'Acad.*, I, 530: '*Désobstruant, ante.* adj. T. de médecine. Il est synonyme d'*apéritif.*'

(2) *désobstruant.* sb.m.

1741 F. A. de Garsault, *Nouv. parfait maréchal*, ed. 1755, p. 186: 'Les désobstruans, comme l'acier et le foye d'antimoine ... ôteront cette indisposition.'

1769 Le Bègue de Presle, *Disc. prélim.*, in *Médecine d'armée*, I, ccvi: 'Quelques-uns des astringens et des fondans ou desobstruans les plus doux. ...'

(3) *désobstructeur.* adj.

1790 *Journ. de Paris*, 26 juin, Suppl., p. iv: 'M. Gerlet ... dont le spécifique vulnéraire balsamique désobstructeur, autorisé par la Société royale de médecine. ...'

(4) *désobstructif.* adj.

1695 Le Clerc, *Chirurgie complette*, p. 229: 'Le sublimé ... est bon pour toutes les maladies veneriennes, il est desobstructif et il tue les vers.'

(5) *désobstructif.* sb.m.

1732 Bremond, quoted by the *Dict. de Trévoux*, ed. 1771, III, 272: 'Des émétiques, des stomachiques, des désobstructifs. ...'

1747 *Essais et observations de médecine de la Soc. d'Édimbourg*, VII, 99: 'Il recommande beaucoup le vin émétique en petites doses, comme un désobstructif et un sudorifique. ...'

1798 ACAD.: '*Désobstructif.* s.m. T. de médecine. Remède qui guérit les obstructions.'

(6) *désobstruction.* sb.f.

1832 Raymond, *Dict. général*, I, 432: '†*Désobstruction.* s.f. Action de désobstruer.—†État de ce qui est désobstrué.'

I think that in discussing the question of the origins of French *désobstruer*, we have to take into consideration both the English *to deobstruct* and the less vigorous English *to disobstruct*. It appears certain that *to deobstruct* is the more usual form in the eighteenth century. On the other hand, French has always used *désobstruer*, a normal compound of *dés-* and *obstruer*.

When I found that the three earliest examples of Fr. *désobstruer* occurred in French translations of English books, I began to suspect influence from English, and that some influence has been exercised is possible. I am, however, less sure; the discovery of French *désobstructif* in 1695 in a book on surgery where no English influence is likely has made me suspend judgment. It is quite possible that earlier books on medicine and particularly on surgery will bring more light.

Old French *laman*, *loman* 'pilot, sea-pilot, coastal- or harbour-pilot'

Littré, in the third volume of his *Dictionnaire*, explained both the French forms *laman* and *locman* as derived from a Dutch compound of *lood* 'lead' and *man* 'parce que les lamaneurs se servent de sondes de plomb pour reconnaître la profondeur de la mer'. Since Littré, the full explanation of the French names of the harbour-pilot, *laman*, *lamaneur*, *locman*, has caused trouble to a number of etymologists, the form *locman* being particularly a stumbling-block.

Littré's explanation is accepted in a modified and faulty form by the *D.G.* (Flem. *lotman*). Behrens, in 1902, in the *Z.R.Ph.*, xxvi, 659, proposed to connect the *loc-* of *locman* with Du. and Engl. *log* in the nautical sense of 'apparatus for ascertaining the rate of a ship's motion, consisting of a thin quadrant of wood, loaded so as to float upright in the water, and fastened to a line wound on a reel' (*O.E.D.*), which is attested in English in the form *logge* in 1574; but Engl. *logman* is not found in the required sense. In 1928, *G.E.W.* 567 gives: 'LOCMAN "lotse", ... aus ndl. *lotman*', and considers Behrens's *logman* from Dutch as less likely from the semantic point of view. In 1931 M. Valkhoff, *Étude sur les mots français d'origine néerlandaise*, pp. 177–8, produced the following:

1806 Q. de Flines, *Scheeps- en zeemanswoordenboek in het Nederlandsch en Fransch*: '*Lochman*, pilote côtier, de havre, pilote lamaneur, locman', but this evidence is too isolated and far too late to explain the history of the French *locman*, and leaves one wondering whether De Flines's Dutch *lochman* may not be borrowed from French *locman*. The French *locman* was first inserted in the *Dictionnaire de l'Académie* in 1762. The starting-point for the more general use of the word is to be found in the famous *Ordonnance sur la marine* of August 1681:

1681 *Ord. s. la Marine*, liv. IV, t. iii, art. 1: 'Dans les ports où il sera nécessaire d'établir des pilotes, locmans ou lamaneurs pour conduire les vaisseaux à l'entrée et sortie des ports et rivières navigables....'

Thus in 1678 Guillet, in his nautical dictionary entitled *L'Art de la navigation*, which forms part of *Les Arts de l'homme d'épée*, gives *lamaneur* but not *locman*. On the other hand, in 1694, in his *Dictionnaire des Arts et des Sciences*, I, 597, in the article *lamaneur*, T. Corneille says: 'On les appelle aussi *locmans* ou *lomens*.' *Locman* also appears in Savary's *Dictionnaire du Commerce* and in the Copenhagen edition we find the following statement:

1761 Savary, *Dict. du Commerce*, ed. Copenhagen, III, 504: 'Il y a apparence que le mot de *lamaneur* vient de *locman*; ce dernier est usité en Bretagne; c'est un mot corrompu de *lootsman*, qui est hollandois....' [After explaining the ordinances relating to the *lamaneurs* and *locmans*] 'Toute cette police des lamaneurs et locmans est tirée de l'Ordonnance générale de la marine du mois d'août 1681 et de l'Ordonnance particulière touchant la marine des côtes de la province de Bretagne du 18 janvier 1685.'

We note the following points from this passage: (*a*) Littré's derivation from Dutch *lootsman* was already in vogue in the eighteenth century; (*b*) *locman* is a word used in Brittany.

The information obtainable from French-Breton and Breton-French dictionaries is as follows:

1732 G. de Rostrenen, *Dict. franç.-breton*, p. 580: '*Loc-man* ou Lamaneur. Ce mot est breton, où il signifie pilote, comme en françois. Il est composé de *loc'h*, qui veut dire barre et de *man* qui signifie homme. *Loc-man*, homme qui tient la barre du gouvernail, qui est le pilote.'— Id., p. 723: '*Pilote—Loman*—lomaned, voyez *locman*. *Pilotage*, lomanaic'h.'

13

1744 L'Abbé Armeyrie, *Dict. franç.-breton*, p. 213: '*Lamanage*
Locmannage.—*Lamaneur, pilote résident, qui introduit les vaisseaux
étrangers dans un port dont l'entrée est difficile*, Locman . . . nett.'—Id.,
p. 220: '*Locman* ou *lamaneur*. Pilote: A zalh er sturt: Loc-man. Le
François a pris ce mot du Breton, ainsi que beaucoup de termes de
marine.' Id., p. 285: '*Pilote cotier* . . . loman.'

1752 Dom Lepelletier, *Dict. de la langue bretonne*, p. 549: '*Locman*,
pilote. Le père Maunoir a mis *loman*, maître de navire, et ailleurs *pilote*,
loman. C'est en Cornwaille *logman*, un pilote et aussi un grand parleur,
un homme qui s'erige en maître dans les conversations. . . .*Loman* est en
abrégé le même que *logman*. M. Roussel m'a donné connaissance que
dans le Haut-Léon *louman* est un pilote. J'ai lu dans un dictionnaire de
1632 imprimé à Morlaix: *Loumman*, pilote.'

Of the three Breton forms, *loman, locman, logman,* the two latter
are found in a French context in documents which come from
Brittany:

c. 1483 Pierre Garcie, alias Ferrande, *Le Grand Routier*, f. 70^r : 'Le
locman prend une nef a mener a Saint Malo. . . .'

1544 Arch. departement, Quimper, in Sneller and Unger, *Bronnen tot
de geschiedenis van den handel met Frankorijk*, I, 377: 'Giles Brolore,
logman du dit navire. . . .'

All the evidence points to the forms *locman, logman* as being used
only in Brittany where they are attested as Breton forms. As the
form *locman* occurs at the end of the fifteenth century in a French
text from Brittany, the question remains as to whether it can be traced
further back, in a Breton, or, as is more likely, in a French context.
The Breton *locman, logman* must, I think, be considered as corrup-
tions of Breton *loman*, due to popular etymology (*ex. g.* from Breton
loc'h 'barre', so that the pilot was considered as a steersman, cf.
French *barre du gouvernail*) or to some other cause.

The Breton *loman* is undoubtedly the original form. As a
Breton word, it is still given by Ernault, *Dict. breton-français du
dialecte de Vannes* (1904), p. 150: '*Loman*, m. pilote côtier; *lomañ-
nereh, -reah*, pilotage.' In 1659 Maunoir, in his Breton dictionary,
translates it by 'maître de navire'. To get further back we must
turn to the various versions of the Sea-Laws of Oleron. The
manuscripts of the Sea-Laws that were written in England are out-

standing, particularly by reason of their being the oldest that have survived. One of the best of these, perhaps the best, is the manuscript called the *Oak Book of Southampton*, written in the early fourteenth century; it was edited by P. Studer for the Southampton Record Society and published in 3 volumes in 1910 and 1911. In the *Oak Book*, article 13 of *La Chartre d'Oylyroun* runs as follows:

c. 1325 *Oak Book of Southampton*, ed. Studer, Vol. II, p. 76: 'Une neff frette a Burdeux ou aillours, et vient a sa charge, et fount chartre partye, towage et petit lodmans sount sour les marchau[nz], *i.e.* 'A ship is freighted at Bordeaux or elsewhere, and comes to her place of loading, and a charter-party is made, towage and petty pilots are a charge upon the merchants.'

We may now turn to such various readings for *lodmans* of the *Oak Book* as are given by Studer from other sources. Studer divided all the sources he knew, either from personal examination or from information to be found in the well-known publications of Pardessus (*Collection des lois maritimes*, 6 vols, 1828–45 and *Us et Coutumes de la mer*, 1847) and Twiss (*Black Book of the Admiralty*, 4 vols., 1871–6), into two groups *x* and *y*, the group *y* containing the continental versions. The readings of these versions are:

(1) *petits lomang servantes* in *Les louables coutumes du pays et duché de Bretaigne*, ed. Rennes, Jehan Macé, 1514. The first edition was published at Paris in 1480.

(2) *petits loesmans* in the version published in 1742 at Paris by Dom Morice in his *Mémoires pour servir de preuves à l'histoire ecclésiastique et civile de Bretagne*, I, 786. The MS. used by Dom Morice is said by Pardessus to be in the Bibliothèque Nationale.

(3) *petis lomaux* in the *Grand Costumier de Normandie* by Nicholas le Roux, published at Rouen in 1539 (*u* in *lomaux* no doubt for *n*).

(4) *petilemanes* in the Spanish version given by Capmanh in his *Codigo de las costumbres de Barcelona*, published in 1791. This version is said by him to be a translation of a Castilian MS. in the Escurial (now lost) the original of which went back to *c.* 1266. *Petilemanes* is for *peti lemanes*; the final -*es* is a hispanicism.

The characteristics of the Continental versions are: (1) All have in one form or another the word meaning 'pilot', *loman*; (2) The

Breton and Norman versions have the certificate of authentication under the seal of the island of Oleron, dated 1266. In this connection it is curious that the original Castilian version in the lost Escurial MS. is stated by Capmanh to go back to *c.* 1266. (3) Among the MSS. in England, the B.M. MS. Sloane 2423 of the late fifteenth century was not examined by Studer, so that I do not know in what form the name of the pilot occurs in it. It is said to be similar to the French group of MSS. and like them it contains the certificate of 1266; from these facts, I gather that it belongs to the group *y.*

The date 1266 appears to me to have considerable importance. It takes one back to the long rule of the Duke of Brittany, John I (1237–86). From 1266 onwards, it is likely that the Bretons had uninterrupted recourse to Oleron for settlement of disputes in matters of the sea. The fourteenth-century *Coutumier de la commune d'Oleron* records a judgment as having been delivered in the Mayor's court at Oleron, on a case in which two Bretons were involved, and then adds the statement that Breton merchants and mariners often came to Oleron and submitted matters of dispute for settlement.

So much for group *y.* The other group, *x,* contains the MSS. written in England; it is divided by Studer into two sub-groups α and β; α^1 includes the *Liber Memorandum* and the *Liber Horn,* both of the early fourteenth century and both in the archives of the Guildhall; α^2 is the *Oak Book of Southampton* which stands by itself. The sub-group β is again subdivided into β^1 and β^2; β^1 contains the version of Bodley MS. 462 of the early fourteenth century; β^2 contains the Cambridge, Corpus Christi College MS. LIX 26, again of the early fourteenth century. The readings of these MSS. which correspond to those given for the Continental MSS. are:

(1) *petite lodmanage* in the *Liber Memorandum.*
(2) *petites lodmanage* in the *Liber Horn.*
(3) *petit lodmans* in the *Oak Book of Southampton.*
(4) *petitz lodmanage* in Bodley MS. 462.
(5) *petit lodmannes* in Corpus Christi MS. LIX 26.

It will now appear that the *Oak Book* and the Corpus Christi MS. have, like the continental MSS., the name of the pilot (*loman*), while the other MSS. have the derivative in *-age* in the sense of 'pilotage'; cf. Breton *lomanaic'h* given by Grégoire de Rostrenen and Breton *locmannage* quoted by the Abbé Armeyrie.

All the surviving MSS. of the Rolls of Oleron that were written in England are in Anglo-French. The readings I have quoted are from the oldest. The fifteenth-century MSS.: (*a*) The *Black Book of the Admiralty*; (*b*) B.Mus. Vespasian B XXII; (*c*) Oxford Selden B 27 have ten articles more than the original Rolls and are further removed from the source.

It is an important fact that MSS. of the Rolls of Oleron are still preserved in the municipal records of London, Southampton and Bristol, the ports most interested in the wine trade to England from La Rochelle, Bordeaux and the West French coast. The *Red Book of Bristol* was not examined by Studer, but it is said to be of the fourteenth century; the others appear to have been written in the reign of Edward II (1307–27). Studer's classification of the surviving Anglo-French MSS. implies that they were copied from four different MSS. now lost. In his edition of the *Oak Book of Southampton*, Vol. I, Introd., p. xxxviii, Studer says:

It is remarkable, too, that the Southampton text contains a twenty-fifth article, not found in any of the other MSS., which reads, not like the previous articles, as a mere statement of a custom, but like an ordinance or some other royal instrument (note especially the use of the first person, *nous en voloms*, and the reference to some definite statute, *le estatut veot*). This article is immediately followed by the opening lines of a letter of Edward I, A.D. 1285. As the handwriting is continuous, and there is apparently no break in the Southampton MS., we must assume as highly probable that these additions already existed in the model of the Southampton text, *i.e.* in MS. α². The latter was in all probability a text of the time of Edward I, the period at which Admiralty jurisdiction first developed in England, and was itself derived from MS. α. It must therefore be admitted that MS. α, which was the original of the oldest English MSS. still extant, could not very well have been written later than the reign of Henry III, and might even belong to an earlier reign.

This statement refers to the MSS. of the Rolls of Oleron written in England and in Anglo-French. The first part of it appears sound; but even if it be admitted: (*a*) that the Oak Book MS. is, of the MSS. written in England, and in fact of all the surviving MSS. of the Rolls of Oleron, the most satisfactory, and further the nearest

to MS. X which is the source of all the Anglo-French MSS.; and
(*b*) that the Oak Book MS. is a direct copy of an Anglo-French MS.
α² written before 1285; there remains the fact that no statute such
as is referred to in art. 25 of the Oak Book version of the Rolls is
known to exist now or to have existed in the past. The second part
of Studer's statement, beginning 'it must therefore be admitted',
is largely in the nature of hypothesis and evidence in support of a
date much earlier than 1285 for any Anglo-French MS. of the Rolls
is lacking.

I propose myself to submit another hypothesis based on certain
historical considerations. Shortly after the middle of the thirteenth
century, the states that had ports on the Bay of Biscay, and were
interested in maritime trade, appear to have adopted a common
code of sea-laws derived from the old customs of the island of
Oleron. The evidence we have given suggests that in or about
1266 Castile and Brittany secured authenticated copies of the
Rolls of Oleron; none of the MSS. of the Rolls written in England
have the certificate of authentication of 1266 or any other certification whatever. Now we know that the King of France, Louis IX,
had, by the treaty of Abbeville in November 1259, ceded to the
King of England the duchy of Aquitaine (including Saintonge),
with the ports of Bayonne, Bordeaux and La Rochelle, and the island
of Oleron. The acceptance by Brittany and Castile of the sea-
customs of Oleron was really the acceptance of customs already
accepted in the King of England's own domain of Aquitaine. The
fact that he was duke of Aquitaine and lord of Oleron may explain
the absence of any kind of certification in the Anglo-French MSS.
The certification of the Castilian and Breton rolls can hardly have
been made without his full knowledge and consent.

Turning now to the name of the pilot with which I am here
concerned: generally speaking, specialists in Germanic consider that
Swedish *lots*, Low Germ. *lots* (whence German *lotse*) are all to be
traced back to Dutch *loods*; that Dutch *loods* is a reduction by
apocope of the full Dutch form *loodsman*, *lootsman*, whence are
derived such full forms as occur farther north: Mid. Low German
lotsman, archaic Danish *lodesmand* etc.; that the starting point for
all the more northern Germanic forms is the Mid. Dutch *loodsman*,
lootsman, which is not attested before 1400; that the Mid. Dutch

lootsman, loodsman, is derived from Mid. Engl. *lodesman,* attested in *c.* 1275 in the meaning 'leader, guide', and in the fourteenth century in that of 'pilot'. Studer claimed that the Flemish version of the Rolls of Oleron was translated from an Anglo-French MS.; and in that connection it is interesting to observe that the oldest surviving MS. of the Flemish version, the *Purple Book of Bruges,* which is assigned to the second half of the fourteenth century, has for the Anglo-French *lodmanage* a form *ledmanage,* possibly due to the influence of Mid. Flemish *leden* 'to lead'.

The French *loman* and the Breton *loman* are not derived from the Mid. Engl. *lodesman,* which has given the Germanic forms. Mid. Engl. *lodesman* is considered by the authors of the *Oxford English Dictionary* to be an altered form of Mid. Engl. *lodeman* due to the analogy of the genitival compounds of the type *doomsman.* Although not attested in the sense of 'pilot' by the *O.E.D.* before 1536, the Mid. Engl. *lodeman* is used *c.* 1385 by Chaucer in the sense of 'leader, guide', and in the sense of 'pilot' is represented by the Anglo-French *lodeman* in the *Oak Book of Southampton* and other Anglo-French MSS. of the Rolls of Oleron. It is clearly to the Mid. Engl. *lodeman* that we must refer not only French *loman,* Breton *loman,* but also the Spanish *limonage,* 'pilotage', still found in Spanish dictionaries, which by its form is of French origin and offers a case of vowel metathesis for **lominage, *lomenage.* In fact, it would appear that along the shores of the Bay of Biscay, a name derived from Mid. Engl. *lodeman* was in general use among mariners from the latter half of the thirteenth century.

The other French name of the coastal pilot with which this note is concerned is *laman.* The two words *lamanage,* 'coastal pilotage', and *lamaneur,* 'coastal pilot', were admitted to the *Dictionnaire de l'Académie* in 1762, no doubt because, like *locman,* they occurred in the *Ordonnance sur la marine* of 1681. *Lamaneur* is apparently derived from an unattested verb **lamaner;* it is found already in a royal document of 1584:

> 1584 Isambert, *Recueil gén. des anciennes lois françaises,* XIV, 584: 'Pareillement seront les lamaneurs reduits en chacun port à nombre competent, par l'advis des dits echevins . . .',

and it seems likely that it superseded the much older *laman* as the name of the coastal pilot during the course of the sixteenth century.

Laman will be found in Godefroy with three examples of 1346, 1355 and 1385. I can quote three more; the latest is of 1510:

1510 Fréville, *Commerce maritime de Rouen*, II, 420: 'Pilottes, lamants, posdeurs ou d'autre estat se sont vantés et efforcés . . . troubler et empescher nostre dit cousin suppliant en ses droictures ou aucunes d'icelles. . . .'

Another is from farther west:

1425 *Docum.*, in *Chron. du Mont-Saint-Michel, S.A.T.F.*, I, 186: 'A Olivier Capuchet et Cardin Tiron, lamans de la hourque dessus dicte, pour leurs gaiges d'un mois entier . . . de gouverner et conduire la dicte hourque avec le maistre et compaignons dessus diz. . . .'

The last is the oldest:

1341 *Privilèges des Portugais à Harfleur*, in Fréville, *Commerce maritime de Rouen*, II, 107: 'Nous . . . voulons que le dit prevost de Harefleu . . . ou son lieutenant, baille laniens [r. *lamens*] pour toutes les nefz et vaisseaux. . . .'

All of these examples come from Normandy. One of Godefroy's examples, however, is from the Picard harbour of Le Crotoy:

1385 *Charte*, in Beauvillé, *Docum. inédits concernant la Picardie*, II, 101: 'Vingt trois lamans mariniers de le dicte ville du Crotoy . . . lequel lamanage ilz ont fait par trois foiz en .iii. marees. . . .'

As early as 1278, *Laman* occurs as a surname in a document derived from the Douai archives:

1278 Espinas, *Vie urbaine de Douai*, III, 498: 'Jehan Laman, de Saint Omer. . . .'

From all this evidence, it seems that French *laman* was a name of the coastal pilot all along the Northern coasts of France from Mont-Saint-Michel to Le Crotoy and beyond. The only Germanic form that can explain the form of *laman* is Old Engl. *ladmann*, attested about the year 1000 by Aelfric in the meaning 'leader, guide' (Num., X, 31). *Ladmann* is merely an older form of Mid. Engl. *lodeman*, 'leader, guide' attested in the sense of 'coastal pilot' by the Anglo-French *lodeman* of the Rolls of Oleron.

It would be useful to know approximately at what period the *a* of *ladman* became *o*. While recognizing the difficulty of fixing any such date, it would appear, from such information as is available in the *O.E.D.*, that no example of *o* appears before 1200. We still have *lade*, 'leading, guidance', *c.* 1200, Ormin 2140. Again *lodesman*, a modified form of *lodeman*, is attested *c.* 1275, *Layamon* 6245 (cf. *c.* 1205 *lædesman*). It seems unlikely then that a Mid. Engl. *lodeman* could have been borrowed before 1200. What is possible is that for some time before 1266 the word may have become generally known to sailors in the Bay of Biscay; and what is relatively certain is that from 1266 it became a technical word known to such mariners as traded to and from the Bay of Biscay; and it is notable that in the fourteenth-century *Coutumes de la Commune d'Oleron* the technical expression *petit lomant* is carefully explained.

As borrowing from English in the thirteenth century is very rare, our particular case requires some explanation. We have to bear in mind that for some 300 years, that is from the marriage of Eleanor of Guyenne and Henry Plantagenet in 1152 to the defeat and death of Talbot at Castillon in 1453, the influence of the king of England was great in Aquitaine, and that his influence was not merely political, but also economic, because there had grown up a great wine trade between the ports of south-west France and England.

The older Northern form, *laman*, on the other hand, must have been borrowed before 1200, and the most likely date seems to be at some time between 1066 and 1204; first, because the word was particularly used in Normandy, whence it seems to have spread eastwards along the coast, and secondly because during that period the king of England was also duke of Normandy.

The names of coastal pilots I have examined in this note have been much discussed by etymologists since Littré. Attempts have been made to connect them, and *locman* in particular, with Dutch; for my part I can see no influence from Dutch at all.

In the following scheme, which represents in brief the views expressed in this note, I use 1762 ACAD. to indicate the admission in the fourth or 1762 edition of the *Dictionnaire de l'Académie* of the three forms *lamaneur, lamanage, locman*:

I O. Engl. *ladman* > North French *laman* (1278–1510), whence *lamanage* (1355–1762 ACAD.), *lamaneur* (1584–1762 ACAD.).

II (a) Mid. Engl. *lodeman* > Span. *limonage*; Fr. *loman*; Breton *loman*; Anglo-French *lodman*.

(b) Breton *loman*, corrupted in Breton itself to *locman*, *logman*, whence Fr. *locman* (1483–1762 ACAD.), *logman* (1544).

(c) Fr. *locman* > Dutch *lochman* (1806 De Flines).

French *patchouli*=*pogostemon patchouli* and the perfume derived from that plant.

D.G., p. 1692:

Patchouli. *s.m.*

[**Etym.** Paraît emprunté de l'angl. *patch-leaf*, mot hybride composé de *patch*, nom indigène de la plante et *leaf* 'feuille'.]

|| *Néologisme.* Admis ACAD. 1878.

|| Plante labiée aromatique originaire de l'Inde. || *Par ext.* Le parfum extrait de cette plante.

In its article on Engl. *patchouli* the *O.E.D.* says:

The spelling *patchouli* appears to be French, and may have arisen in the French possessions on the Coromandel coast. If there is anything in the conjecture in Hatz.-Darm. [i.e. the *D.G.*], that it is a phonetically spelt adaptation of Eng. *patch-leaf*, this would necessarily carry back the name in French to a period anterior to the earliest English examples. But in French dictionaries it was entered as a neologism by Littré in 1875, and was admitted by the Académie in 1878, long after it was known in English.

The *O.E.D.*'s first example of Engl. *patchouli* as a name of the plant (*pogostemon patchouli*) is of 1851 and of *patchouli*, as the name of the perfume derived from the essential oil in the plant, of 1845. Now in French, in the year 1845, the word occurs in a dictionary:

1845 Bescherelle, *Dict. Nat.*: '*Patchouli. s.m.* Parfum, nouveau cosmétique dont on ignore l'origine.'

The word was used by Balzac:

1844 Balzac, *Béatrix*, ed. C. Lévy, p. 107: 'Elle chargea la cheminée de patchouli. . . .'

Some fifteen years earlier, light is thrown on its origin in French:

1829 Chevallier, Richard et Guillemin, *Dict. des drogues*, IV, 133: '*Patchouly*. Sous ce nom vulgaire, on a rapporté, de l'île Bourbon, une plante sèche dont l'odeur est forte, analogue à celle de la valériane. Mise dans les étoffes de laine, elle en éloigne les insectes. M. Virey (*Journal de Pharmacie*, 1826, p. 61) croit que le patchouly est le *plectranthus graveolens* de R. Brown, espèce appartenant à un genre de labiées fort voisin du genre *ocymum* nommé en français basilic.'

The judgment of the authors of the *O.E.D.* is then confirmed: *patchouli* is a French form and is not derived from Engl. *patch-leaf*; Engl. *patchouli* is derived from French. Our knowledge of the French form is taken back from 1869, the date of Littré's third volume, for some forty-three years; we have learnt that the dried plant called *patchouli* was imported into France from Mauritius and that in 1826 it was the subject of an article in the *Journal de Pharmacie* by Dr J. J. Virey (1776–1847). It is very likely that the name was used in Mauritius, and if we can accept the statement that *patchouli* is 'the vernacular name of the plant over the greater part of the Madras Presidency' (Sir G. Birdwood in *Athenaeum*, 22 Oct. 1898), the name may have been imported into Mauritius from Pondichéry.

PROUST AND HARDY: INCIDENCE OR COINCIDENCE

BY

L. A. BISSON

*Professor of French and Romance Philology
in the Queen's University of Belfast*

IN July 1926 Thomas Hardy made an interesting observation in
his Diary: 'It appears that the theory exhibited in *The Well-
Beloved* in 1892 has since been developed by Proust still further.'
As proof, he notes a passage from *A l'ombre des jeunes filles en fleur*:

> Peu de personnes comprennent le caractère purement subjectif du
> phénomène qu'est l'amour, et la sorte de création que c'est d'une personne
> supplémentaire, distincte de celle qui porte le même nom dans le monde,
> et dont la plupart des éléments sont tirés de nous-mêmes. (*JF* I, 40.)

And the Diary goes on to quote a second passage as a summing-up
of the 'theory' thus 'developed' by Proust:

> Le désir s'élève, se satisfait, disparaît—et c'est tout. Ainsi la jeune fille
> qu'on épouse n'est pas celle dont on est tombé amoureux. (*JF* II, 158-9.)[1]

Hardy's note is clearly open to two interpretations: it may merely
record his perception of the correspondence between Proust's
formula for the experience and his own in *The Well-Beloved*; or it
may convey a suggestion that Proust took the Platonic thesis of
the successive incarnations of the Beloved from Hardy's novel and
expanded it in *A la recherche du temps perdu*.

But Proust had anticipated Hardy's discovery of the correspondence by sixteen years. In the summer of 1910 he wrote thus
to his friend, Robert de Billy:

> Je viens de lire une très belle chose qui ressemble malheureusement un
> tout petit peu (en mille fois mieux) à ce que je fais: *La Bien-Aimée* de
> Thomas Hardy. Il n'y manque même pas la légère part de grotesque
> qui s'attache aux grandes œuvres.[2]

Proust's statement leaves no doubt as to its meaning. He has
recognized the same resemblance as Hardy, but his conception and

24

treatment of love were anterior to his reading of *The Well-Beloved*. The general truth and the sincerity of both statements are not in question; yet the mere juxtaposition of them does not dispose of a problem which is not as simple as they suggest. Is Hardy's assumption, with all its possible implications, that Proust developed the theory of *The Well-Beloved* 'since', to be rejected entirely? How, if at all, can the two statements be reconciled with each other and with the facts?

In taking as our starting-point the 'theory exhibited' in *The Well-Beloved*, it will be well to define it as closely as possible, and in Hardy's own words. The most striking and comprehensive statement of the successive appearances of the Platonic phantasm occurs in Part I, Chapter vii, at the moment when the hero, Jocelyn Pierston, becomes fully conscious of his experience, and seeks relief by expounding it to his friend, Soames:

> The Beloved of this man, then, has had many incarnations—too many to describe in detail. Each shape or embodiment has been a temporary residence only, lived in a while, and made her exit from, leaving the substance, so far as I am concerned, a corpse, worse luck![3]

When Pierston tells him some of her various and manifold avatars, his friend diagnoses his condition as 'fickleness', although 'a perceptive fickleness'. But Pierston protests that the flitting of the Beloved has always been independent of his volition, and 'anything but a pleasure':

> To see the creature who has hitherto been perfect, divine, lose under your very gaze the divinity which has informed her... turn from flame to ashes . . . has been nothing less than a racking spectacle to my sight. Each mournful emptied shape stands ever after like the nest of some beautiful bird from which the inhabitant has departed and left it to fill with snow.[4] I have been absolutely miserable when I have looked in a face for her I used to see there, and could see her there no more.

At an earlier stage Pierston had thought that the first episode was also the last; when he describes his experience to his friend, he has long realized the continuity, or rather the repetitive nature of the process:

> When the whole dream came to an end ... I thought my Well-Beloved had gone for ever (being then in the unpractised condition of Adam at sight of the first sunset). But she had not. Laura had gone for ever, but not my Beloved.[5]

Beyond any doubt, these were among the passages that struck a familiar chord in Proust's mind when he read *The Well-Beloved* in 1910, almost certainly in the translation by Eve Paul-Margueritte, published in the preceding year.

At this point two further questions arise. Was this Proust's earliest acquaintance with Hardy; and is there any evidence, other than his statement in the letter to Robert de Billy already quoted, that he had arrived at his conception of love before meeting it in Hardy's novel?

The answer to the first of these questions is fairly simple. Proust's knowledge of English was so slight and uncertain that it is impossible for him to have read *The Well-Beloved* before its appearance in a French translation. 'Entendait-il assez l'anglais pour lire un livre dans le texte? Je ne le crois pas', wrote his artist friend, Jacques-Émile Blanche;[6] and Georges de Lauris is still more precise: 'Il ne lisait pas en anglais d'autres auteurs' [*i.e.* other than Ruskin].[7] But Proust had certainly heard of Hardy, and may have read translations of other novels by him, before 1910. In this earlier, and probably first contact, Blanche was his guide. In June 1906,[8] while working for a period in London, Blanche painted Hardy's portrait, and the painter and his sitter became friendly. On his return from this London venture he was therefore full of Hardy's work, and ready to answer Proust's eager questions about the contemporary English novel—questions which he summarizes thus:

> Monsieur, dites-moi, est-ce que M. Henry James est plus grand que M. Meredith? M. Thomas Hardy, dont vous parlez, est-il grand comme Balzac, ou comme ces messieurs de Goncourt, ou comme M. Anatole France? Que faut-il lire de M. Thomas Hardy?[9]

And the inevitable reply was: 'Lisez *Jude l'obscur.*' If Blanche's recollection is to be trusted, therefore, it was in 1906 that Proust first gained some definite knowledge of Hardy,[10] probably read *Jude the Obscure*,[11] and heard something about other novels which had made a deep impression on his friend, notably *The Trumpet Major*, *The Return of the Native* and *The Mayor of Casterbridge*. Blanche, it may be noted, makes no mention of *The Well-Beloved*, and in *Jude* Proust could have found neither statement nor illustration of the theory of a Platonic 'Idea', the successive incarnations of an adored divinity.

On this evidence, however inconclusive, it is difficult to put Proust's introduction to Hardy before 1906, so that it may very well have been in 1910, as his letter to Robert de Billy states, that he read *The Well-Beloved*, and, for the first time, discovered that in it Hardy makes use of a 'theory' curiously like his own: the passionate adoration of a particular beloved, inevitably followed by 'l'indifférence et l'oubli', followed as inevitably by adoration of another, and the repetition, in recurring phases, of the process. But on the larger question of how and when Proust's conception of love began to take this form and direction, the evidence is to be found in Proust himself, in *Les Plaisirs et les Jours*. The essential elements are already there; and the *contes* and sketches that make up the book were written between 1891 and 1895, and published in this collected form in 1896,[12] a year before the first English edition of *The Well-Beloved*. If any doubt remain, *L'Inconstant*, which appears in *Les Plaisirs et les Jours*, seems to have been written in 1891, well before the serial publication of *The Well-Beloved* in 1892. There can be no possibility, therefore, of Proust's indebtedness to Hardy for an initial suggestion; and when we put his treatment of the process of love, even in the embryonic stage of *Les Plaisirs et les Jours*, alongside that of Hardy, certain differences emerge as striking as the common formula. In Hardy, it is, and remains, a 'theory', deliberately and methodically 'exhibited' in *The Well-Beloved*, perhaps implicit, though not stressed, elsewhere in his favourite theme of woman's inconstancy. It is tempting to suppose that the idea may have been born of his reading of Shelley, and given form and feature by his observation of human behaviour. But whatever its source and inspiration, in Hardy it never strikes, as it does in Proust from the beginning, the note of acutely felt and personal experience, or becomes a key to the whole life and death of the affections. Already in 1929, Benjamin Crémieux noted that Proust had found his formula by the time he wrote the stories in *Les Plaisirs et les Jours*:

Dans la *Mélancolique Villégiature de Madame de Breyves*, le caractère purement imaginatif de l'amour, la non-coïncidence de l'être aimé et de l'être réel auquel on donne son amour, l'irréalité par conséquent de l'être aimé sont déjà nettement aperçus et affirmés.[13]

And when, a few pages later, he calls the whole book 'des confessions à peine déguisées',[14] every reader will be disposed to agree that M. Crémieux has defined the theme that binds these stories into some kind of unity, and that, whenever that theme is touched upon, the book reads like a transcript, a notation of a personal experience and pain.

Some characteristic passages from *Les Plaisirs et les Jours* will serve to show the striking resemblance to *The Well-Beloved*, and the equally striking difference in tone and emphasis. In *L'Inconstant* we find the formula in abstract, as it were, the full cycle of 'l'amour' —'l'indifférence'—'l'oubli', and successive migrations of the Beloved to new dwellings, exactly as in Hardy's novel:

> Fabrice, qui veut, qui croit aimer Béatrice à jamais, songe qu'il a voulu, qu'il a cru de même quand il aimait, pour six mois, Hippolyta, Barbara ou Clélie. . . . Mais sa passion pour Béatrice finie, il reste deux ans sans aller chez elle, sans en avoir envie, sans souffrir de ne pas en avoir envie. . . . C'est qu'il rêve nuit et jour à Giulia.[15]

But Proust's analysis, especially of the process of disintegration, of the stages on each successive journey towards 'l'indifférence et l'oubli', is closer and more searching than Hardy's. He describes them gently in his portrait of the dying officer, who daily reads his old love letters, finding in them a kind of fresco of his life. For a time, as he lives the past over again, he gathers a sense of warmth; then the inevitable changes set in:

> Chaque fois était plus difficile. . . . Et chaque fois, il avait moins de peine de les avoir perdus, ces baisers. . . . Et il eut de la peine d'avoir moins de peine, puis cette peine-là même disparut.[16]

A few pages later, Proust is sadly reflecting on the bitter prescience, the 'désolation enchanteresse' of love and love's decay, in terms that foreshadow those of *A la recherche du temps perdu*. The passage must be given at some length:

> Ce contraste entre l'immensité de notre amour passé et l'absolu de notre indifférence présente, dont mille détails matériels . . . nous font prendre conscience que ce contraste, si affligeant, si plein de larmes contenues, dans une œuvre d'art, nous le constatons froidement dans la vie, précisément parce que notre état présent est l'indifférence et l'oubli;

que notre aimée et notre amour ne nous plaisent plus qu'esthétiquement tout au plus, et qu'avec l'amour, le trouble, la faculté de souffrir ont disparu. . . . Souvent, en effet, quand nous commençons d'aimer, avertis par notre expérience et notre sagacité, nous savons qu'un jour celle de la pensée de qui nous vivons nous sera aussi indifférente que nous le sont maintenant toutes les autres qu'elle. . . . Nous entendrons son nom sans une volupté douloureuse, nous verrons son écriture sans trembler, nous ne changerons pas notre chemin pour l'apercevoir dans la rue, nous la posséderons sans délire. Alors cette prescience certaine, malgré le pressentiment absurde et si fort que nous l'aimerons toujours, nous fera pleurer.[17]

In that and other passages of *Les Plaisirs et les Jours* we surely begin to distinguish Proust's theme of 'les intermittences du cœur', his private clue to the tragic instability of human affection, the ineradicable frailty of human nature.

In the early nineties, then, before the first appearance of *The Well-Beloved* in any form, Proust had crystallized from his own experience a conception of love, as a purely subjective phenomenon and recurrent process, which bears a remarkable resemblance to that found in Hardy's novel. The evidence is clear: before 1910 the two writers present at most a curious parallelism. But the story of their relationship does not end there. Proust's reading in contemporary English literature was limited to a very few authors. He refers to Stevenson, to Barrie, and, as we have seen, to Meredith and Henry James; but none of them left a mark upon him. Emerson, if we may include him here, was an incident, at most a passing one. There remain Ruskin, George Eliot and Hardy. The first two are of capital importance in Proust's development;[18] and in a passage in *La Prisonnière* Hardy, too, appears, ranked with Dostoievsky, as a genuine inspiration, at once poetic and creative. Proust's characteristic theme is what he calls 'phrases types' in literature, analogous to the 'petite phrase' of the Vinteuil sonata; and he dwells on the significant, recurrent parallelisms he has noted in Barbey d'Aurevilly, in Stendhal, above all in Dostoievsky, and here in Hardy:

Rappelez-vous les tailleurs de pierre dans *Jude l'obscur*; dans *La Bien-Aimée*, les blocs de pierre que le père extrait de l'Ile viennent par bateaux s'entasser dans l'atelier du fils où elles deviennent statues; dans *Les Yeux bleus* le parallélisme des tombes, et aussi la ligne parallèle du bateau, et les wagons contigus où sont les deux amoureux et la morte; le parallélisme entre *La Bien-Aimée* où l'homme aime trois femmes et *Les Yeux bleus* où la femme aime trois hommes, etc., et enfin tous ces romans superposables les uns aux autres, comme les maisons verticalement entassées en hauteur sur le sol pierreux de l'Ile.[19]

The particular point that Proust is illustrating does not concern us here. The passage is quoted as helping to fix the probable extent of his first-hand knowledge of Hardy, and as proof that, possibly between 1910 and 1914, certainly by 1922, he had read *A Pair of Blue Eyes*, and reflected on all three of the novels he mentions. The list may not be complete, but a significant point emerges from his insistence on *A Pair of Blue Eyes* and *The Well-Beloved*, as compared with the slighter reference to *Jude the Obscure*. It is a commonplace in the history of literary relationships, and indeed of every contact between one mind and another, that we tend to assimilate those elements for which we are already prepared, which have some affinity with our own thought and feeling. Of all Hardy's novels, it is in *A Pair of Blue Eyes* that he would have found, repeated and emphasized, the resemblance that had already struck him in *The Well-Beloved*. If, by any chance, he had happened on the Preface of 1912, he would have found, too, that Hardy himself was conscious of it:

The first edition of this tale, in three volumes, was issued in the early summer of 1873. In its action it exhibits the romantic stage of an idea which was further developed in a later book [*The Well-Beloved*].[20]

Throughout the story runs the theme of love's successive incarnations, and the familiar formula is crisply stated in the opening sentence of Chapter XXVII: 'Love frequently dies of time alone—much more frequently of displacement.'[21]

If it were possible to observe all the complicated alchemy of Proust's thought, we should probably find that this was what drew him to Hardy, and became the most powerful agent in his own work. But there were other strains in *The Well-Beloved* which he could hardly miss, and which may have operated on him. The transformations wrought by time on human beings Proust had early noted, and reflection upon them is in his natural vein, and crept into *Le Temps perdu* from the start.[22] But it is suggestive to compare Hardy's description of the havoc that Time and Age had made on the face of Marcia in *The Well-Beloved* with Proust's of the now aged duc de Guermantes at the famous 'matinée' in the last volumes of his book.[23] The passage is a late interpolation, and may owe something to the novel which had made so strong an impression upon him, and which contained yet another strain which he must have at least perceived. When the idea of *The Well-Beloved* first occurred to Hardy in February, 1889, it was not the Platonic theory finally exhibited in it that was uppermost in his mind. In his Diary the entry runs:

> The story of a face which goes through three generations or more would make a fine novel or poem of the passage of Time. The difference in personality to be ignored.[24]

In *The Well-Beloved* the Time-motif ultimately became subordinate to others, but enough of it remains to present certain analogies with the general idea of *A la recherche du temps perdu*, and, we may be sure, to awaken Proust's attention.

These strains, however, are less central and organic in Hardy's book than that which startled Proust by its resemblance to his own conviction of the subjectivity of love and the bitter thesis of 'les intermittences du cœur'. When, finally, we seek to determine how far, if at all, the theme already apparent in *Les Plaisirs et les Jours* was appreciably modified or intensified by his reading of *The Well-Beloved*, whether to the initial coincidence of these two writers must be added the actual 'incidence' of Hardy on Proust, the impact of the cognate theme, the evidence is complicated, as always in Proust, by his involved and complicated dealings with the text of his book. We know that by 1910, when he read *The Well-Beloved*, *A la recherche du temps perdu* was substantially complete, for he was already in search of a publisher. But we know, too, that what remained unpublished of the Grasset version was enormously expanded between 1914 and 1922 into the book as we now have it. And Feuillerat has made it possible to identify these expansions and interpolations with a large degree of accuracy. It therefore becomes extremely significant when some of the most characteristic developments of the Platonic theme are found among them. Here, for example, are two passages from *A l'ombre des jeunes filles en fleur* as striking in their way as those noted by Hardy in his Diary:

On construit sa vie pour une personne et quand enfin on peut l'y recevoir, cette personne ne vient pas, puis meurt pour vous et on vit prisonnier dans ce qui n'était destiné qu'à elle.[25]

In the second, still more significant, which occurs later in the same volume, the 'romancier' whom Proust mentions may be an indirect allusion to Hardy and 'la vie de son héros' to *The Well-Beloved*:

Si, en ce goût de divertissement Albertine avait quelque chose de la Gilberte des premiers temps, c'est qu'une certaine ressemblance existe tout en évoluant, entre les femmes que nous aimons successivement, ressemblance qui tient à la fixité de notre tempérament parce que c'est lui qui les choisit, éliminant toutes celles qui ne nous seraient pas à la fois opposées et complémentaires, c'est-à-dire propres à satisfaire nos sens et à faire souffrir notre cœur. Elles sont ces femmes, un produit de notre tempérament, une image, une projection renversée, un négatif de notre sensibilité. De sorte qu'un romancier pourrait au cours de la vie de son héros, peindre presque exactement semblables ses successives amours, et donner par là l'impression non de s'imiter lui-même mais de créer, puisqu'il y a moins de force dans une innovation artificielle que dans une répétition destinée à suggérer une vérité neuve.[26]

But it would be misleading to quote from *A l'ombre des jeunes filles en fleur* only, and leave the impression that such developments of the theme are confined to that section of Proust's book. They occur elsewhere, as here in two interpolations in *Le Temps retrouvé*:

L'amour nous montre la beauté fuyant la femme que nous n'aimons plus et venant résider dans le visage que les autres trouveraient le plus laid. . . . Mon étonnement à chaque fois que j'avais revu aux Champs-Élysées, dans la rue, sur la plage, le visage de Gilberte, de Madame de Guermantes, d'Albertine, ne prouvait-il pas combien un souvenir ne se prolonge que dans une direction divergente de l'impression avec laquelle il a coïncidé d'abord et de laquelle il s'éloigne de plus en plus.[27]

And, finally, a firm statement of the central theme, the subjectivity of love:

Si notre amour n'est pas seulement d'une Gilberte, ce n'est pas parce qu'il est aussi l'amour d'une Albertine, mais parce qu'il est une portion de notre âme plus durable que les moi divers qui meurent successivement en nous.[28]

Passages such as these do not necessarily prove that anything in Proust's conception of love or his treatment of it was the direct outcome of his reading of *The Well-Beloved*; but it is difficult to resist the conclusion that the finding of a kindred perception in a living English novelist strengthened his consciousness of this particular strand in the queer web of human destiny. Whether Hardy exercised any larger or more general influence upon his art is not as easy to determine as it is to distinguish the inspiration he certainly drew from George Eliot, between whom and Proust even the verbal resemblances are striking at crucial points in the work of both. But in these later years of isolation from the everyday world, of absorbed and tortured concentration on his book, Proust's outlook on life takes on a colouring not unlike Hardy's; the frustrations of his 'Marcel' recall those of Jude, his pessimism that of Jude's creator. It is important to remember that, in proportion as he was cut off from the living world, the world of art was often called upon to supply the stimulus of life. If the past was indeed ready to emerge from the depths in which time had buried it, the magic evocation of painter, composer or writer was needed to awaken and vivify the experiences lying dormant in his memory. For that subtle process, the present writer has elsewhere deprecated the use of the word 'influence' as a term 'too gross and palpable', and suggested that it may be compared to 'the deposit of a fine patina on an object, attenuating and modifying its outline, giving it a new texture, a delicacy of tint and surface, beyond the power of any conscious agency'.[29] The task of isolating it is delicate, its analysis elusive; but there can be little doubt that Hardy, like George Eliot, had his share in Proust's great and composite creation, has left something of himself in *A la recherche du temps perdu*.

NOTES

(1) F. E. Hardy, *The Life of Thomas Hardy*, vol. II, p. 248; cf. ibid. p. 59.

(2) R. de Billy, *Marcel Proust*, pp. 180–1.

(3) Hardy, *The Well-Beloved*, Macmillan's Pocket Edition, pp. 50 sqq.

(4) Here, as often, Hardy is remembering Wordsworth. His image recalls Wordsworth's symbol for the desolate heart, 'a forsaken bird's nest filled with snow', the sight of which inspired the lovely sonnet beginning:

> Why art thou silent? Is thy love a plant
> Of such weak fibre that the treacherous air
> Of absence withers what was once so fair?

(5) Hardy, op. cit. p. 52.

(6) J.-É. Blanche, *Mes Modèles*, p. 139.

(7) G. de Lauris, 'Marcel Proust', *Revue de Paris*, 15 June 1938. That the text even of Ruskin presented formidable difficulties to him is amply shown in *Lettres à une amie*.

(8) Blanche suggests 1905, but 1906 is the date given by Mrs Hardy, who is usually accurate on such points of detail: cf. F. E. Hardy, op. cit. II, 119.

(9) J.-É. Blanche, op. cit. p. 80.

(10) This is partly confirmed by Madame Riefstahl, who remembers discussing Dostoievsky and George Eliot with Proust prior to 1906, but not Hardy.

(11) Most likely in the translation by F. Roz, which had appeared in 1901.

(12) They had already been published piecemeal in *Le Banquet* from March 1892 onwards, in the *Revue Blanche* in 1893.

(13) B. Crémieux, *Du côté de Marcel Proust*, p. 23.

(14) Ibid. p. 31.

(15) Proust, *Les Plaisirs et les Jours*, p. 71.

(16) Ibid. pp. 189–90.

(17) Ibid. pp. 197–9. Cf. also ibid. p. 157, p. 220 *passim*, and pp. 266–72 for the description of similar experiences.

(18) The Ruskin-Proust relationship has produced a large and well-known 'literature'; for the interesting and perhaps more central one between him and George Eliot, see my article: 'Proust, Bergson and George Eliot', *M.L.R.* XL (1945), pp. 104–14.

(19) Proust, *La Prisonnière*, II, 237.

(20) Hardy, *A Pair of Blue Eyes*, Wessex edition, p. viii. French translation, *Deux Yeux bleus*, by E. Paul-Margueritte, Plon, 1913.

(21) Ibid. p. 288.

(22) A. Feuillerat, *Comment Marcel Proust a composé son roman*, p. 237, note 5.

(23) Proust, *Le Temps retrouvé*, II, 218–9.

(24) F. E. Hardy, op. cit. I, 284.

(25) Proust, *A l'ombre des jeunes filles en fleur*, II, 49.

(26) Ibid. II, 175; cf. also ibid. II, 143.

(27) Proust, *Le Temps retrouvé*, II, 69.

(28) Ibid. II, 51.

(29) L. A. Bisson, 'Proust, Bergson and George Eliot', *M.L.R.* XL (1945), p. 114.

NAPOLÉON ET SES ADMIRATRICES BRITANNIQUES

BY

J. DECHAMPS

*Professor of French Language and Literature
in the University of London
(Queen Mary College)*

CONTRAIREMENT à une opinion accréditée, Napoléon n'avait pas que des adversaires dans le Royaume-Uni. Au plus fort du conflit qui divisait la France et l'Angleterre, il trouvait des laudateurs, voire des panégyristes, dans les milieux que nous appellerions aujourd'hui libéraux: Hazlitt lui demeura fidèle jusqu'à son dernier souffle.

Il était même un centre de référence pour certains esprits qui refusaient de se laisser influencer par la propagande officielle.

En 1810 Miss Anne Plumptre, fille du Président de Queens' College, à Cambridge, publiait un ouvrage intitulé: *A Narrative of Three Years' Residence in France, principally in the Southern Departments from the year 1802 to 1805, including some authentic particulars respecting the early life of the French Emperor, and a general enquiry into his character.* Le livre, loin d'être celui d'une écervelée ou d'une sentimentale, a pour auteur une femme intelligente dont les jugements reposent sur des faits, observés par elle sur place. Elle reconnaît qu'il existe une grande liberté de parole en France, que la législation y est sagement progressiste, que la tolérance religieuse y règne. Dans les pays soumis à l'influence française, les classes non privilégiées voient en Napoléon leur libérateur:

In all the governments where Bonaparte has any influence he has uniformly been the means of procuring relief to the people from some of the most grievous of their oppressions. He has carried on a determined warfare against feudal and ecclesiastical tyranny, and this has rendered him odious among those whose exclusive privileges have been abrogated; but it has rendered him popular among the orders relieved; and if their voices were as much to be heard as those of the other class, we should from them probably hear a very different representation of his character.

Pendant les Cent-Jours, Hobhouse, le futur Lord Broughton, osa faire son apologie avec une grande force de conviction et une chaleureuse éloquence. Après sa chute, même chez ceux qui l'avaient honni et vilipendé, il y eut un assez prompt revirement. Les ministres de Sa Majesté s'en rendirent compte, et au lieu de l'autoriser, après Waterloo, à se fixer en Angleterre, comme il l'aurait voulu, ils résolurent de l'éloigner à deux mille lieues. Analysant les raisons qu'ils pouvaient avoir de se prononcer pour la détention à Sainte-Hélène, l'auteur de *The Last Phase*, Lord Rosebery, écrit ce qui suit:

Lastly, and we suspect that this weighed most with our rulers, he would have become the centre of much sympathy and even admiration in England itself. . . .

There was indeed an extraordinary glamour about the fallen Monarch, of which he himself was quite aware. He said with confidence at St Helena that had he gone to England he would have conquered the hearts of the English. He fascinated Maitland, who took him to England, as he had fascinated Ussher, who had conducted him to Elba. Maitland caused enquiries to be made, after Napoleon had left the *Bellerophon*, as to the feelings of the crew, and received as the result: 'Well, they may abuse that man as much as they please: but if the people of England knew him as well as we do, they would not touch a hair of his head.' When he left the *Northumberland*, the crew were much of the same opinion: 'He is a fine fellow, who does not deserve his fate.'

The crew which brought Montchenu[1] held similar views. When he had left the *Undaunted*, which conveyed him to Elba, the boatswain, on behalf of the ship's company, had wished him 'long life and prosperity in the island of Elba, and better luck another time'. After two short meetings, both Hotham, the admiral, and Senhouse, the flag-captain, felt all their prejudices evaporate. . . .

There was a more sublime peril yet. 'Damn the fellow,' said Lord Keith, after seeing him, 'if he had obtained an interview with his Royal Highness (the Prince Regent) in half an hour they would have been the best friends in England.'

Après la mort de Napoléon en 1821, le mouvement de sympathie qu'il provoquait prit une incroyable ampleur, et dans un discours du mois d'août 1822, Lord Holland s'écriait:

The very persons who detested this great man have acknowledged that for ten centuries there had not appeared upon earth a more extraordinary character. All Europe has been mourning the Hero; and those who contributed to that great sacrifice, are devoted to the execrations of the present generation as to those of posterity.

Au captif, Lady Holland avait fait parvenir des livres et des douceurs de toute sorte. C'est une Anglaise, Lady Malcolm, femme de l'amiral, qui recueillit les confidences de l'exilé, et c'est en présence de la fille du général Dillon, Madame Bertrand, qu'il rendit le dernier soupir.

Longue serait la liste de leurs consœurs britanniques qui, comme elles, subirent son ascendant, soit pour l'avoir approché, soit à distance. Tout au long du Consulat et de l'Empire, le charme n'avait cessé d'opérer. Celui qu'on appelait dans les cours et les chancelleries d'Europe un Attila ou un Minotaure, avait su, en effet, s'attirer les cœurs féminins. Bien des compatriotes de Castlereagh, appartenant au beau sexe, lui vouaient un culte, semblables à cette Allemande, la comtesse de Kielmansegge dont les mémoires sont si curieux.

La mère de Leigh Hunt le regardait comme une sorte de Messie. Miss Mary Berry déclarait en 1802 que son sourire était incomparablement *sweet*. Mrs Damer, Whig militante et artiste de mérite,[2] lui fit la promesse, tenue en 1815, de lui envoyer un buste de Fox. Il avait le suffrage de la duchesse de Gordon et celui de Lady Cholmondeley qui avait, écrit la duchesse d'Abrantès, 'un accent si parfaitement bienveillant lorsqu'elle me parlait de la gloire du Premier Consul'.

Mais ce sont surtout les récits de Sainte-Hélène qui firent monter comme un chœur de voix éplorées et ferventes, autour du roc fatidique. Rien ne serait plus instructif que de suivre la fortune, dans les Iles Britanniques, d'un livre comme celui de Barry O'Meara, le chirurgien irlandais qui donna ses soins à Napoléon. Ce livre, intitulé *A Voice from St Helena*, forme le sujet d'un long passage dans la lettre adressée par Thomas Carlyle, fin juillet ou au début d'août 1822, à sa future épouse, Jane Welsh, ardente napoléonisante:

O'Meara's work presents your favourite under somewhat of a new aspect: it has increased my respect for Napoleon ....
Since the days of *Prometheus vinctus*, I recollect no spectacle more moving and sublime, than that of this great man in his dreary prison-

house; given over to the very scum of the species to be tormented by every sort of indignity, which the heart most revolts against;—captive, sick, despised, forsaken;—yet rising above it all, by the stern force of his own unconquerable spirit, and hurling back on his mean oppressors the ignominy they strove to load him with. I declare I could almost love the man. His native sense of honesty, the rude genuine strength of his intellect, his lively fancy, his sardonic humour, must have rendered him a most original and interesting companion; he might have been among the first writers of his age, if he had not chosen to be the very first conqueror of any age. Nor is this gigantic character without his touches of human affection—his little tastes and kindly predilections—which enhance the respect of meaner mortals by uniting it with their love.

Il ajoute qu'il enverra le second volume à Miss Welsh dès que Mrs Butler en aura terminé la lecture.

This lady likes Napoleon even better than you do; made a pilgrimage to his grave, stole sprigs of willow from it, etc.; and called him the greatest of men in the presence of Mr Croker[3] himself.

La réponse de Miss Welsh est vraiment caractéristique:

Mrs Butler likes Napoleon better than I do! How do you know that? I do not think any human being can love and admire him more than I do. When a mere child I could have sacrificed my life to free him from captivity, and win for my name a line in the history of his life. Do not in future make such gratuitous assertions.

Il n'est pas jusqu'à la cour d'Angleterre qui n'ait été sensible à l'attrait que Napoléon exerçait sur plus d'une dame haut placée ou distinguée par ses talents.

La princesse Charlotte, héritière présomptive de la Couronne, était une de ses admiratrices et elle témoigna plus d'une fois de sa tendre commisération pour le prisonnier de Sainte-Hélène. Celui-ci fondait beaucoup d'espoirs sur elle, comme le prouvent ses entretiens avec Las Cases et Gourgaud. Mais une catastrophe emporta la princesse le 5 novembre 1817, sans qu'elle eût régné.

En 1832 Lady Anne Hamilton, dame d'honneur et amie de la reine Caroline, publiait, sans vouloir s'en avouer l'auteur, une *Histoire secrète de la Cour d'Angleterre* où Napoléon est défendu

avec une énergie surprenante, en une série de chapitres dont voici
la conclusion:

> There is every reason to believe that his great name will be finally
> rescued from that misrepresentation with which interested writers have
> endeavoured to surround all his actions.

Dans le *Journal* de la reine Victoria, pour les années 1832 à
1840, il y a une page significative à propos de Lady Holland qui,
suivant Melbourne, 'was half on his (Napoleon's) side, if not
more',—et sur une autre de ses adoratrices, Lady Emmeline Wort-
ley, cinquième fille du duc de Rutland. La reine elle-même prenait
beaucoup d'intérêt à l'histoire de l'Empereur et cite fréquemment
des anecdotes se rapportant à sa personne ou à son époque.

Dans les souvenirs du maréchal Canrobert, aide de camp de
Napoléon III, on trouve la relation de la visite qu'elle fit à Paris en
1855. Après une grande revue des troupes au Champ-de-Mars,
elle alla visiter le tombeau de Napoléon aux Invalides. Elle était
accompagnée de l'empereur, du prince Albert en habit rouge de
feld-maréchal, et du prince de Galles en highlander, avec sa veste
de velours, sa sacoche de fourrure, et le kilt. La scène qui suivit
est racontée avec beaucoup de pathos par Canrobert, et plus
prosaïquement dans la biographie de la reine.

> Napoleon's fate moved her to compassion, and she bade the Prince of
> Wales, who, clad in Highland costume, had accompanied his mother to
> the Hôtel des Invalides, kneel at the hero's tomb. A thunderstorm broke
> out at the moment, and the impressive scene moved to tears the French
> generals who were present. A picture of the scene, now at Windsor,
> was painted for the Queen by E. M. Ward, R.A.[4]

. . . .

Personne ne s'est jamais avisé d'étudier la légende napoléonienne
en Grande-Bretagne. Pourtant ce ne sont pas les matériaux qui
manquent. Cette légende y a parcouru une longue carrière, moins
agitée, plus unie qu'en France, parce qu'elle n'y fut pas l'alliée de
partis politiques ni l'auxiliaire de la propagande bonapartiste. Elle
a donné lieu à une belle floraison poétique; on la trouve au théâtre,
dans le roman, dans les manifestations de la vie artistique.

Il n'est pas sans intérêt de faire voir que les femmes, y compris
la souveraine, n'ont pas été les dernières à en favoriser l'essor.

NOTES

(1) Le Commissaire français, envoyé à Sainte-Hélène par le gouvernement de Louis XVIII.

(2) Un autre artiste, Sir Benjamin West, qui fut Président de la Royal Academy, était grand partisan du Premier Consul et de l'Empereur. Leigh Hunt en parle dans son *Autobiographie*. 'I believe he retained for the Emperor the love that he had had for the First Consul, a wedded love, "for better, for worse". However, I believe also that he retained it after the Emperor's downfall—which is not what every painter did.'

(3) L'homme d'État qui passe pour avoir donné le nom de conservateur au parti tory.

(4) Voir *Queen Victoria, a Biography*, new and revised edition, 1904. Voir aussi le chapitre "Homage to Napoleon" du livre récent d'Edith Saunders, intitulé: *A Distant Summer*, récit de la visite royale, en 1855, à Paris.

A SEMANTIC GROUP IN ALPINE ROMANCE

BY

W. D. ELCOCK

Professor of Romance Philology and Mediaeval French Literature in the University of London (Westfield College)

Rheto-Rom. *agŏr, adigŏr.*   Bearn. *agǫ́r, abǫ́r.*
Arag. *agüerro.*   Basque *agǫ́r.*

THE existence of close lexical and semantic affinities between the local Romance speeches of the Pyrenees and those of the Alps, suggested on various occasions by earlier scholars (certain publications by V. Bertoldi will in particular come to mind), has of late been re-affirmed by J. Coromines in a contribution to the *Festschrift Jacob Jud*, becomingly entitled *Dis Aup i Pyreneu.*

The Catalan philologist here asserts his belief that these affinities are more numerous, and of deeper linguistic significance, than has hitherto been conceded; with a promise of more in the future, he adduces and analyses a number of common features, gleaning principally, for his information concerning the Rheto-Romance area, from the abundant documentation now afforded by the *Rätisches Namenbuch* and the first fascicules of the *Dicʒiunari Rumantsch Grischun.*

We may note in passing that recent years have seen a great increase in the work of exploration conducted in both areas; the initiative taken by Coromines is therefore a logical step, and implies a stimulus to further research. His examples, certain of which are extant only in place-names, point in some cases to a common archaic Latin, while others are apparently pre-Latin in origin. The discovery of common Latin forms, surviving only in the seclusion of these two mutually isolated domains, where displaced populations have sought refuge, and where local words, yielding to the new-found favour of migratory synonyms, linger a while before they are finally discarded, is in itself interesting enough, suggesting as it does the possibility of providing a clearer picture of the lexical variety of rustic vernacular in the early period of Romanization: but of still greater interest, perhaps, to whoever has experienced the fascination of the substratum, is the prospect of reconstructing elements of a pre-Romance vocabulary common to the Pyrenees and eastern Switzerland, and which may once have been in use in the territory intervening.

Toponymists and historians, it is true, are no strangers to such a conception; but the modern dialectologist, handicapped in the past by lack of adequate material, has still his contribution to make. Systematic investigation of the two areas, based on this premise, may eventually lead to a notable development in our knowledge, at present so vague, of pre-Romance speeches in western Europe. More immediately, the speech of either area may be used as a means of sifting the non-Romance element in the speech of the other. Thus, if we seek in the Rheto-Romance area for words cognate with the elements of pre-Latin vocabulary to be found in the Pyrenees, we may well find that a considerable part of that vocabulary belongs, not, as is so often and somewhat arbitrarily alleged, to Iberian, but to a speech (Ligurian?) extending from the Pyrenees to the Alps.

It was with such ideas in mind that, in 1938, I turned aside from the Pyrenees to pay a brief exploratory visit to the Rheto-Romance area. The years between have given little opportunity for further investigation, but there is one small problem which has remained obstinately lodged in a recess of memory, and which seems worthy of statement, and, in so far as it permits, of elucidation, as a contribution to research on these lines.

The starting-point, as for so much in Pyrenean studies, lies in the slight but highly original work of J. Saroïhandy. With the main thesis of his now well-known article, 'Vestiges de Phonétique Ibérienne en Territoire Roman' (*Revue Internationale des Etudes Basques*, Oct.-Déc. 1913), I have elsewhere found occasion to disagree, but the information there collated remains most valuable, and from it is culled the following quotation:

... on trouve encore aujourd'hui dans les montagnes du Béarn et de l'Aragon quelques mots d'usage courant, dont la parenté avec les mots euskariens correspondants semble incontestable. A ceux que l'on a cités oserai-je ajouter le béarnais *agor* signifiant 'automne', que je retrouve sur le versant espagnol, à Plan, à Benasque, et à Castejón de Sos, sous la forme *agüerro*? Il n'y a rien dans le Latin qui puisse expliquer *agor* (*agüerro*), et l'on ne peut s'empêcher de songer à l'adjectif basque *agor*, qui a le sens de 'sec', et de remarquer en outre que *agor* est employé pour désigner le mois de septembre en biscayen et en guipuzcoan, et que le nom du mois d'août est *agorril* dans le Labourd, dans la Basse-Navarre, dans la Haute-Navarre, et dans la vallée de Roncal. Les formes basques et romanes pouvaient ne pas avoir autrefois la signification précise qu'elles ont aujourd'hui, et désigner simplement l'époque de l'année où la sécheresse commence à se faire sentir.

Thus we have, in the Romance dialects of both slopes of the Pyrenees, and in Basque dialects, also on both sides of the present Franco-Spanish frontier, a type *agor* (*agüerro*) which employed as an adjective means 'dry', and as a noun, the 'late or dry season'.[1] Certainly, one may agree with Saroïhandy that these words would appear to have a common origin, and that no Latin etymon is immediately available to explain them.

Turning now to Rheto-Romance, we find there a word which is employed over a wide area with the single meaning of 'aftermath', and which shows a bewildering variety of forms; particularly since the publication of the *A.I.S.*, it has come under the microscope of a number of specialists in the dialects of that region, though none has ventured to proffer an etymological explanation. Professor J. Jud selects the words designating 'aftermath' as an example when describing the possible applications of the information provided by the *A.I.S.* ('La valeur documentaire de l'A.I.S.', *Revue de Linguistique Romane*, IV, p. 272): from among the many forms here collated, he picks out (*a*)*digör* as representative of one particular category. In this he is followed by R. A. Stampa, in the latter's valuable *Contributo al Lessico Preromanzo dei Dialetti Lombardo-Alpini e Romanci*, where the word is definitely considered as pre-Romance. The authors of the *Dicziunari Rumantsch Grischun* select, however, as type, a form *agör*, and, allowing for the possibility of agglutination of prefixes, this form would certainly appear to be the more primitive. The similarity in form between this word and the Pyrenean words quoted above is at least sufficiently arresting to retain our attention, while the meaning 'aftermath' bears an obvious relation to the meaning 'season when the aftermath is gathered in'. In passing, it may also be observed that in the examples of usage in popular sayings quoted by the authors of the *D.R.G.* (*fain giuven ed agör vegl*, 'hay fresh and aftermath old'; *il fain in flur, l'agör in colur*, 'hay in flower, aftermath browned by the sun', etc.), there is a general tendency to indicate that the aftermath is the *dry* crop, as opposed to the hay, which must not be allowed to lose its freshness. The sense of 'dry', attributed by Saroïhandy to the Basque *agór*, thus appears here intimately associated with the sense of 'aftermath'.

I may now make a personal contribution by indicating that in the Pyrenees the word *agór* is also employed in a sense virtually identical to that which we have found for *agör* in Rheto-Romance.

In the course of pre-war explorations I recorded at Fabian, in the upper Vallée d'Aure, which until recent years (it is now the site of a hydro-electric plant) has been one of the least frequented of French valleys in the Central Pyrenees, beside the word *arredalh* (the orthography is standard Bearnese) employed in the sense of 'aftermath', the form *agór*, currently used to designate the third crop of hay, the *pâture d'automne*. A recent exchange of letters with my informant at Fabian, M. Georges Fourcadet, a local farmer and guide of unusual intelligence, tends to confirm the impression that the word is unknown outside the valley; such publications as I have been able to consult, including Simin Palay's comprehensive *Dictionnaire du Béarnais et du Gascon Modernes*, show no trace of its use in this sense. Unsolicited, M. Fourcadet supplies the following examples from the speech of Fabian (the orthography is his own): *Aquet agor m'a et creba eras oueillos*, 'that *pâture d'automne* has killed the sheep'; *qu'aouem u bet péchiou dat aquet agor*, 'we have a fine fodder with that *pâture d'automne*'.[2] Comparison of these examples with those quoted by the authors of the *D.R.G.* leaves me in little doubt of the genuineness of that affinity which I am seeking to establish.

There are, moreover, certain indications which suggest that the word *agór* was formerly more widely used in the French Pyrenees, and that it probably had the actual sense of 'aftermath'.

A glance at the *A.L.F.* (Map No. 1139, 'regain') will show that the word *arredalh* (a repetitive substantive formed on the verb *dalhà*, 'to mow with a scythe') occupies a compact area, and has all the appearance of a word until recently in flux, a word which may well have submerged others; Fabian lies in the south-east corner of this area; to the north and east are local varieties of *regain*, obviously an invader from the north, and of a type *revivre*, found in Central French. In other parts of the Romance area where the practice of cutting grass more than twice in a season is usual, the third and successive crops are designated either by some such general term as *pâture d'automne*, or by a diminutive of the local word for 'aftermath' (cf. E. Tappolet, 'Le Regain et la Pâture d'Automne dans les patois Romands', *Bull. du Gloss. des Patois de la Suisse Romande*, 1911). Why then should Fabian, not otherwise outstanding for lexical wealth, possess a word so strongly individualized to designate the third crop, unless it is that the word was formerly applied to the more important second crop, and was relegated to its present position of semantic inferiority under pressure of the Bearnese *arredalh*?

One is further tempted to see evidence of a more widespread use of *agór*=aftermath in the existence of the variant *abór*, beside *agór*, in the sense of 'autumn'. The passage of *agór* to *abór* is almost certainly to be explained by the attraction of *ibér* (< HIBER-NUM), but why should this analogical attraction have taken place, or more precisely, once a form *abór* had been spontaneously created, why should this form have been preferred to the already existing *agór*? May not the preference have been dictated by a desire to differentiate the symbol for 'autumn' from *agór* in the sense of 'aftermath'? Nowhere in the modern dialects have I come upon an instance of the same word being used to express both these senses in one and the same locality. Thus the area of *abór*='autumn' may well correspond to a submerged area of *agór*='aftermath'.

Even though these 'indications' be dismissed as deriving from the realm of fancy, yet the remnants to be observed in the modern dialects seem in themselves to stand in such close semantic relation that one may be justified in assuming a common origin for the two domains. With regard to this origin, we may note that the words have already been examined, in the light of the known etyma of Romance, by specialists in the dialects of both areas, working independently, and all those etyma have been rejected. The author of the article on *agör* in the *D.R.G.* (it is initialled by C. Pult) is quite categoric: 'Das etymologische Problem von *agör* ist noch nicht gelöst; RECHORDUM genügt nicht den heutigen Dialektformen des Wortes, das vom Unterengadin, Munstertal und Puschlav süd- und ostwärts in mannigfachen Varianten sich bis ins Friaul hinzieht.' The form RECHORDUM seems to call for further examination. In mentioning it, M. Pult probably had in mind the situation in western Switzerland. Here, Romance dialects show two different types employed to express the sense of 'aftermath'. In the Bernese Jura we have *vouayín*, of which the source is *weida*, and which is thus cognate with the *regain* of northern France, and the *guaime* of Italian; elsewhere, the usual form is *rekór*, deriving from RECHORDUM (see E. Tappolet, *op. cit.*). Now, RECHORDUM is merely the repetitive form of CHORDUM (cf. *regain*, O.Fr. *reaoust*), implying the sense of second crop; the basic word is the Latin adjective CŎRDUS (CHŎRDUS), used by Latin writers on agricultural topics with the sense of 'late': thus *frumentum cordum*, 'late wheat', *uvae cordae*, 'late grapes', and applied to animals it may have the sense of 'late-born' (and by extension 'new-born', whence Span. *cordero*). The aftermath is thus *foenum cordum*, also described in Latin as *foenum autumnale*; it therefore appears that in the rustic Latin of certain areas the word CŎRDUM became specialized as a noun with the sense of 'aftermath'.[3]

If I dwell on this form at some length it is because a type *AD CŎRDU would appear to explain satisfactorily all the Pyrenean forms. The tonic vowel offers no difficulty, and the correspondence *-rd-*: *-rr-* is a characteristic feature of Aragonese phonology. In face of the unanimity with which students of Rhetic concur in rejecting this root—C. Tagliavini, W. Th. Elwert and R. A. Stampa are all of the same mind as Pult—I hesitate to suggest it again as the source of the Rheto-Romance forms. Yet *agör* would seem to derive quite normally from the type I postulate; and particularly suggestive among the forms collated by Professor Jud (see above) is *agǘér*, so reminiscent of the *agüerro* of Benasque, and showing an intermediate stage in the development of stressed *ŏ > ö*, as paralleled in French. With this as a basis, it may well be possible, allowing for the intervention of common linguistic phenomena—

metathesis, assimilation and dissimilation, and, above all, contamination with other words—to explain the many remaining variants. May we then hope that, in the light of the Pyrenean forms, the words for 'aftermath' in Rheto-Romance may be considered worthy of further consideration by specialists in that area? If derivation from *AD CORDU (through a verb *ADCORDARE?) still appears unlikely, then we must again think in terms of a pre-Romance root, possibly, as Saroïhandy hints, with the sense of 'dry'.

Whatever the final result of such inquiry, the first purpose of this article will have been attained if only the kinship between the Pyrenean forms and those of the Alps can be admitted. It will then be apparent, since the Iberians did not penetrate into the Alps, that the theory of an Iberian origin for Pyrenean *agor* (*agüerro*), as postulated by Saroïhandy (and repeated, incidentally, by G. Rohlfs, *Le Gascon*, and by W. von Wartburg, *Französisches Etymologisches Wörterbuch*), becomes untenable, and the word *agor* in Basque is in all probability, like so many other Basque words, a borrowing from the neighbouring Romance.

As Coromines writes: 'Les romanistes, des Pyrénées aux Alpes, ne peuvent que gagner en s'efforçant de mieux connaître réciproquement les domaines particuliers qu'ils cultivent.'

NOTES

(1) From personal observation I can confirm the use of the form *agüerro* in the valley of Benasque, and add that it extends to Bielsa, in the neighbouring valley to the west.
On the French side, G. Rohlfs, *Le Gascon*, records *agór* at Aramits, and in several localities in the valley of Aspe; and *abór* to the east of this region, in the valley of Ossau, at Gavarnie and other localities in the same valley, and at Pontacq. The *A.L.F.* (Map No. 75, 'automne') also shows a form *gór* at three points in the northern Landes and in the Gironde.

(2) I am indebted to Mr J. Cremona, who is investigating the dialect of the Vallée d'Aure, for the following note: At Le Plan, the last hamlet in the valley, *agór* stands for the aftermath which has been bonified by the sheep, in moveable enclosures; it is thus of better quality than the normal aftermath. At Fabian and Guchen, on the other hand, *agór* stands for the second aftermath, which is not harvested, but left for the sheep to graze, and is of much inferior quality to the first aftermath.

(3) It is presumably this same word, uncompounded, which survives as *kórt*, employed with the sense of 'aftermath' in certain localities in northern Italy (see *A.I.S.* No. 1402, 'il guaime').

A BIBLIOGRAPHY OF
EIGHTEENTH-CENTURY TRANSLATIONS
OF VOLTAIRE

BY

H. B. EVANS

Sub-Librarian in the
University of Birmingham

I T is an extraordinary fact that in the field of comparative literature, the attention of researchers, as far as the eighteenth century
is concerned, has been confined to the influence of English writers
on the French public and men of letters. Hitherto little has been
written of the part played by the French encyclopaedic writers in
shaping English thought, and even the translations of their works
published in England during the century have been well-nigh
neglected. The one notable exception to this has been the article
of J. S. Warner entitled 'Bibliography of 18th-century English
editions of J. J. Rousseau, with notes on the early diffusion of his
works' (*Philological Quarterly*, XIII (1934), 225–47); with 'Addenda
to the bibliography of 18th-century English editions of J. J.
Rousseau' (ibid. XIX (1940), 237–43).

It is particularly surprising that the fortunes of Voltaire in England
during his life-time have received so little attention, for the number
of translations extant bears ample witness to the popularity of his
works and, to quote Bruce in his *Voltaire on the English stage*
(University of California Publications in Modern Philology,
VIII (1918), 1–152): 'From the day in 1726 that he came to London
an exile, to that day in 1778 when they (the English) heard how his
bust was crowned with garlands and roses at the Théâtre français,
Voltaire was never entirely out of their minds.'

Georges Bengesco, the author of the standard bibliography of
Voltaire (*Bibliographie Voltairienne*, 4 vols., Paris, 1882–90), had
intended to devote the third volume of his work to translations of
Voltaire made in other countries, and states in the preface to the
first volume that much of his material for it was ready: 'Ce troisième

volume, dont nous avons déjà réuni tous les éléments, et dont la rédaction est commencée, sera le complément nécessaire de notre "Bibliographie Voltairienne".' But, alas, when Bengesco has reached the end of a fourth volume he announces that his task is over: 'Ce serait allonger celui-ci outre mesure que d'y ajouter, comme nous en avions d'abord conçu le projet, la nomenclature des Traductions que l'étranger a faites de Voltaire, et celle des ouvrages relatifs à sa personne et à ses écrits. . . .'

The fortunes of Voltaire's plays in England have been adequately treated by Bruce in the article already quoted, and so it has seemed wiser to confine the scope of the present bibliography to the non-dramatic works, and a short table will serve to show how quickly translations of these were issued by enterprising booksellers:

TITLE	FRENCH	ENGLISH
Poetry:		
La Henriade	1728	1729 (first canto)
		1732 (in full)
Sept discours sur l'homme	1738	1738 (three only)
		1764 (in full)
Tales:		
Zadig	1748	1749
Candide	1759	1759
Philosophy and polemics:		
Lettres philosophiques	1734	1733 (issued first in English)
Éléments de la philosophie de Newton	1738	1738
Traité sur la tolérance	1763	1764
Dictionnaire philosophique	1764	1765 (in abridged form)
		1786 (complete)
History:		
Histoire de Charles XII	1731	1732
Siècle de Louis XIV	1751	1752
Essai sur les mœurs	1756	1758
Histoire de la Russie sous Pierre le Grand	1761	vol. 1, 1761; vol. 2, 1764
Précis du règne de Louis XV	1768	1770

In all over 250 eighteenth-century translations of Voltaire (including the dramatic works) are still extant and the following table illustrates how these fall into the various decades of the century:

YEARS	NO. OF EDITIONS
1730–1740	29
1741–1750	18
1751–1760	62
1761–1770	56
1771–1780	60
1781–1790	23
1791–1799	20
Total	268

As we should expect, the table shows an awakening of interest in Voltaire during, and immediately after, his visit to England. During the forties the issue of translations flags, coinciding with a very peaceful period in Voltaire's life when he was the guest and friend of the Marquise du Châtelet, 'la divine Émilie', and was secure in the favour of the court of France, being appointed royal historiographer, gentleman-in-waiting to the king, and a member of the Academy. Although this part of Voltaire's life was extremely fruitful in literary production and greatly increased his prestige in his own country, it was not of a kind to make him better known in England, for in general the popularity of the French writers of the period in this country depended either on their personal visits here or on the more stormy periods in their lives and on the scandal of any quarrels, literary or otherwise, in which they indulged. In 1742, 1746, 1748 and 1751 no translations of Voltaire occur: this in itself is a significant fact, which is only repeated for three other years throughout the period from 1730 to 1799.

With the stay of Voltaire at the court of Frederick II the lime-light of public interest in England was once more focused on his work, and his fame was stimulated rather than impaired by the stormy breaking off of his relations with the famous enlightened despot. In fact, Voltaire's popularity probably reached its acme in 1759 and 1760 when we have traced respectively twelve and fifteen editions in English of various works. From then until about 1780 there is no break and little diminution in the long line of translations and adaptations.

He died in 1778, in the same year as Rousseau, and, although some interest was aroused by his apotheosis in the same year, 1778 is the beginning of a marked decline in the number of English editions of his works, a decline which continued to the end of the century.

If any further proof were required of the popularity of Voltaire's works in the eighteenth century, it may be found in the researches of Professor Ronald S. Crane of Northwestern University on 'The diffusion of Voltaire's writings in England, 1750–1800' (*Modern Philology*, xx, part 3). Professor Crane examined the sale catalogues of 218 English private libraries of the period, chosen at random. He found editions of Voltaire, originals and translations, in 172 libraries, as compared with Pope in 115, Young in 62, Thomson in 51, Rousseau in 50 and Gray in 43.

The translators of Voltaire have, for the most part, elected to hide under a cloak of anonymity—of those who have left their names to posterity the majority appear to be hack-writers and hangers-on of literature. The name of Smollett appears linked with that of Thomas Francklin in the great translation of Voltaire's work, but we are told that in all probability he had no part in the translation and that Francklin's only contribution was the 'Orestes'. The anonymity of the majority is, however, easily understood when we come to read the comments they produced in the literary reviews of the time. Here is a selection of them: 'The translation has little, in point of elegance or accuracy, to recommend it.' 'The infidelity of translations is become so trite a subject of complaint that we are heartily weary of repeating it. As to the work before us; if the proof positive did not immediately stare us in the face, we should hardly have thought it possible that such a spirited and entertaining piece, in the original, could so totally lose its distinguishing qualities, by means of any version or paraphrase whatever .... The translation is one of the most dull, heavy and disagreeable performances that ever was read.' 'A stiff and stupid translation.' 'Should this translator, as he dares to call himself, be capitally indicted in the Muse's high court of Justice, there is not the least doubt, but he would be found guilty of wilful murder.' The *Monthly Review* for October, 1765, vol. XXXIII, p. 276, contains a lengthy diatribe against translators, occasioned by the abridgment of the *Dictionnaire philosophique* entitled *The Philosophical Dictionary for the Pocket*.

Lest, however, we should end this survey on too gloomy a note, we will quote two versions of a part of Canto I of *La Henriade*, both of which appear to be faithful and elegant. Here is the original verse of Voltaire:

> Descends du haut des cieux, auguste vérité,
> Répands sur mes écrits ta force et ta clarté:
> Que l'oreille des rois s'accoutume à t'entendre,
> C'est à toi d'annoncer ce qu'ils doivent apprendre.
> C'est à toi de montrer, aux yeux des nations,
> Les coupables effets de leurs divisions.
> Dis comment la discorde a troublé nos provinces;
> Dis les malheurs du peuple, et les fautes des princes.
> Viens, parle: et s'il est vrai que la fable autrefois
> Sut à tes fiers accents mêler sa douce voix,
> Si sa main délicate orna ta tête altière,
> Si son ombre embellit les traits de ta lumière;
> Avec moi sur tes pas permets-lui de marcher,
> Pour orner tes attraits, et non pour les cacher.

This is the version of the anonymous translation of 1797:

> Descend, bright Truth! from Heaven's ethereal vault,
> Guide my weak pen, give vigour to my thought,
> Accustom kings thy warning voice to bear,
> 'Tis thine to dictate as 'tis theirs to hear;
> 'Tis thine to bid contending nations know,
> 'What dire effects from civil discord flow'.
> Tell how her standard on our plains she spread,
> How princes err'd, and hapless subjects bled.
> And, heavenly Truth! if e'er thou did'st descend
> Thy voice with Fiction's silver sounds to blend;
> If e'er that lofty forehead stoop'd to wear
> The flow'ry wreath her graceful hands prepare;
> If from her shade thy lustre brighter shine,
> Let her with me her magic garland twine,
> And lend what sportive Fancy can devise
> Thy modest charms to deck, but not disguise.

Finally, this is the translation of the same passage from the collected edition of Voltaire's works, vol. I (1762):

> O heaven-born truth, descend, celestial muse,
> Thy power, thy brightness in my verse infuse.
> May kings attentive hear thy voice divine,
> To teach the monarchs of mankind is thine.

'Tis thine to war-enkindling realms to shew
What dire effects from curst divisions flow.
Relate the troubles of preceding times;
The people's sufferings and the princes' crimes.
And O! if fable may her succours lend,
And with thy voice her softer accents blend;
If on thy light her shades sweet graces shed,
If her fair hand e'er decked thy sacred head,
Let her with me thro' all thy limits rove,
Not to conceal thy beauties, but improve.

BIBLIOGRAPHY

ABBREVIATIONS USED

A. Bibliothèque de l'Arsenal.
BM. British Museum.
BN. Bibliothèque Nationale.
BO. Bodleian.
BR. Birmingham Reference Library.
BU. Birmingham University.
E. Edinburgh University.
G. *Gentleman's Magazine.*
L. Lowndes; *Bibliographers' manual* . . . 6 vols.
       London, 1865.
LC. Library of Congress.
LL. London Library.
M. *Monthly Review.*
S. Sorbonne.
W. Watt, *Bibliotheca Britannica* . . ., 4 vols.
       Edinburgh, 1824.

COLLECTED WORKS

(*a*) The works of M. de Voltaire.   Translated from the French.
   With notes, historical and critical.   By Dr Smollett and others.[1]
   36 vols.   London, 1761–65
   —— 2nd edition, 1762–1767–1769?
   3rd edition, 1770–71–?   BM. (two sets); LC.; BR
   Vols. 37–38 added 1774
   —— New edition 1778–1781

(*b*) The works of the late M. de Voltaire. Translated from the French, with notes, critical and explanatory. By the Rev. David Williams, Hugh Downman, M.A., Richard Griffith, Elizabeth Griffith, William Campbell, Ll.D., James Parry, M.A., John Johnson, M.A., under the direction of W. Kenrick, Ll.D. 14 parts [incomplete]. London, 1779–81. BM. (Supplement).

SELECTIONS

(*a*) Babouc, or the world as it goes. By . . . Voltaire. To which are added letters concerning his disgrace at the Prussian court. With his letter to his niece on that occasion. Also, the Force of Friendship, or Innocence Distress'd, a novel. London, 1754. BM.; G., 1754; M., 1754; W.
—— Another edition. Dublin, 1754. BM.

(*b*) Select pieces . . . Translated by Joseph Collyer. London, 1754. BM.; G., Jan. 1754; M. Feb. 1754; W.

(*c*) Dialogues and Essays, Literary and Philosophical . . . Glasgow, 1764. BM.

(*d*) Fragments relating to the late Revolutions in India, the Death of Count Lally, and the Prosecution of Count Morangies. London, 1774. G., Apr. 1774.

(*e*) Romances, tales and smaller pieces. 2 vols. London, 1794. BM.; LC.

(*f*) Critical Essays on Dramatic Poetry . . . With notes by the translator. London, 1761. BM.; BO.; E.; M., Mar. 1761; W.
—— Glasgow, 1761. BM.

LETTERS

(*a*) Letters addressed to his Highness the Prince of * * * * *, containing Comments on the writings of the most eminent writers who have been accused of attacking the Christian religion. London, 1768. BM.; M., 1769.
—— Another edition. Glasgow, 1769. BM.

(*b*) Genuine Letters between the Archbishop of Anneci and Mons. de Voltaire, on the subject of his preaching at the Parish Church at Ferney without being ordained . . . London, 1770. BM.; M. Jan. 1771; G., Nov. 1770.

(*c*) A Letter from M. de Voltaire to M. d'Am, dated March 1st, 1765, upon two tragical incidents in France, at the same time: that of Calas, and that of Sirven; both on account of Religion. London, 1765. G., Mar. 1765; M., Apr. 1765.

(*d*) A Letter from M. Voltaire to the French Academy, containing an appeal to that society on the merits of the English Dramatic Poet Shakespeare . . . London, 1777. BR.; BO.; M., May 1777.

(*e*) A Letter from Mons. de Voltaire to Mr Hume, on his dispute with M. Rousseau . . . London, 1766. BM.; M., Nov. 1766.

(*f*) A Letter from Mr Voltaire to M. Jean Jacques Rousseau (Appendix: Extracts from book just published, entitled: Anecdotes relative to the persecution of J. J. Rousseau). London, 1766. BM.; BN.; G., Apr. 1766; M., May 1766.

SEPARATE WORKS

Annales de l'Empire (1753)

Annals of the Empire from the reign of Charlemagne . . . 2 vols. London, 1755. M., Aug. 1755; W.

Candide (1759)

(*a*) Candid, or all for the best. London, 1759. BM.; BO.; M., July 1759; G., May 1759; W.; L.
—— Another edition. London, 1796. BM.

(*b*) Candidus; or, the Optimist. Translated by William Rider, M.A. London, 1759. BM.; G., May 1759.

(*c*) Candidus; or, All for the Best . . . A new translation. Edinburgh, 1759–61. BM.
The spurious second part, attributed to Thorel de Campigneulles, was published in English in 1761, the year it appeared in French.

Défense de Milord Bolingbroke (1752)

A Defence of the late Lord Bollingbroke's Letters on the study and use of History . . . London, 1753. BM.; M., Feb. 1753; W.

Défense de mon Oncle (1767)

A Defence of my Uncle . . . London, 1768. BM.; LC.; M., Dec. 1768; G., June 1768; W.

Dictionnaire philosophique (1764)

The philosophical dictionary for the pocket. Written in French by a Society of Men of Letters, and translated into English from the last Geneva edition . . . With notes, containing a refutation of such passages as are any way exceptionable in regard to Religion. London, 1765. BM.; LC.; M., Oct. 1765.

Dictionnaire philosophique

> Another edition [published J. Carman] [1767?] BM.
> L. also has two further editions. Glasgow, 1766 and London, 1786, 4 vols., but there is no further proof of these.

Discours en vers sur l'homme (1738)

> (*a*) Epistles translated from the French of Mr Voltaire. On Happiness, Liberty and Envy. London, 1738. BM.; W.
> (*b*) Three epistles in the ethic way. From the French: viz. 1. Happiness. 2. Freedom of Will. 3. Envy. London, 1738. BM.; G., Sept. 1738.

Eléments de la philosophie de Newton (1738)

> The elements of Sir I. Newton's Philosophy ... Translated from the French. Revised and corrected by J. Hanna, etc. London, 1738. BM.

Various 'Epistles'

> An Epistle of Mr de Voltaire, upon his arrival at his estate near the lake of Geneva, in March, 1755 (French and English). London, 1755. BM.; M., Oct. 1755; W.
> —— Another translation; in blank verse. London, 1765. M., Jan. 1756.
> Epître de M. Voltaire au Roi de Prusse. With a translation. London, 1757. M., Feb. 1757; G., Feb. 1757.

Essai sur les mœurs (1745–)

> (1) The general history and state of Europe, from the time of Charlemain to Charles V, with a preliminary view of the Oriental empires. 6 parts. London, 1754–7. BM.; E.; M., 1754–7.
> (2) The general history and state of Europe. 3 vols. Edinburgh, 1758. BM.
> (3) An essay on universal history, the manner and spirit of nations, from ... Charlemaign to ... Lewis XIV. Translated ... by Mr Nugent. 2nd edition, revised, etc. 4 vols. London, 1759–61. E.
> —— Third ed., revised. 4 vols. Dublin, 1759. BM.
> L. has also two editions, London, 1777. 4 vols.; 1782. 4 vols.
> A supplement to the Essay on general history, the manners and spirit of nations from the reign of Charlemaign to the present time. 2 vols. London, 1764. E.; M., Sept. 1764; G., Nov. 1764.

Essay upon the civil wars of France (1727) (written and published in English by Voltaire; afterwards translated into French).

An essay upon the civil wars of France, extracted from curious manuscripts. And also upon the epick poetry of the European nations from Homer down to Milton. London, 1727. BM.; BO.; W.

—— 2nd edition. London, 1728. BM.; BN.; S.

—— 4th edition. To which is now prefixed, a discourse on tragedy; with reflections on the English and French drama. 2 parts. London, 1731. BM.

—— Another edition. London, 1745. BM.; G., Oct. 1745.

—— To which is prefixed a short account of the author. By J[onathan] S[wift] . . . Dublin, 1760. BM.

La Guerre civile de Genève (1768)

The civil war of Geneva; or the amours of Robert Covelle, an heroic poem. Translated . . . by T. Teres. London, 1769. BM.; M., Aug. 1769; W.

La Henriade (1728)

(*a*) No. 1 of the Herculean Labour . . . At the end is subjoyn'd the first canto of Voltaire's Henriade turned into English verse [by John Ozell]. 2 vols. London, 1729. BM.

(*b*) Henriade, an epick poem in ten cantos. Translated . . . into English blank verse by [John Lockman]. London, 1732. BM.; LC.

(*c*) The Henriade . . . translated into English rhyme, with large historical and critical notes. London, 1797–8. BM.; BN.; BO.; E., etc.

Histoire de Charles XII (1731)

(*a*) The History of Charles XII, King of Sweden . . . 2 parts. London, 1732. BM.

—— 2nd edition. London, 1732. BM.

—— 3rd edition. London, 1732. BM.

—— 5th edition. London, 1733. BM.

—— 6th edition. Dublin, 1732. BN.

—— 7th edition. London, 1740. BM.

L. has also 4th edition, London, 1732, and two others 1735 and 1798.

(*b*) The History of Charles XII (an abridgment of the 1732 translation). London, 1734. BM.
—— Another edition. London, 1739. BM.
—— Another edition. Glasgow, 1750. BM.
(*c*) [Spurious extract.] The History of Frederick, King of Sweden ...
Translated and improved from the French of M. de Voltraie [sic]
by Andrew Henderson. London, 1752. BM.; M., Feb. 1752.

Histoire de l'Empire de Russie sous Pierre le Grand (1759)

The History of the Russian Empire under Peter the Great. 2 vols.
London, 1761–4. M., Feb. 1761, Mar. 1764; G., Feb. 1761; W.
L. has editions in 1769 and 1789.

Histoire de la guerre de 1741 (1755)

The history of the war of 1741 ... in two parts. London, 1756.
BM.; M., Feb. 1756; W.
—— 2nd edition. London, 1756. BM.
—— 2nd edition. Carefully revised. Dublin, 1756. BM.
—— [Another edition.] [London?] 1756. BM.
L. has another edition, with appendix. London, 1758.

Histoire des voyages de Scarmentado (1756)

The History of the voyages of Scarmentado. A Satire ... London,
1757. BM.; LL.; M., Feb. 1757; G., Feb. 1757.

L'Homme aux quarante écus (1768)

The Man of Forty Crowns ... London, 1768. M., Aug. 1768;
G., July 1768.
—— [Another edition.] Dublin, 1770. BM.

L'Ingénu, ou le Huron (1767)

(*a*) L'Ingénu; or the Sincere Huron, a true History ... London, 1768.
M., Aug. 1768.
(*b*) The Pupil of Nature; a true History, found among the papers of
Father Quesnel. London, 1771. BM.; E.; M., Oct. 1771; W.
(*c*) The Sincere Huron. A true History. Translated ... by Francis
Ashmore. London, 1786. BM.
Also issued as vol. 21 of Ashmore's 'Novelists' Magazine',
1786. BR.; LC.

Jenni, ou le Sage et l'Athée (1775)

Young James, or the Sage and the Atheist. An English Story.
From the French of M. de Voltaire. London, 1776. BM.; M.,
June 1776; G., July 1776.

Letters concerning the English Nation (1733).[2]

> [First edition.] London, 1733. BM.; BR.; BU.; LC.; S.; W.
> —— [Another edition.] Dublin, 1733. BM.
> —— 2nd edition. London, 1741. LL.; G., Apr. 1741.
> —— 4th edition. Dublin, 1740. BN.
> —— 3rd edition, corrected. Glasgow, 1752. BM.
> —— 4th edition, corrected. Glasgow, 1759. BM.
> —— New edition. London, 1760. BM.
> —— New edition. London, 1767. BM.
> —— [Another edition.] London, 1773. BN.
> —— [Another edition.] London, 1778. BN.

Mémoires (1784)

(1) Historical Memoirs of the Author of the Henriade. With some original pieces. To which are added, genuine letters of M. de Voltaire. London, 1777. BM.; E.; BO.; M., Jan. 1777; G., Feb. 1777.

(2) Memoirs of the life of Voltaire, written by himself. London, 1784. BM.; M., Sept. 1784; G., Jan. 1784; W.

(3) The Life of Voltaire, by the Marquis of Condorcet. To which are added, Memoirs of Voltaire, written by himself . . . London, 1790. BM.; E.; M., Mar. 1791; W.

Métaphysique de Newton (1739)

The Metaphysics of Sir Isaac Newton; or a comparison between the opinions of Sir Isaac Newton and Mr Leibnitz . . . Translated . . . by D. E. Baker. London, 1747. BM.; BO.; LL.; BN.; G., Jan. 1747. L. has also Glasgow, 1764.

Micromégas (1752)

Micromegas: a comic romance. Being a severe satire upon the philosophy, ignorance and self-conceit of mankind. London, 1753. BM.; LC.

Les Oreilles de Lord Chesterfield (1775)

The Ears of Lord Chesterfield and Parson Goodman. Translated . . . by J. Knight. Bern, 1786. (Imported by G. Kearsley, London.) BM.; M., Sept. 1786; G., Nov. 1786.

Panégyrique de Louis XV (1748)

Panégyrique de Louis XV. Sixième édition. Avec les traductions latine, italienne, espagnole et anglaise. n.p., 1749. LC.

Le Philosophe Ignorant (1766)

> The Ignorant Philosopher. With an Address to the Public on the Parricides imputed to the families of Calas and Sirven. London, 1767. M.; W. L. also has Glasgow, 1767 and London, 1779.

La Philosophie de l'Histoire (1765)

> The Philosophy of History. London, 1766. BM.; M., May, 1766; W.

Précis du siècle de Louis XV (1748)

> The age of Louis XV, being the sequel of the age of Louis XIV. 2 vols. London, 1770. W.; G., Sept. 1770.
> —— [Another edition.] 2 vols. Glasgow, 1771. E.

La Princesse de Babylone (1768)

> The Princess of Babylon. London, 1768. BN.; G., July, 1768; M., Aug. 1768.

La Pucelle (1755)

> (a) The Maid of Orleans . . . 2 vols. n.p., 1758. BM.; M., Sept. 1758.
> (b) The Maid of Orleans . . . Canto I. London, 1780. M., July, 1780.
> (c) The Maid of Orleans. Canto the first. n.p., 1782. M., Oct. 1782.
> (d) La Pucelle, or the Maid of Orleans . . . 2 parts. London, 1785–6. B.M; M., Dec. 1785; G., July, 1785.
> —— 2nd edition. 2 parts. London, 1789. BM.; M., Nov. 1789; G., July, 1789.
> (e) La Pucelle; or, the maid of Orleans . . . (By Catherine Mary Bury, Countess of Charleville.) 2 vols. (Privately printed) 1796–7. BM.

Siècle de Louis XIV (1751)

> (a) An essay on the age of Louis XIV by Mr de Voltaire, being his introduction to the work. Translated . . . by John Lockman.[3] London, 1739. BM.; BO.; E.; G., Dec. 1739; W.
> —— Dublin, 1760. BM.; BO. (BM. suggests probably a misprint for 1740.)
> (b) The Age of Lewis XIV . . . 2 vols. London, 1752. G., July, 1752; M., Aug. 1752.
> —— 2 vols. Dublin, 1752. BM.
> —— A new edition, corrected by Mr Chambaud. 2 vols. London, 1753. BM.
> —— [Another edition.] 2 vols. Glasgow, 1763. E.

Le Taureau Blanc (1774)

(a) The White Bull; an Oriental History . . . [by J. Betham]. 2 vols.
BM.; M., July, 1774; W.

(b) [Another translation.] Le Taureau Blanc; or the White Bull . . .
Translated from the Syriac by M. de Voltaire. 2nd ed. BM.;
LC.; M., July, 1774; G., July, 1774.

Le Temple du Goût (1734)

The Temple of Taste. By M. de Voltaire. London, 1734. BM.;
LC.; G., Feb. 1734.

Traité sur la Tolérance (1763)

(a) A Treatise on Religious Toleration. Occasioned by the execution
of the unfortunate J. Calas for the supposed murder of his son.
Translated . . . by the translator of Eloisa [William Kenrick] etc.
London, 1764. BM.; M., Oct. 1764; G., Sept. 1764.
—— [Another edition.] Edinburgh, 1770. LC.

(b) A Treatise upon Toleration . . . Carefully corrected. Glasgow,
1765. BM.
L. has also London, 1772 and Edinburgh, 1776 and 1779.

Zadig (1747)

Zadig; or, the Book of Fate. An oriental history. London, 1749.
BM.; G., Jan. 1749.
—— Translated by Francis Ashmore. London, 1780. BM.
—— 'Novelists' Magazine' (vol. 2). London, 1790. BR.
—— London, 1794. BM.
The Hermit: an Oriental Tale. [A chapter of 'Zadig'.] London,
1779. BM.

Miscellaneous Pieces:

1. The conversation between Mademoiselle Clairon, a celebrated
actress at Paris, and the fathers of the church, occasioned by
the excommunication denounced in France against all dramatic
writers, actors, singers . . .4 London, 1768. BM.; W.

2. An Essay on Taste, by Alexander Gerard, M.A., Professor of
Moral Philosophy at Aberdeen, with three Dissertations on the
same Subject, from the French of M. de Voltaire, M. D'Alembert,
F.R.S. and M. De Montesquieu. 1759. (John Nichols: 'Anecdotes of William Bowyer' in 'Literary Anecdotes of the Eighteenth
Century'.5)
—— 2nd ed. Edinburgh and London, 1764. BM.; BN.

3. Original Pieces relative to the trial and execution of Mr John Calas. With a preface and remarks . . . by M. de Voltaire. French and English. London, 1762. BM.; M., Nov. 1762.

4. The Memorial of Mr Donatus Calas . . . concerning the execution of his father, Mr John Calas . . . With remarks by M. de Voltaire. In John Lockman's 'History of the cruel sufferings of the Protestants . . .' Dublin, 1763. BM.

5. The history of the misfortunes of J. Calas, a victim to fanaticism; (with) . . . a letter from M. Calas to his wife and children. London, 1772. BM.; LL.

—— Edinburgh, 1776. BM.; BO.; LL.

6. Thoughts on the pernicious consequences of war. By the celebrated Mons. Voltaire. [179–?] BM.

Work edited by Voltaire

An Essay on Crimes and Punishments . . .[6] with a commentary attributed to Monsieur de Voltaire. London, 1767. M., Apr. 1767.

—— 2nd edition. London, 1769. BM.

—— 3rd ed. London, 1770. BM.

—— 4th ed. London, 1775. BM.

—— New ed. Edinburgh, 1778. BM.

—— New ed. Edinburgh, 1778. BM.

NOTES

(1) The name of T. Francklin, M.A., was added in the second and subsequent volumes.

(2) This translation, by John Lockman, was published before the first French edition.

(3) A translation of a pamphlet published at Amsterdam in 1739, containing the Introduction and Book I of the later work.

(4) Translation of 'Conversation de l'Intendant des Menus en exercice avec M. l'abbé Grizel'.

(5) London, 1812–1815.

(6) By the Marquis Cesare Beccaria Bonesana.

GUILLAUME D'ANGLETERRE

BY

E. A. FRANCIS

Fellow of St Hugh's College,
Oxford

THIS poem is a stumbling-block in the path of critics. F. Michel first edited the text without adding his customary notes and comments.[1] R. Müller published a thesis, in 1891, to prove the identity of the style and language with those of Chrétien de Troyes. In a short notice P. Meyer observed 'avant d'en regarder le résultat comme acquis, il convient d'en attendre un examen contradictoire'.[2] This was forthcoming in 1931.[3] In the interval there had appeared Förster's edition (1914), Wilmotte's article and edition (1927) and G. Cohen's monograph (1931).[4] The three scholars treated the poem as authentic work of Chrétien de Troyes, but each made a slightly different approach to the two main issues—the questions of authorship and literary value. Could the author of *Erec*, *Cligès*, *Ivain*, *Lancelot* and *Percival* have departed so far from his usual choice of subject-matter and mode of narrative? Curiously, it fell to Wilmotte, who had stressed so greatly the contribution of hagiographical writing to French literature, to deny this title to a work, at first sight, so suggestive of that type of composition, both in matter and mediocrity. Wilmotte, as likewise Nitzke and Cohen, considered that here, as elsewhere in the 'romans' of Chrétien de Troyes, the aim of the author was to fashion his materials to illustrate a particular theme.[5] This explanation, however, still left untouched anomalies of style and subject-matter. It is plain to the most casual of readers of this poem that, at the beginning, the style is quite unlike that of Chrétien de Troyes and the manner of telling the story is stilted. It is not until we reach the point where the king and queen, in their resolve to obey divine commands, escape from their palace window, that any of the animated spirit characteristic of the celebrated 'Champenois' novelist can be detected. Thereafter, some features of style and vocabulary could justify an identification of the poet with Chrétien de Troyes.

Indeed, even the harshest of the critics, Tanquerey, is constrained to admit to some extent the claim of the author to match the famous Chrétien, since on that fact depends his own theory. In his view the poem was composed as 'une tentative d'exploiter la popularité de Chrétien de Troyes' and 'l'auteur fait preuve d'une dextérité assez remarquable puisqu'il a réussi à induire en erreur un aussi bon juge que M. Wilmotte'.[6]

It is not proposed, here, to intervene in so long-standing a debate, but merely to add a few observations which have been provoked by a chance re-reading of the poem. It is not a *conte pieux*, but a *roman d'aventure* and a *roman à thèse*—and, again, not these but a *conte moral*.[7] The last verdict, that of Tanquerey, appears the most justified, but may it not be more accurate still to revert to the first epithet, while broadening the term 'pieux' to include both religious and feudal piety?

The source of the tale before it reached the author, either in written or oral form,[8] has long been recognized as of the type represented by *Apollonius of Tyre* and the Placidus-Eustace legend. To this Chrétien (or his unknown namesake) undoubtedly added the many passages descriptive of twelfth-century social life, the characterization and the development of the particular aspects which appealed to the author and his audience.[9] In the years when the poem would have been 'composed', a different spirit, or perhaps it should rather be said a changed spirit, was affecting the relations between the religious and lay sections of upper-class society. What the earlier attitude was can be conveniently illustrated by the history of the foundation at Bec. Here a layman, a seasoned warrior but an unlettered man, founded a religious house, entered it himself and summoned to rule over it an able Italian-trained ecclesiastical lawyer and administrator, with results far-reaching for religious affairs in northern France and the British Isles. At this period, also, laywomen, royal princesses, found in the cloister a life of spiritual harmony and intellectual inspiration.[10] But the religious world was consciously differentiated from the lay world. In contrast, Bernard of Clairvaux and his brothers, in the flower of youth, came straight, it might be said, from the feudal 'mêlée'. The type of Benedictine reform known as Cistercianism was at its height in the middle years of the twelfth century and the power of its preachers can be indicated by a comparison of three familiar figures of the society of the time. One is the ordinary knight, fully occupied with the duties involved by tenancy of a fief (or fiefs). The next is the knight vowed to a Crusade, who, in consequence, delegated, or partly ignored, his duties as a layman. The third is the Templar. The novelty of the last is apparent—less so is the subtle permeation of a lay society which produced him.[11] G. Cohen has already suggested that *Perceval*, with its exceptional emphasis on knightly code and ritual, may owe something to the Templars.[12] The same critic has also stressed, more than his predecessors, the conspicuous reputation for chivalry assigned to Philip of Flanders, to whom the poem is dedicated and from whom came the 'book' in which Chrétien de Troyes found the tale. Nevertheless, Cohen implies that Chrétien was not catering for an audience which cared especially for religious sentiment.[13] Wilmotte agrees and considers that Chrétien did not scruple to take an entirely religious 'tract' and secularize it, in order to produce a fantastic and amusing tale. 'Le livre confié au poète par Philippe d'Alsace était une histoire de la relique du Saint-Sang' (*Le poème du Gral*).

The prologue to *Perceval* gives us some information which, I think, has not been fully appreciated in comments made on that passage. It is agreed that the unusual feature is the praise of a patron, not found elsewhere in Chrétien's work, and, for that reason, judged by Cohen to be sincere. 'Phelipes de Flandres miauz vaut ne fist Alexandres . . . cui ne chalut de charité.' The word 'largesse', for which in mediaeval literature the name of Alexander is almost a synonym, is never mentioned in the prologue. But 'charité' (which Alexander lacked) is defined and elaborated,[14] 'Li don sont de charité, que li bons cuens Phelipes done'. *Charité*,[15] in the Cistercian sense, meant 'a way of life', and the word surely has that value when it is used in the prologue to *Perceval*, and also in *Guillaume d'Angleterre*. How far the narrative of Perceval's 'aventures' was intended as an illustration is not a question to be considered here. The theories of Cohen and Wilmotte discount any real religious preoccupation. Turning to *Guillaume*, Chrétien writes of this fictitious English king—'Li rois fu plains de carité: moult ot en lui d'umilité', and of his queen—'Se cil fu de carité plains, en celi n'en ot mie mains; s'il ot humelité en lui, en l'estoire trovai et lui k'autant en ot en la roïne'. It has been remarked that the humiliation of this royal pair constitutes the main plot of the story, thus bringing the poem into line with those in which Chrétien de Troyes builds up a tale round a main theme. What has not been sufficiently noted is the aptness of the whole scheme of incidents in the tale to exemplify what Cistercian theology understood by 'humilité'. 'L'humilité peut se définir la vertu par laquelle l'homme, se connaissant exactement tel qu'il est, se rabaisse à ses propres yeux.' The attainment of self-knowledge is represented in various fashions in this story—the king's first realization of his impotence to defend wife and children—his humiliation as a servant.[16] The queen's natural pride is not only abased by circumstances: she mortifies herself by pious and horrifying lies. 'En atteignant le faîte de l'humilité nous atteignons aussi le premier degré de la vérité qui est de reconnaître sa propre misère.'[17] In contrast to their parents the twin sons, who have never known any other social rank than that of their foster-parents, instinctively and energetically rebel against what cannot be a self-humiliation for them. The restoration of the whole family to their proper stations in life, and the gratitude they display to their lowly benefactors, in the form of material rewards and aggrandisement, are not inconsistent with the central theme. It may be argued that those who have schooled themselves have the right to govern others.[18] Nor is the severely aristocratic attitude, shown throughout the narrative, out of keeping with the preaching of Christian charity and humility, when such a view is interpreted in terms of twelfth-century feudal society. Cohen expressed surprise: 'même le gros marchand, semble-t-il, ne trouve pas grâce devant Chrétien et ceci est étonnant pour qui montre, comme lui, sa familiarité avec les foires de Champagne . . . dont était fait le luxe de ses futurs maîtres'. But the poem itself gives the explanation. The sons of the merchant of Galloway are knighted, married to rich heiresses and given 'chastel et tor'.[19] They become, thus interpreted, the king's 'new men'. The Galloway merchant himself is made 'ses primes consilliers'[20] and the Bristol child, who kept the king's horn as a plaything, now, at man's estate, becomes a 'chamberlain'.[21] All these have now been brought within the charmed circle. Thus the tale is plainly a tract in support of the gentry.

The poem is enlivened by much description which even Tanquerey admits to be clever.[22] The materials for these embellishments are certainly borrowed, but effectively introduced. Indebtedness to Wace's *Brut* for the storm has been noted, although Tanquerey argues in favour of first-hand experience.[23] Although at first glance it did not seem to me likely that significance should be attached to the mention of saints whose lives had also been celebrated, in verse, by Wace[24] (since similarity in terms would be so probable), I am now fully disposed to think these poems were known to the author. The queen, during the first pangs of childbirth, invokes St Margaret, with obvious appropriateness. But it should be noted that Wace's French version is the first work in which that particular detail of the cult appears.[25] In the poem there is no special reason given for the invocation but, on the other hand, the context makes the cause recognizable.[26] The argument of unavoidable similarity of wording applies very strongly to the literature of devotion to the Virgin. But Wace's poem was a careful compilation and propaganda for the Feast of the Conception. Now the short prayer, before the second birth, combines the most characteristic—even essential—features of various passages in Wace's poem.[27] Lastly, so wide was the veneration of St Nicholas by travellers and seafarers that this fact also diminishes the value of similarities. Indeed, some positive likeness in the seascapes of both Wace's poems and the storm in *Guillaume* might be expected, and this is lacking. However, the sailors' cry and prayer 'Sains Nicholais, aidies, aidies...' might have been suggested to a reader of Wace's poem by the similar incident. There is skill, also, in the poet's choice (for a rhyme) of this saint when the king's nephew thinks he has found his uncle again.[28]

Turning to other more general characteristics in style and composition, it is interesting to observe the devices used to avoid monotony.[29] The author's skill is displayed especially in the portrayal of the twin children. One of them, though at first carried off by a wolf, is rescued by the arrival of a party of merchants in the animal's path. The other child is found, by the same merchants, apparently cast away in a boat. Both these scenes are well elaborated. The traditional tale, as well as artistic symmetry, required some resemblance between the children, not only physically but in

situation and temperament.[30] The narrator adroitly presents the
two boys enduring the same ordeal, at the same moment, but
unknown to each other. Yet the poet differentiates. The foster-
parent of each boy decides he should be apprenticed as a skinner.
Both resist, exclaiming, 'ja n'i ira, se Marins ses compaigns n'i va...
Dist que ja n'ira en escriene, se Loviax ne va avoec li'. But Lovel
(so named from the incident of the wolf) is presented in the more
sympathetic fashion. He, with innate courtesy, it may be surmised,
does not ignore his obligations to his foster-parent. The latter,
finding the boy is not to be swayed, sends him off with friendly help,
supplying money, equipment, clothes, and a 'squire' and two
horses.[31] This turn of the tale introduces a slightly dramatic episode.
Marins (so named from the rescue from the boat) has set out on
foot, after a brief, downright quarrel with his foster-father.[32]
Hearing horsemen, he fears that he is being pursued, and tries, in
vain, to hide in the forest. The 'friends' thus meet again and happily
continue their journey together, attended by the squire. Lovel
displays inborn skill with his bow, shooting a deer.[33] This introduces the account of their crime against the forest laws, which
brings them, through their arrest by the friendly, but dutiful,
forester, to a pardon from the king of Caithness, and service in his
household, where as befits knights they are trained in venery.

The details of the narrative do not show which of the children
is the first-born—that matter of supreme importance for feudal
inheritance. There are, however, many signs that the poet intended
to give more attention to Lovel than to Marins, although this fact
does not seriously disturb the impression of similarity and equality
appropriate to twins. Lovel always takes the initiative. The rescue
of Lovel from the wolf is, in the nature of things, a more striking
episode than the discovery of a foundling in a boat. It should also
be noted that the carrying off of the child by the wolf is more
closely involved with the psychological delineation required in the
tale. The king's vain pursuit of the animal, his subsequent
exhaustion, are all part of the complicated lesson of humiliation.[34]
To the astonished merchants who see the wolf drop its prey this is a
'miracle'.[35] The bereaved Guillaume wildly apostrophizes the wolf
in a monologue described by Wilmotte as curious.[36] This obvious
stressing of the rôle of Lovel seems to me to warrant a suggestion.

In this re-telling of a widely known folk-tale, elaborated by pictures of twelfth-century life and attached to an imaginary king of England, may we not find some kind of reflection of 'family' history or legend? 'The surname Lovel, Luvel, Lovet (Lupellus —little wolf) was not uncommon in Norman times, and there is no likelihood that families possessing it came from a common stock.'[37] Two family groups in particular may be considered. One is the family of Ascelin Goel d'Ivry.[38] His son Robert joined the revolt against Henry I, but almost immediately went over to the king.[39] William Lovel (Lupellus), brother and heir of Robert, married a sister of Waleran de Meulan. William, again, had a second son, William Lovel, who was endowed by his father and brother with lands, and with the property of Minster Lovel by his mother. He joined the Third Crusade in 1190, the Abbot of Bury St Edmunds being pardoned his scutage.[40] He gave 110 marks fine for seisin of the manor of Southmere (Norfolk), probably as heir. The second group are descendants of Ralph of Castle Cary (Somerset), tenant of William Count of Mortain, half-brother of the Conqueror. A grandson, Ralph, in 1138, held Castle Cary against Stephen, but was compelled to make peace. He married Margaret, an heiress in county Roxburgh. Her son, Henry Lovel, gave land at Branxholme to St Andrews, and Hawick was said (in 1347) to have been held from the Crown by Richard Lovell and his ancestors 'from time immemorial'.[41]

Before further considering these facts it is necessary to examine, briefly, the geography of *Guillaume d'Angleterre*. William and his queen are in the castle of Bristol when the tale begins, and this town is later described at its 'fête'. The children are born in a cave in a forest near Yarmouth. The king is taken to Galloway, the children to a 'port' in Caithness—and journey to the abode of the kings of Caithness. The queen is taken to the castle of 'Sorlinc', whither comes, eventually, Guillaume, driven out of course by a storm. Bristol, Yarmouth, 'Galloway' are all shown as places of trade, and for that reason would probably have been well known. Tanquerey, however, regards the geographical accuracy of the poem as an argument against attributing it to Chrétien de Troyes.[42] A problem remains. The successive editors have provided no satisfactory comment on Sorlinc. Förster alone deals with the point briefly.[43] Sorlinc is clearly intended to be in Scotland and on the borders of the kingdom of Caithness. The ruler of the castle (who claims harbour dues as a feudal right) is not

> rois, ne dus, ne cuens,
> Mais chevaliers estoit moult buens;
> Onques miudres ne fu Rollans

and his name is Gleolaïs. The border, in relation to Caithness, is not merely convenient proximity to facilitate the encounter of William and his lost sons. There seems to be some echo of disputed property, or grant of lands. The queen, widow and heir of Gleolaïs, with Guillaume's consent, transfers the fief to the king of Caithness in gratitude for his care of her sons.[44] In accepting it, she alludes to long-standing claims to it, although the only cause of warfare in the story is his suit in marriage.[45] There are other references to territorial boundaries. When Guillaume disappears his kingdom is ruled by a nephew, who loyally regards himself as a deputy. Perceiving the likeness of the visiting trader to his lost uncle he begs the merchant, Gui, to stay at court as his seneschal. He would thus, he says, hold sway 'jusqu'a la u Tamise court et jusqu'a la u ele faut'. The earldom of Gloucester (or, as it was otherwise denominated, of Bristol) being held by Robert, half-brother of Empress Matilda, during the wars with Stephen, this would correspond to his sphere of influence.[46] The water the stag crosses, in the second hunting episode, is on the border-line of the fief of Sorlinc and the realm of Caithness.[47] The forest itself is subject to the forest laws, of which details are given.[48] The precise description of these feudal and royal enactments balances that already noted of the trading communities. The period of this poem is that of the rise of the 'royal burghs' of Scotland. May it be hazarded that 'Sorlinc' could represent Stirling?[49]

Many characters of the tale are unnamed—the merchant of Galloway and his sons, the king's nephew, the king of Caithness and the Bristol youth. Rodain, the 'squire', has a name which might correspond to that of a twelfth-century Northumberland family.[50] The names of the foster parents are appropriately commonplace. Therfes, the shipmaster, is, strangely, not rewarded as others are. On the whole the fullest description appears to be reserved for Gleolaïs, who receives family and territorial designation.

> Onques miudres ne fu Rollans.
> Or estoit si vix et crollans
> Que de lui n'estoit mais parole,
> Car del tot destruit et afole
> Biauté d'ome et force et proece
> Ancïenneté et viellece.

He sends for all the 'preudome' and 'chevalier' to do homage to his second wife, and heiress (Gratienne).

> Tot maintenant a court asamblent
> Tel gent qui moult mal s'entresamblent,
> Chevalier, serjant, jougleour,
> Et fauconier et veneour,
> Gent d'ordre, canoine demaïne.

A Scottish-Bristol combination would favour the Castle Cary Lovels, but the reference to the Thames Valley and Bury St Edmunds those of Minster Lovel (and Southmere). The cave at Yarmouth is made a place of special ceremony. The king waits there to receive the crown from his nephew:

> Quant li rois a la roce vint
> Le roi de Catanesse tint
> Par la main; et si li a dit
> Sire rois, veés ci le lit . . .

Perhaps some local natural feature in the locality of Yarmouth is made a basis for this detail of the tale. Pilgrims to Bury St Edmunds were numerous and important—notably Henry I to carry out a vow made in a storm at sea and John immediately after his coronation. One of the miracles of Saint Edmund describes a wolf guarding the lost 'relic', the Saint's head.[51] The 'book' of St Edmunds used by the author of *Guillaume d'Angleterre* seems to suggest itself as perhaps including a 'miracle of a wolf', possibly hinted at in the hagiographical writing which this abbey fostered.[52]

Finally, this despiser of merchants, by name Chrétien, who wrote this poem, must surely have had 'friends' among the knights, just as Lovel and Marin were 'compagnons'. From some such source he could have gained some of his oral information. The Rogiers li Cointes known to all 'prodome' may perhaps be looked for in such a quarter. Placing this *conte pieux* in such a context, it would become an early and incomplete example of what can be found later in *Gui de Warewic* and *Fulk Fitz Warin*.

NOTES

(1) *Chroniques Anglo-Normandes*, III, Rouen, 1840, "par Chrétien de Troyes". From a MS. containing *Cligès* and *Erec et Enide*.

(2) *Romania*, XXI, 139.

(3) *Romania*, LVII, 75–116. F. J. Tanquerey, *Chrétien de Troyes est-il l'auteur de* Guillaume d'Angleterre?

(4) *Christian von Troyes*, IV, Halle, 1899; 'Classiques français du moyen âge', *Romania*, XLVI, 1–38; *Chrétien de Troyes*, Paris, 1931.

(5) '*Guillaume* est un conte aristocratique, au même degré que *Cligès*, *Yvain* et *Lancelot*. Littérature de classe . . . mais ce qui distingue Chrétien . . . c'est l'importance doctrinale des thèses que cette notion de classe lui a inspirées' (Wilmotte, p. 8). '*Lancelot* et *Guillaume d'Angleterre* s'accordent en ceci du moins, qu'ils sont l'un et l'autre une étude de formes différentes de l'humilité: humilité courtoise dans un cas, monastique dans l'autre' (Nitzke, *Romania*, XLIV). 'Mais il a travaillé l'aventure qui, réservé son point de départ, n'a plus rien de religion' (Cohen, p. 108).

(6) 'Le Chrétien de *Guillaume d'Angleterre* me semble avoir été le Pierre Camus du XIIe siècle, comme Chrétien de Troyes a été son Honoré D'Urfé.' For arguments in full, see pp. 114–16. The aside 'mais s'appelait-il réellement Chrétien?' implies impersonation presumably. No criticism was as devastating as the brief comment of G. Paris: 's'il l'a écrit pour ses péchés, c'est pour les nôtres que nous le lisons'.

(7) 'Au fond ce n'est donc pas un conte pieux que *Guillaume d'Angleterre*, c'est un roman d'aventure. Förster a raison sur ce point, mais où il a tort c'est d'y voir un récit de la vieillesse de Chrétien et non, comme Wilmotte, une œuvre de jeunesse' (Cohen). '*Guillaume d'Angleterre* est par-dessus tout un conte moral' (Tanquerey, p. 89).

(8) Crestiiens se veut entremetre,   Por çou que plaisans est e voire,
Sans nient oster et sans nient metre,   On troveroit a Saint Esmoing;
De conter un conte par rime,   Se nus en demande tesmoing,
U consonant u lionime,   La le voise querre s'il veut.
Aussi com par ci le me taille;   Chrestiiens dist, qui dire seut,
Mais que par le conte s'en aille,   . . . (1–18).
Ja autre conte ne prendra,
La plus droite voie tenra   . . . .
Que il onques porra tenir,   Tex est de cest conte la fins.
Si que tost puist a fin venir.   Plus n'en sai, ne plus n'en i a.
Qui les estoires d'Engleterre   La matere si me conta,
Vauroit bien cerkier et enquerre,   Uns miens compains, Rogiers li
Une qui moult bien fait a croire,   Cointes,
                                     Qui de maint prodome est acointes.

(9) Müller; Wilmotte, pp. 17–19, 22–23, etc.; Tanquerey, pp. 79–82, etc.; Cohen, p. 101, etc. Apart from rhetorical ornament (e.g. 150–58; 3042–3045) the following passages may be noted. The courtiers ransack the palace (377–422); the king and the merchants (566–752); the Tantalus simile (903–927); the second party of merchants (955–984); the rich burgess of Galloway's service (988–1036); the queen's fate (1037–1325); the children's fate (1328–1945) and their fight with their father (2716–2773); trading at Bristol (1946–2264); the sea voyage (2265–2348); the harbour (2368–2509); entertainment at the castle (2516–2626); the chase (2621–2716); the comic merchants (3155–3220).

(10) Bezzola, *Romania*, LXVI, 40–4.

(11) Cf. St Bernard, *De laude novae militiae ad milites Templi*. Migne, *Pat. Lat.* 182, 926. The Order was recruited from adults.

(12) Cohen, p. 456.

(13) 'Il [Chrétien] recueille, quand il les trouve plaisants et riches, des récits, et il les mêle à ses propres inventions. . . . Chrétien de Troyes a certainement mêlé plus de religion qu'il n'a fait jusqu'alors à cette œuvre. . . . On ne peut pas, à cet égard, invoquer le début puisque la citation de Saint Paul sur la charité n'a pour but que d'exalter les vertus du comte Philippe d'Alsace. Mais on peut faire état des avertissements de la mère à son fils, etc. . . . c'est tout un tableau de la chevalerie, de ses usages, de sa doctrine' (Cohen).

(14) *Perceval*, 43–50.

(15) For the significance of the name of *Carta Caritatis* see Migne, *Pat. Lat.* See also Gilson, *Etudes de philosophie médiévale*, Paris, 1934, p. 95.

(16) The conduct and character of Gratienne are severely reprobated by the critics: Tanquerey (pp. 97–99), Cohen (pp. 99–100), Wilmotte (pp. 16–17).

(17) Gilson, *La philosophie au XIIe siècle*. Paris, 1922, p. 81.

(18) It can be noted that Guillaume wins esteem and becomes a successful trader and that Gratienne shows ability in getting and managing a fief. Tanquerey acidly remarks: 'Il semble beaucoup mieux à sa place comme domestique ou comme marchand que sur le trône.'

(19)   Et li rois avoit retenus
        Avoec li les fix as borgois;
        Et si lor promet comme rois
        Qu'il lor donroit castiax et tors. (3237)

        Ses fix fist andeus chevaliers
        Ses maria, ce dist li contes,
        As filles a deus rices contes
        Si furent andoi castelain. (3297)

Cf. Round, *Tower and Castle, Geoffrey de Mandeville*, 328–346.

(20) His status is not clear: the inference seems to be that a change of rank is reserved for the younger generation.

(21)   Du vallet fist son chambrelain
        Qui a le feste de Bristot
        Les deniers, que por le cor ot,
        Departi as povres por s'ame;
        Si li dona moult rice fame,
        Car de rente mil mars i prist. (3303)

This description and the details (2080–2112) are hardly accurately indicated by Tanquerey's disdainful comment: 'Même le valet qui avait volé le cor du roi reçoit sa récompense, on ne sait trop pourquoi' (p. 86).

(22) Tanquerey, p. 103: 'de petites habiletés'.

(23) Tanquerey, p. 102: 'un réalisme excellent, une description faite par quelqu'un qui connaît et aime la mer'.

(24) *Vie de Sainte Marguerite, La Conception Notre Dame, La Vie de Saint Nicolas.*

(25) *Vie de Sainte Marguerite*, XIII (E. A. Francis).

(26)   Angoisse ot moult, Dieu en apele
      Et la gloriouse pucele.
      Sainte Margerite reclaime;
      Tos sains et totes vergenes aime,
      Et tos les doute et tos les croit:
      Tous deprie, si qu'ele doit,
      Qu'il pricent por sa delivrance
      Dieu, qui de tot a le poissance. (464)

Förster punctuates with a comma after 'pucele' (458), Wilmotte with a full stop. F. Michel prints the text with inversion of lines 459–60, as in MS. *P*: as they are not in MS. *C*, Förster regarded them as interpolated in *P*.

(27)   'Glorïeuse Sainte Marie,
      Qui vostre fil et vostre pere
      Enfantastes, et fille et mere,
      Regardés, glorïeuse dame,
      De vos biax iex le vostre fame.' (500) (*Guillaume*)
      Saches que, por veir, peut hom dire . . .
      La fille est devenue li mere,
      Et devenus est fis li pere. . . .
      Jesus, cist non ço est sauviere:
      A sa mere ert et fis et pere. (*Notre Dame*)

(28) 2170, etc. Cf. *Jeu de Saint Nicolas* for help given by this saint in finding what is lost.

(29) See Cohen and Wilmotte, *passim*, and Tanquerey for recapitulation and criticism of points made by Wilmotte.

(30)   Il sont tot doi d'une façon;
      Et lor parole est tote une
      Que, se par lui oiiés cascune,
      Mais les enfants ne veïssiés,...
      Quant oïs les ariés andeus
      Que n'aroit parlé que uns seus;
      Et de si grant amor s'entraiment
      Por poi frere ne s'entreclaiment:
      De tex enfans est çou mervelle;
      Et li uns a l'autre conselle,
      Ne des autres enfans n'ont cure;
      Je cuic qu'il lor vient par nature,
      Et si croi que il les desdaignent,
      K'avoec aus nul n'en acompaignent.

(31) 1562–1642. Perhaps the opening of *Perceval* may be compared.

(32) 1462–94.   (33) 1743–63.

(34)   Mais trové i a une beste
Grant comme leus, et leus estoit.
A cele beste tenir voit
L'enfant en sa goule engoulé:
Es vos le roi moult adolé
Quant au leu vit l'enfant tenir.
Ne set que il puist devenir;
Si grant duel a, ne set qu'il face.
Li leus s'en fuit, et il le cace
Au plus isnelement que il puet;
Mais por nïent après se muet,
Que il ne le porra ataindre;
Mais por çou ne se vaut refraindre,
Ains s'esforce tant qu'il recroit
Et de son leu mie ne voit;
Ains se recroit en tel maniere
Que il ne puet avant n'arriere:
Si l'estuet dalés un rochier
Par force asseïr et couchier.
La s'endormi, la se coucha;
Et li leus, qui en sa boche a
L'enfant, nel quaisse ne ne blece;
Fuiant vers un cemin s'adrece ... (796)

(35)   Si l'escrïent et si le huent
Et bastons et pierres li ruent.
Tant que li leus en mi la voie
Lor a deguerpie la proie ...
Que tout sain et riant le voient;
Miracle i entendent et croient. (810)

(36) 'Ce curieux morceau ... intercalation assez baroque ici (il s'adresse à un loup ravisseur, non à la mort)', *Romania* (1914), p. 110.

(37) *The Complete Peerage*, 1937, p. 207.

(38) Ascelin Goel was son of the blessed Hildeburge and Robert d'Ivry: 'de Percival' also appears in references (cf. Round, p. 94, note).

(39) *Ordericus Vitalis*, IV, 343.   (40) Pipe Roll, 3 Richard I.

(41) *D.N.B.*: King William of Scotland, in 1165, confirmed a gift, by Margaret, which Henry Lovel ratified.

(42) 'Enfin l'exactitude très réelle de *Guillaume* est-elle une preuve qu'il est de Chrétien de Troyes? J'y verrais plutôt une forte présomption du contraire.' Other places mentioned are London, Winchester, Lincoln and York (or perhaps Warwick—MS. *P*, 'Wiric'), (Bury) St Edmunds.

(43) 'Einen Hafenort Sorlinc oder etwas ähnlich klingendes habe ich dort nicht gefunden. Jedenfalls sind es nicht die Scilly Inseln ... und franz. *Sorlingues* heissen. Auch andre ähnliche Namen wie Surlingham in Norfolk u. ä. müssen abgewiesen werden' (p. clxxxi).

(44)   Sire rois, et je vous merci
De mes deus fix moult hautement.
A cest premier mercïement

Avés vos sor moi conquesté
Çou dont j'ai lonc tans dame esté;
Mais tant i mec jou tote voie,
Se me sires li rois l'otroie . . .
Lors l'en ravest, et cil le prent.   (3106)

(45)   L'orgilleuse dame caitive,
Qui ja n'ara tant com jou vive
A moi pais, s'ele ne me prent
U se sa terre ne me rent.   (2918)

(46) Cf. Adams, *History of England*, p. 217, for the raids from Bristol in which the Lovels took part; also *Victoria County History* (Somerset), II, 180–3.

(47)   Sire, uns rois qui a moi marcist...
Cix bos est entre lui et moi...
D'une aige qui cest bos depart.

A legend of the Sinclair family associates grant of lands with a pursuit of a stag (*D.N.B.*).

(48)   Ains lor dist: 'Pris estes a mort;
Arrivé estes a mal port,
Par celi Dieu en cui je croi!
Je vos menrai devant le roi;
Si vos fera pendre u desfaire,
Les puins colper u les iex traire,
Por son dain que vos avés pris.'   (1843)

In the famous prosecutions of 1176 Henry Lovel was fined for infringement of forest law. A century later (1235), the keeper of Cheddar forest was ordered to allow H. de Candover and William Lovel to take all bucks and does which they could find, and the sheriff of Somerset was to cause all the venison to be salted.

(49) Some other versions of place-names found in the work of Chrétien de Troyes are the familiar Nicole (Lincoln), Cardeuil (? Carlisle), Cotoatre (Scotwater), Tenebroc (? Edinburgh). The proximity of Cambuskenneth might be suggested by a detail: Gleolaïs at the feast receives 'sa feme des mains un abé'. Rodain gets supplies at an abbey—perhaps the same.

(50) *History of Northumberland*, XIV, 281. Eleanor Roddam is said to have been wife to Robert Umfraville, 'Earl' of Angus, in 1184.

(51) *Vie de Seint Edmund*, Denis Piramus. Common features are the harmlessness of the animal to the object held (i.e. supernatural animal piety in the case of St Edmund) and the abandoning of the 'prey' when the animal is scared. Actual details of the texts do not suggest borrowing.

(52) Cf. Osbert of Clare. Abbot Anselm strove to obtain recognition of the Feast of the Conception. Wace's poem was a result of this movement. In this connection it may be remembered that St Margaret was specially venerated in East Anglia. St Margaret's, Lynn, and St Nicholas', Yarmouth, were both founded by Bishop Herbert Losinga of Norwich before 1119. Subsequently Bury St Edmunds became of chief importance.

A CONTEMPORARY DRAMATIST:
RENÉ BRUYEZ

BY

H. J. HUNT

Professor of French in the University of London
(Royal Holloway College)

IN setting down these impressions of a literary personality whose work has not as yet received the wide attention it deserves, I am put in mind of the Gidian paradox: 'J'estime que l'œuvre d'art accomplie sera celle qui passera d'abord inaperçue, qu'on ne remarquera même pas.' Certainly it has always been easier for the Pradons of literature than for the Racines to win immediate recognition from a public addicted to fashions and 'snobismes'. It is not for me to put forward extravagant claims on René Bruyez's behalf, though assuredly he runs no risk of being relegated to the Pradon category. Critics of such fine discernment as Henry Bidou and Gabriel Marcel have paid enthusiastic tribute to the distinction and originality of his conceptions. Their appreciations were addressed to French readers. In addressing mine to English ones, I am not so naïve as to suppose I can right a wrong or start a vogue. But I willingly testify to the intense interest and pleasure which the inspection of M. Bruyez's works has afforded to one who can claim to be little more than an arm-chair student of contemporary French drama.

M. Bruyez is the author of some sixteen dramatic pieces, most of them one-act plays, though three or four have attained the dimensions of full-blown dramas. By far the greater number of them have been performed, and with great success, though usually at experimental theatres or by 'irregular' companies. One play in particular, probably his greatest, has not only been produced in France, but has travelled also to the Antipodes: *Jeanne et la Vie des Autres* (1938). A great part of M. Bruyez's life has been spent in close connection with the theatre. For many years he assisted Charles Dullin as *secrétaire-général* at the Atelier Theatre. In 1934, with M. Pierre Aldebert, he conducted a French company of actors

77

to Italy to perform *Horace* and *Britannicus* in the Roman Forum: an interesting experience, that of submitting the patriotic Horatii, the vehement anti-totalitarian Camille and the sadistic Nero to the appraisal of that would-be 'antic Roman', Benito Mussolini. M. Bruyez has a flair for the production of great plays in novel but appropriate *décors*. As *commissaire-général* of the *section française* delegated to the World-Theatre Exhibition held at Frankfort in 1937, his glance fell on the Frankfort Town Hall as a suitable setting for *Le Cid*, and on a Rhine castle for *Les Burgraves*. Laval had already turned down, in 1936, as being too expensive, his idea of staging *Le Cid* in the Basilica at Burgos—M. Bruyez's quasi-ambassadorial missions involved him in frequent contact with the Fascist countries, as it was then still the official policy to cast pearls before swine in the hope that the latter might belie the proverb. In 1939 we find him busy organizing a performance of Racine in the arena of Nîmes for the Racine tercentenary; the onset of war brought all such schemes to an end.

It is not therefore surprising that, in his own theatrical compositions, René Bruyez should have shown a marked inclination for experiment. But the Bruyez with a pen in his hand is very different from the Bruyez devising spectacular *décors* for classical masterpieces. His meditations on new dramatic possibilities have led him, not to scenic flamboyancy, but to the mysterious hinterland of psychological and metaphysical experience. For this purpose he has usually chosen modern life as his field of investigation, though he has made an occasional sally into other ages and climes. His witty verse-play of 1926, *La Coqueluche des Précieuses*, stages a day in the life of Molière, and throws the budding genius into contact with a medley of social eccentrics who are very eager to provide him with 'copy' at the expense of friends and acquaintances, but unable to perceive that they themselves are sparing him the necessity of searching further. In his one-act tragedy of 1930, *Le Triomphe du Silence*, he migrates to ancient Hellas and, in *Jeanne et la Vie des Autres*, to fifteenth-century France.

But these are exceptions standing out against a more sober texture of milieu and subject. M. Bruyez has advanced along a trail first blazed by Marivaux and Alfred de Musset, the Musset who composed such 'proverbs' as *Un Caprice, Il faut qu'une porte soit ouverte ou fermée, On ne saurait penser à tout.* But, in harmony with an age which from Nerval to Proust and Giraudoux has pressed on ever further and further into the tangled undergrowth of human psychology, he has carried his investigations to the point where Freud and the other psycho-analysts come into the picture. At the same time his work remains agreeably free from those obsessions and systematizations to which psycho-analysts are normally prone. For, beside being sane and lucid (and clean), he is also a poet; something of a metaphysician to boot, and even something of a mystic, within those same limits of sanity and lucidity. When he probes into the troubled shadowland of the subconscious, it is not merely in order to seek explanations and rationalizations of mental disorder, but to find points of contact between psychic intuitions and suprasensible reality whose very existence remains unsuspected by the normal mind but is dimly perceptible to the victims of apparent mental aberration. That is why Villiers de l'Isle-Adam has occasionally been spoken of in connection with René Bruyez. Indeed the ideal world—*l'imaginaire*—evoked in particular in *L'Ève future* (livre VI, chapters vi–viii) is not without kinship with that hidden universe to which M. Bruyez often penetrates, though the latter can afford to dispense with the pseudo-scientific substructure on which Villiers de l'Isle-Adam found it necessary to build. M. Bruyez has more cogent justification for opposing 'les lumières du rêve aux ténèbres du sens commun'.

Maeterlinck has also been quoted as an evident precursor for M. Bruyez. But in the main Maeterlinck's dramas are fantasias, his creatures are symbols, tokens, not specimens of flesh-and-blood humanity. M. Bruyez is no symbolist, his fantastic creations emanate from the real. And lastly, in an effort to 'place' his curiously original work, we might be inclined to remember that, while Bruyez was writing many of his plays, Pirandello was rising to his zenith. Both authors discover dramatic possibilities in speculation on the subjective substratum in 'reality'; both are apt at propounding an enigma and leaving it unsolved. But the likeness is superficial. Pirandello's chief interest lay in a problem inherent in the concept of individuality: the inscrutability, perhaps the instability of the human person; or at any rate the disparity between the self as it is and the conflicting views which outside observers obtain of it.

79

M. Bruyez has quite different preoccupations. In attempting at the outset to suggest the drift of his thought and to convey the atmosphere with which his work is pervaded, I can scarcely do better than steal a sentence or two from M. Henry Bidou, who has summed up M. Bruyez's outlook in the following terms:

Derrière le glissement des phénomènes se meuvent les réalités véritables. Elles nous parlent le langage le plus usuel, et nous ne les comprenons pas. Elles se manifestent par des symptômes quotidiens et nous n'y prenons pas garde. Une infinie complexité de rouages relie notre âme à l'univers. Et ces rouages sont encore de notre âme. Dès qu'on y touche, nous sentons un ébranlement profond, une angoisse, une horreur sacrée. Dans les profondeurs du monde, ils déclenchent les destins. Dans le monde des apparences, ils produisent d'étranges fantômes et des réalités inexpliquées: des faits pareils à tous les autres, mais affectés . . . d'un indice de transcendance. C'est sur ces confins que vit René Bruyez, à demi ravi, à demi épouvanté.[1]

However, to peer too closely at this stage into the more abstruse aspects of M. Bruyez's dramatic creation would be to begin at the wrong end. It is the *marivaudesque* element which is the most prominent in the normal run of his plays—especially those in one act. I use the term as a rough means of classification, and not in order to suggest that M. Bruyez is, either consciously or unconsciously, a 'disciple' of Marivaux or Musset. A glance at the subjects he treats and the problems of psychology he investigates can easily demonstrate his independence of these authors, whose technique only bears some resemblance to his.

A few of M. Bruyez's plays I must leave in the shade—I have not been able to read all of them. They are among his earlier ones, though they are characteristic of his manner. *Crime rituel* (1910) examines a peculiar case of remorse—that of a man who, in complicity with a woman of stronger character than his own, has committed a murder. To prevent him from owning up when official suspicion has begun to fall on him, the woman probes into the circumstances of their common crime, and contrives to persuade him of his own innocence. The next two plays, *Le Père Ilote*[2] and *Le Sceptique ébloui*,[3] have more of a moral bearing. In the former, a father, mindful of the ancient Spartan method of disgusting young men with drunkenness by making them watch the antics of an intoxicated helot, plunges into vice in order to instil into his sons the love of virtue. In the second an atheistical and cynical priest is shaken in his scepticism by the example of noble disinterestedness shown him by a woman who has loved him; but once converted he is oppressed with the sense of his own unworthiness and seeks to doff the cassock he had not scrupled to use as a cloak for vice in his unregenerate days. The interest in curious psychological cases is already evident; it becomes still more so in such one-act plays as *Le double Simulacre*[4] (written in collaboration with Yvon Noë) and *Le Paradoxe de la Comédienne*.[5] The scene of *Le double Simulacre* is a masked ball, and its subject is the ingenious deceit of a woman who assumes the mask of a duenna and, to mystify an intrigued and already susceptible partner, enlarges on the theme of her own ugliness. The point is that she is in fact as ugly as sin, but has chosen the most subtle way of disguising the truth. *Le Paradoxe*, gleaning most profitably in a field which Diderot had incompletely harvested, treats the case of a mediocre actor who, by the very fact of playing the part of lover opposite an actress who is falling in love with him, casts the slough of his mediocrity and becomes quite an accomplished actor; and the woman in question admires his acting all the more in proportion as her infatuation for him increases.

This takes us to 1924. After the interlude of *La Coqueluche des Précieuses*,[6] M. Bruyez set to work on one of his most original plays, *La Puissance des Mots*,[7] which will claim special attention later on. But three admirable examples of M. Bruyez's own particular type of short comedy occur in *Il faut qu'une cage . . .*,[8] *Les Ténèbres de la Charité*,[9] and *Le Mur qui tombe*.[10] In the meantime he had produced two outstanding pieces, *Le Triomphe du Silence*,[11] and *Le Conditionnel passé*.[12] These two help to carry him to the summit of his performance; but the three one-act pieces just listed are first of all worth attentive study inasmuch as they reveal the essential quality of our author's subtle and penetrating insight into human motives and states of mind.

There are only two characters in *Il faut qu'une cage . . .*, Michel and Madeleine, a bachelor and a married woman of the same age, friends since childhood. Madeleine has a meanly unfaithful husband from whom she cannot succeed in detaching herself in spite of the humiliation in which she stands. To Michel, who has loved her from youth up, falls the equally torturing role of disinterested confidant and counsellor. Madeleine's indignation has reached a pitch at which she is ready to elope with Michel, who in fact has made all the necessary preparations for a flight to Guadeloupe. At the rise of the curtain, he is waiting for her in his flat. She arrives; and he realizes at once that Madeleine, 'si docile aux moindres influences', has already come to regret her decision; that the impulse to leave her husband is strong only at moments of intense exasperation and is as soon succeeded by the resolve to defeat the other woman. Mastering his own disappointment, Michel resumes his role of adviser: Madeleine's best chance, as he makes plain to her, is to afford her husband all facilities for flight with her rival and at the same time to give him in his turn apparent cause for suspicion and jealousy. Her visit to Michel's flat will admirably serve this purpose; and Michel's sole reward will be the innocent complicity which binds them together; in her husband's eyes, and in the world's eyes, Madeleine will be a guilty spouse, while Michel alone will know 'que nos lèvres ne se sont jamais jointes'. And the action of this little play shows the accomplishment of this design. Madeleine's husband is seen prowling round in the street below. He enters the house and takes the lift, which remains suspended in mid-air because Michel has adopted the simple device of opening the lift-door at his flat. When eventually the husband is released, he will find Madeleine gone and the flat empty; but his wife's scent will pervade the room. And this dénouement emphasizes the theme of the play and justifies its title. 'Tu vois', says Michel before showing Madeleine out by an alternative door,

Tu vois, Madeleine; c'est quand la cage est ouverte, que l'occupant de l'ascenseur y reste prisonnier. Qu'on la referme . . . il n'a plus qu'à déguerpir. . . . Tout être a le choix entre deux solutions: retenir de force celui qu'il aime et lui devenir odieux. Ou le rendre libre . . . soit en le laissant partir soit en se retirant lui-même. . . . Il faut qu'une cage . . .
    MADELEINE. Soit ouverte ou fermée.

By its title this excellent little play invites comparison with Musset's *Proverbes*. Each author gains and loses by the comparison. Musset is superior by the wit, the topical allusion, the incidental detail, the picturesqueness of touch and the scintillation of style which distinguish his work. Bruyez's sensitive handling of a long conversation between a nobly selfless lover and an involuntarily selfish woman is a model of discretion and discernment; and the action of the play, so completely interior, is at once ethereal and solid: it rests on Michel's ability, born of sympathy and strength, and supported by an acute assessment of Madeleine's every word, gesture and intonation, to pierce through to her inmost soul and to make tactfully but irrevocably the only decision worthy of an *honnête homme*.

The note of delicate sadness predominant in *Il faut qu'une cage...* is intensified to tragedy in *Les Ténèbres de la Charité*; and in it he returns to that contemplation of religious fervour which had already prompted *Le Sceptique ébloui* and which perhaps bespeaks the persistence of religious questionings, of unresolved misgivings, within his own *for intérieur* A man of thirty, André, is in hospital recovering from an attempt at suicide prompted by two motives: a war-wound (the date of the action is 1924) which has necessitated a trepanning operation and left him the victim of intolerable headaches; and a personal tragedy which has left him without the zest for life: he had been reported killed during the war, and his young fiancée, Violine, had taken the veil as Sœur Élisabeth de Jésus.

Leave from her superior to visit her mother brings Sœur Élisabeth to Paris just at the time of André's attempted suicide. Learning of this with horror, she takes it upon herself, without authorization, to go to André's bed-side, certain that she alone can extract from him the promise never again to attempt his own life. The play stages their interview. During the first moments Violine is chiefly concerned to make the desperate but lucid André respect the fact that she is now *another person* than the one he knew, the nun consecrated to God. But in the spiritual struggle she has with him she realizes that he has weapons strong enough to force her from the position she had thought impregnable. She discovers (and appropriates) a phial of poison concealed under his mattress, thus becoming aware that he still contemplates suicide. A new onset of the intolerable headaches, and André's obduracy in wishing for death, force her to a terrible decision: she will mix the poison with a sedative, administer it to him, and so kill him to save his soul. For this purpose it is imperative that he shall die reconciled with life: hence apparent capitulation on her part—the admission that she came to him, not out of charity or pity, but out of love for him, that Sœur Élisabeth de Jésus is after all Violine.

The study of the woman is more searching and sustained than that of the man: it is indeed an analysis of the obscure subconscious motives prompting an act of charity which is at once sublime and appalling. Before revisiting André, Violine believes she has attained stability and serenity. She has committed her breach of religious discipline in complete lucidity of determination:

> J'accepte toutes les conséquences d'une telle démarche. La question n'est pas, pour moi, de savoir si je compromets mon salut, mais si je suis en mesure de sauvegarder celui d'une âme en péril. Que le péché souille la mienne, qui aura toute la vie de la terre pour faire pénitence; puissé-je encourir toutes les disgrâces, même spirituelles; puissé-je vivre pécheresse plutôt que d'apprendre un jour que celui qui reçut en même temps que moi-même la divine Eucharistie, plutôt que d'apprendre que celui-là s'est damné!

By the end of the play this self-possession is gone. Her anxiety to save her former lover from the blasphemy of self-slaughter drives her from concession to concession: she will not leave his bed-side, she gives up her nun's nuptial ring, she consents to apply for annulment of her vows. In his dying moments André divines the atrocious act she has committed, and, threatening to forestall its effects by instant suicide, makes her confess that all she has done has been for love of him, and not out of zeal for his soul. And as she does so she becomes aware that it is not a charitable lie, but the truth that is being forced out of her. So the *De Profundis* she utters over his corpse is as much for herself as for him. And the play closes with the resurgent Violine trying to convince herself that she is still Sœur Élisabeth de Jésus:

> Je m'en retourne vers vous, Seigneur . . . Seigneur! Éclairez-moi. Non! Non! . . . Je ne sais pas . . . Je ne sais plus qui je suis! . . . Je . . . Je ne veux pas savoir! (*elle a fait un pas en arrière et, reculant vers la porte, répète avec ferveur et sans arrêt comme pour s'étourdir l'âme*) Je suis la servante du Seigneur! Je suis la servante du Seigneur! Je suis la servante du Seigneur!

Le Mur qui tombe brings us back to more mundane regions, but is no less delicate in its psychological probings. A woman just widowed, Pauline de Gastel, is unable to find even the consolation of tears and conventional gestures in mourning her husband, for in his life-time she had sensed an intrigue between him and another woman. Pride and the fear of driving him from secret disloyalty to despicable prevarication had prevented her from taxing him with infidelity; and so suspicion had poisoned her conjugal life and now adds bitterness to her grief. An old friend, Georges Anceiet, comes to visit her; his sympathy and discernment break down Pauline's reserve and he learns the cause of her bitterness. He is able to dispel her doubts and convince her she has wronged her husband, by revealing that it was he himself who had been the lover of the woman in question. The purpose of his visit is in fact to recover the letters he had written to this woman and which he had entrusted to Pauline's husband for safe keeping. Pauline's mind is set at rest, for suspicion of her husband is now replaced by a more bearable feeling—that of grief for happiness irretrievably lost. The plot, as always with M. Bruyez, is of the simplest, but the working-out of it is extremely clever. As is the case with *Il faut qu'une cage . . .* a conversation between a cultured and sensitive man and woman becomes a sort of subtle duel whose thrust and parry is an exchange of thoughts and reticences which make a wholly interior action both palpable and dramatically tense. But all risk of dullness is conjured away by the knack our author has of working his action up to a material and tangible climax. In this case his dénouement has an almost sardonic twist. Having obtained possession of the casket in which his love-letters had been stored, Anceiet finds that it has other and unsuspected contents—letters which his erstwhile mistress had written to the husband, who had thus betrayed both his wife and his best friend. Mercifully, Anceiet leaves Pauline happy in her illusion.

Discussion of these shorter plays should have served to give an idea of a technique which M. Bruyez has used to even better purpose in his longer ones, in which his psychology takes on a metaphysical quality and lifts his drama on to a truly poetical plane. *La Puissance des Mots*[13] has not the unilinear simplicity of the plays considered above. It has been qualified by M. Henry Bidou as a 'drame cérébral'; both as a drama and as an investigation into the mental activity of an abnormal man (a painter and novelist of high quality) it is of the closest and most complex texture. Here more than anywhere up to this date, M. Bruyez probes into the no-man's-land which stretches between the conscious and the subconscious—as one critic has said, with perhaps a note of unjustified disparagement, 'M. Bruyez ouvre des personnages morbides pour découvrir les secrets de la nature'. As a metaphysician, he carries his inquiry further and examines the relation between the imaginary and the real, between illusion and fact; and because he is himself an artist, a draughtsman and sculptor as well as a writer, the metaphysical problem is also, quite naturally, an aesthetic one.

The psychopathic case is that of the artist Raymond Daryelles, estranged from his wife Clothilde not (at first), as she thinks, because he is enamoured of a woman within their family circle, Hélène Paquelet, but because his paintings reveal an obstinate effort to imprison on canvas a certain 'blonde éclatante' with amethyst eyes. Taxed with positive infidelity, he lies to divert suspicion from Hélène; but the woman about whom he begins to weave circumstantial details is still the ideal which haunts his imagination. To banish this illusion, he does actually make the reluctant Hélène his mistress, but to no avail. A friend, Griseville, tumbles to the truth and tries to persuade him of the unreality of the vision. Daryelles obstinately refuses to yield. Eventually the re-appearance of a boyhood friend, the blind Noël Aveline, awakens his memory to a fact long forgotten: the remarkable eyes of Noël's mother with which he had been fascinated when a boy, and which had set him on this striving to reveal them in painting, and, later, to achieve by the medium of his art the total person with whose lines and colouring these eyes should be consonant. But he is not cured by this discovery; his reverie, at once aesthetic and erotic, lingers on in exasperated contemplation of his dream.

M. Bruyez's aesthetic theory is bound up with these data, and reposes on the fact that artistic vision, however ideal, is never entirely a fiction. It has its point of departure, however unconsciously so, in something really perceived. It leads to—or strives vainly for—the fixation of that ideal in a representation—in this case a portrait, which Daryelles had attempted some ten years before: 'le Visage de l'Idéal'. A portrait without model, one would say: a portrait, as Daryelles would maintain, not without model, but *anterior* to the model. And it is here that René Bruyez's metaphysical inquietude steps in—does not in fact this insistent dream evoke, may it not *create*, the reality after which it was striving? Is nature docile to that extent? At the end of the play the former Mme Aveline's daughter by a second marriage, Gisèle Courtin, stands on the threshold of the Daryelles salon. Raymond will not be allowed to see her; but his son Georges recognizes in her the living incarnation of his father's dream.

Envisaged afresh from the aesthetic angle, but this time in the literary rather than the pictorial sphere, the same problem is embodied in the title of the play—*La Puissance des Mots*: the power with which words are endowed (*car le Mot c'est le Verbe* . . .), when communicated through the living resonance of a remembered voice, may also be evocative and creative. It is certain that, *retrogressively*, 'les mots font vivre les êtres dont ils parlent'.

> Tu as quarante-quatre ans [says Raymond Daryelles to the sceptical Noyselin].[14] Tu dois bien accueillir, parfois, le souvenir inattendu de quelque événement. . . .
>
> NOYSELIN, *avec une condescendance souriante.*—Si ça peut te faire plaisir.
>
> CLOTHILDE, *à Raymond.*—'De quelque événement' . . . sentimental?
>
> RAYMOND, *à Clothilde.*—Si tu veux. Par exemple. (*A Noyselin*) Eh bien! Au cours d'une telle évocation, quand des guillemets s'ouvrent tout à coup dans ta mémoire et que des fragments de confidences parlées . . . des lambeaux de phrases vivantes surgissent . . . Est-ce que cet 'événement sentimental,' ta tendresse, ton désir ne ressuscitent pas? Quand tu te rappelles ce que ta maîtresse et toi vous avez *fait*, tu es ému! Mais est-ce que tu n'es pas autrement bouleversé au souvenir de ce qui a été dit, au soudain écho des paroles entendues? Entendues il y a longtemps, et qui. . . .

And perhaps *progressively* as well. A phrase or two recalling Raymond's youth sets in train the process by which he conjures up a physiognomy, a head, a torso and a whole figure from the unconscious memory of the 'amethyst eyes'. As he broods on this, at various moments in the course of the action, his word-pictures gain in precision. The woman's voice, perceptible only in sleep, as rich in reverberation as the note of a piano, provokes a luminous vision. And again, though Raymond does not know it, this vision is realized in Gisèle.

Such are the unaccustomed regions in which René Bruyez's imagination wanders. It must be admitted that this is metaphysical phantasy, not metaphysical thought. Bruyez is of the great throng of subjective idealists, but his idealism goes no farther than suggesting strange possibilities, and builds no system. This is all the more favourable to artistic creation; and *La Puissance des Mots* is indeed an artistic creation. But the subtlety of his ideas, and the psychological exchanges between the characters moving in the limited Daryelles circle (normal themselves with the exception of the central one, though conscious and articulate *à souhait*), do not make the play easy reading. M. Bruyez himself avers that the play gains—and did gain—by representation on the stage, and the general acclamation of critics in 1928 strengthens that contention. Another difficulty which renders the most attentive reading necessary is the author's tendency to weave many threads together. The analysis I have given of the plot is over-simplified to the point of crudeness. There are subsidiary financial interests, and amorous entanglements which are perhaps too discreetly handled are hinted at rather than plainly stated, and in fact only become clear as the action reaches its dénouement. One of them is the incipient love-affair between Raymond and Hélène which only takes shape thanks to the suggestion which the anxious Clothilde involuntarily puts into her husband's mind—yet another instance of 'la puissance des mots'. The secondary characters are shown in penumbra rather than limelight—hence no doubt the necessity for that preliminary assessment of their potentialities which is set forth in the initial pages of the printed play. But the main characters—Raymond, Clothilde, Hélène and Georges—achieve greater firmness and distinctness as the play proceeds. M. Bruyez has the quality— which in certain circumstances and subjects may be a strength, in others a weakness—of moving gradually from indeterminate complexity through half-light to clarity and simplicity. His psychology is a gradation.

So is his action. It moves slowly at first, even imperceptibly. Then it gets under way and reaches moments of increasing dramatic tension. The rise of dramatic temperature is plainly sensible in the second act. In the third act, within the limits of M. Bruyez's essentially classical mode and consistently with the interior nature of his action, the region of the *sensational* is reached: Clothilde's restrained bitterness at the end of the first tableau of this act; the incurability of Raymond symbolized by the piano incident in the first and second scenes of the second tableau;[15] and, in the second and third scenes, Clothilde's vehement repetition '*Je la tuerai!*' as her conviction that she really has a flesh-and-blood rival grows in force. In the succeeding and final tableau the action gains more and more momentum until it finds its climax in the closing scene, when the mysterious Gisèle stands at the door and the reader (also, no doubt, the spectator) shares the almost hysterical anxiety of Georges to keep her from his father's view.

It is with regard to *La Puissance des Mots* (as later in *Le Conditionnel passé*) that the affinity of outlook between Villiers de l'Isle-Adam and René Bruyez leaps to the eye, for the evolution of the real from the imaginary is the essential theme of *L'Ève future* as it is of the drama in question; and Daryelles's 'blonde radieuse' is virtually materialized in Gisèle Courtin as Edison's Hadaly is materialized in the 'replica' of Alycia Clary—with this difference that M. Bruyez is content to *suggest* the miraculous objectification and in truth leaves the basis of rationality intact, whereas Villiers de l'Isle-Adam throws verisimilitude to the four winds from the start. M. Bruyez's subsequent speculation with regard to the *femme idéale*, or rather the masculine myth of the *femme idéale*, transports him to ancient Thebes and inspires *Le Triomphe du Silence*, with its epigraph borrowed from Paul Gauguin, and addressed to the opposite sex *in toto*: 'Soyez mystérieuses.'

Is Bruyez the first in poetry to have voiced curiosity about the nature and meaning of the Sphinx and the gist of its (or her) colloquy with Œdipus? He was certainly four years ahead of Jean Cocteau, who developed this almost virgin theme in *La Machine Infernale*. The bare legend tells how a monster, half human, half animal, propounds a riddle which seems elementary to those who know the answer. No doubt a bright child could guess it. And Œdipus was a bright young man. But the legend also tells of a large number of unsuccessful candidates before him. All of them cannot have been fools. Why did they fail? The answer is: destiny. And the narrator can proceed with the rest of the story. But it needs a Frenchman's turn of mind to enquire how that destiny is worked out in terms of human psychology, and a Frenchman's ingenuity to discern in it a battle of the sexes. Before Cocteau, Bruyez stages this episode as a duel of wits: a semi-amorous duel in which each combatant wields the rapier of a curiosity half sexual and half metaphysical. Œdipus is a young and handsome man whose dangerous enterprise has already won him the tender pity of a Theban maiden, Eunaïka; the Sphinx is three parts woman, with her consciousness as yet unawakened to anything but the necessity for carrying out her sinister mission. Œdipus is only moderately interested in the reward which victory will bring him—the hand of Jocasta and the throne of Thebes. Relying on his Grecian subtlety, but not over-sanguine about his ability to solve a riddle which has baffled so many others, he embarks upon the fateful interview with a two-fold subterfuge: he pretends to a clairvoyance which makes the riddle and its answer a matter of slight moment:

Ne dis rien. C'est mieux. La seule chance que tu aies de me demeurer mystérieuse, c'est de te taire . . . Prononce un seul mot et tu te livres. Propose-moi cette fameuse énigme et ta voix même m'en dicte la solution . . . A supposer que j'aie besoin que tu me le dictes.

And he feigns, then feels genuinely, an interest in this enigmatic monster which becomes intensified into desire, and finally love. 'Tu es étrange. Et belle.' He has known many women, and is weary of finding in each one of them a replica of the species. The Sphinx is unique.

Tu es belle. Surtout, tu es seule! C'est pourquoi je te donne cette curiosité que nulle femme de la Terre n'aura plus de moi.
Que si l'on cesse d'en regarder une première, l'on peut apprécier chez la seconde un galbe plus exact, un aspect plus harmonieux.
Mais sous un extérieur qui varie à peine, de l'une à l'autre, n'est-ce pas toujours le même système qui règne? Car enfin, qu'est-ce que la beauté humaine, sinon *le masque de l'Espèce* (un masque susceptible de prêter à l'Etre un prestige d'exception . . .). La femme qui se pare et se peint le visage ne cherche-t-elle pas ainsi à répudier l'Espèce? A mentir . . .
Or, te voilà belle, toi, sans mensonge; énigmatique sans artifice!

The Sphinx herself, doomed to devour or perish, is grimly self-assured at first, then intrigued, then impatient, then alarmed. Once she has propounded the riddle, Œdipus adopts the tactics of bluff: he claims to know the answer, but is in no hurry to tell it; he is all-absorbed in contemplation of this strange creature, and subject to surges of sensuality in which the incest-complex can already be discerned. When this bluff is worn threadbare, he covers it with a double bluff: to be victorious, to return to a world where every woman is the same woman, is a dreary prospect.

Femelle unique et pourtant humaine! . . . Après tant de femmes, toutes semblables, voici donc enfin le monstre resplendissant! Oui. Et je n'ai plus qu'un désir. Celui d'être contenu en toi, mais à jamais: comme en un sarcophage . . . Dévore ma chair, ô Sphinge; contiens-la . . . Je n'ai pas deviné.'

Reduced to an anguish of uncertainty, the Sphinx unwittingly leads Œdipus to the threshold of discovery, and the answer to the riddle at last flashes across his mind.

The duel is over. Œdipus gloats an instant over the success of his stratagem, but is caught in the toils of his own ruse. He would arrest the hand of Fate, and preserve for himself this unforgettable being who has found a soul through his cajolery and perfidy. But her destiny is fixed. Already an inert mass of blood, flesh and scales lies at the foot of the cliff . . . Only the fading voice comes to him of her who was his enemy and is now his love, who, pacified and aloof, forgives him his unworthy triumph, and, with a tenderness free from irony, shows him that the real victory is hers: by silence he has conquered her, by silence she will conquer him.

. . . Je te possède à jamais, Œdipe! C'est *moi* que tu chercheras désormais, sur les créatures de la terre. Tu ne vécus que pour rencontrer un jour une femelle en dehors de l'espèce. La grâce t'en a été accordée. Aussi vas-tu vivre dans l'irréductible nostalgie de l'Idéal entrevu. Ton investigation sera vaine. Mais tu la poursuivras. C'est ainsi que tes paumes chercheront, entre les muscles polis des Thébaines, la cuirasse naguère bruissante de mes écailles et, dans leurs yeux, candides ou pervers, mes prunelles à moi, qui sont entrées dans les tiennes et qui, allumées à jamais au fond de la mémoire, vont se mettre à veiller ta vie.

ŒDIPE. Ma Sphinge!

LA VOIX DE LA SPHINGE. Tous les êtres ne cherchent-ils pas sur les autres êtres le reflet de ce qui leur manque?—Ne t'enorgueillis pas, Œdipe, d'avoir conquis la reine de Thèbes. Tu ne seras jamais que son Laïus. Elle ne sera jamais que ta Sphinge.—Vous êtes veufs tous les deux!

ŒDIPE. Ton spectre ne désertera pas ma vie!

LA VOIX DE LA SPHINGE. Je te manquerai d'autant plus. Et qui sait si les Immortels, afin que la Terre ne soit point une distraction susceptible d'effacer en toi mon souvenir, ne fermeront un jour tes paupières au soleil?

The terrible secret of Œdipus's birth is already becoming plain to this discarnate spirit, but, as will be the case with the ghost of Cocteau's Laïus, her voice is withdrawn before it can be divulged. Desolate, Œdipus turns away. He would take the road back to Corinth were it not for the Thebans who come to acclaim his triumph and lead him away to their city—and to Jocasta, in whose eyes he at the last moment remembers that he had discerned, at a first encounter, a strange look which now reminds him of the Sphinx's eyes . . . 'ne dirait-on pas de ces prunelles humaines, ne dirait-on pas des prunelles de Jocaste qu'elles enferment, elles aussi, un secret?'

A very arresting evocation this, in which the Hellenic 'colour' goes deeper than the mere use of names like Eunaïka and Agarix. None the less, M. Bruyez's preoccupation is not with antiquity, but with the material the myth provides for the study of the 'Œdipus-complex'; and, not less perhaps, with the disquieting problem about the part the human soul may be deemed to play in helping destiny to its chosen ends. It is a problem which reappears in what are to me his two greatest plays: *Le Conditionnel passé* and *Jeanne et la Vie des Autres*.

The first act of *Le Conditionnel passé* is set in a *pensionnat de jeunes filles* at Parthenay. Mme Darsenne, a widow and mother of two children, has brought her daughter Blanche, aged seven, to board there, and is recommending her to the care of Mme Neveu, the *directrice*. The war of 1914 has been in progress for a few weeks. Although she does not yet know it, Mme Neveu has already lost her son Marcel, Blanche's 'grand ami' who had given her her favourite doll; Mme Darsenne is about to lose her son Michel. Blanche is a sensitive and impressionable child, suspected of abnormal religious devotion, since she has been detected buying a votive candle and offering it to Notre-Dame des Victoires. She has had an indulgent father; she has a selfish mother. Mme Neveu is kind, but capable of testy reprimands. 'Comment tiens-tu ta poupée, toi?' she says to Blanche, impatient at seeing her holding her doll horizontally all the time. 'Une poupée qui ferme les yeux n'est pas faite pour dormir tout le temps. Mets-la un peu debout; qu'elle se réveille! Ces yeux fermés, depuis un quart d'heure, ça t'amuse? Allons, ne pleure pas.' Blanche is grave and quiet, and asks timid questions about the war when she hears the grown-up women talking of the soldiers who will not return from it. 'C'est sûr, qu'il reviendra, mon grand ami, Marcel?'

In the second act, the scene is laid in the manor of Kerlen, overlooking the Breton coast. Blanche, now nineteen years old, is brought there by her fiancé Paul to be presented to the *châtelaine*, his aunt, the Baronne de Kerlen, a widow who has lost two sons, Raphaël and Lucien de Kerlen, in naval action during the recent war. Though their portraits are kept in full view in the Kerlen salon, it is an understood thing that no one refers to the war or to her sons in the Baronne's hearing; and the most tragic fact of all, that Raphaël's ship had been sunk just off the coast at Kerlen, has been kept from her. Blanche is kindly welcomed, but finds herself plunged into an eerie atmosphere. Paul de Kerlen, a gay and somewhat unreflecting young man, has been taking her round the neighbourhood, showing her sinister spots and apprising her of the grim legends connected with them. She is warned not to allude to the Baronne's sons. She learns that the local bishop, Mgr Gréjean, forms a link between Kerlen and her own childhood, for he is none other than the former chaplain of her old school at Parthenay. She discovers that the Baronne is reluctant even to talk of her dead husband, an amateur painter whose landscapes and portraits are hung round the salon. The manor itself makes an indefinable impression on her; the paintings of the late Baron interest her, and her glance repeatedly turns to the defunct Raphaël's portrait in spite of Paul's efforts to distract her attention from it.

Mgr Gréjean arrives and converses with Paul of local superstitions; and Blanche timidly admits that she too is superstitious. Is it a venial sin, she asks, to attribute 'certains malheurs à quelque mauvaise action qu'on a soi-même commise'? She also relates how, three years before, she had consulted a palmist, who had 'read' in her hand the Christian name of the man she was to marry. She hesitates to reveal this name. 'Vous ne vous appelez pas que Paul?' she asks her fiancé. 'Paul, Claude, Robert, Jacques, Raphaël de Kerlen', he replies. 'Robert, Jacques, Raphaël', she repeats musingly . . .—'Raphaël'. As in a trance she is automatically reiterating this name when the Baronne re-enters the salon, and Paul hastily informs her that the Baronne's eldest son was called Raphaël.

A philosophical discussion arises between Paul and Mgr Gréjean over the case of a friend of the Baronne who, at a turning-point in her life, had taken a decision which had led her to an unbroken series of misfortunes, when happiness was hers for the grasping if she had chosen a different course. Confronted with this mystery, the bishop offers the pious and orthodox explanation: 'Les événements qui ne se sont pas produits, ce sont ceux que la Providence n'a pas cru devoir permettre.' But he recalls the theory of a free-thinking youth he had known at school. 'La destinée . . . disait-il, à de certains moments, bifurque. De même que, selon l'Église, nous choisissons sans cesse entre le bien et le mal, nous optons, en toutes circonstances selon notre philosophe, entre plusieurs destins.' 'Somme toute', comments Paul a moment later, 'votre ami comparait l'homme au mécanicien d'une locomotive, qui, à la différence des mécaniciens de locomotive, ferait prendre lui-même à son engin la direction voulue.' The discussion continues in spite of the bishop's efforts to close it. Blanche listens, and ponders on the bishop's truism: 'Il est incontestable que notre vie actuelle est un ensemble de conséquences différentes de celles que nous aurions déterminées si nous avions agi autrement que nous n'avons fait.' She dwells on the idea of 'le mal . . . que nous aurions pu ne pas commettre', and Mgr Gréjean detects in her an excess of scrupulosity which he regards as disquieting. 'Il faudra que je vous voie, vous', he says smilingly: 'vos yeux, vos regards, ne sont pas de ceux qui se fixent sur la réalité des choses.'

The motive for Blanche's scruples is explained in the next scene, when Blanche and Paul are alone together, the former still turning her gaze instinctively to the portrait of Raphaël de Kerlen. She confesses a 'crime' of her childhood. At seven years of age, after her father's death, her unsympathetic mother had been on the point of sending her away to live with an aunt at Épinal, a prospect which had filled the child with horror. The outbreak of war alone could frustrate her mother's plan. Blanche hoped for war, and rejoiced when it came:

> La guerre: ça a été pour moi la délivrance! J'ai cru que la Sainte Vierge ne l'avait permise, la guerre, que pour me protéger! J'ai consacré mes économies à l'achat d'un cierge, pour la remercier. Vous ne croiriez pas cela! Ma mère l'a su, que j'avais acheté un cierge. Elle a supposé que j'étais heureuse d'entrer dans une pension de la ville. Mais que je fusse heureuse qu'il y ait la guerre, qui s'en serait douté?

Then, to her ecstasy of joy had succeeded a realization of what war involved. Her brother had been killed, with a host of his and her friends. In her sense of guilt and remorse she tried to avoid making her first communion, but the abbé Gréjean had brushed aside her scruples:

> Il y a une chose abominable et qui, depuis, me hante: le souvenir de cette messe, à l'issue de laquelle des dames sont venues m'embrasser. . . . Ces mères en deuil de leurs fils, pour la plupart, et dont le crêpe enveloppait ma mousseline blanche, à moi; à moi qui, peut-être, avais porté malheur à leurs enfants, à moi, qui m'étais réjouie de la guerre! Pendant deux ou trois ans, j'ai rêvé d'une communiante toute blanche, environnée d'une quantité de mères toutes noires! . . . Il m'arrive encore d'en rêver! . . .

Paul is disturbed, but he has neither the understanding nor the opportunity to set her mind at rest; he urges her to forget. Then, from Yvonne, the old servant of the manor, Blanche learns more of Raphaël and Lucien, that they too had fallen in the war. Her distraction becomes complete. She moves and talks like a sleepwalker. She goes upstairs to her bedroom, murmuring: 'C'est ici que j'aurais dû vivre' as she looks round the place. It is a long time before she reappears. Paul gets anxious and goes up to her room to find her. She had been standing on the balcony watching the sea.

Act III represents M. Bruyez's most inspired venture into the realm of the phantasmagoric. The scene is laid in Blanche's bedroom, where, at the beginning, in the flicker of a bedside candle, she can be seen lying in fitful slumber. Outside a wild storm is raging, and at sea ships' sirens are heard wailing. The nightmare through which Blanche is passing gradually takes shape before the spectators' eyes. Gréjean and the Baronne first appear, then other figures: young men killed in the war—Raphaël and Lucien de Kerlen, Blanche's brother Michel, her 'grand ami' Marcel Neveu. Blanche is seen in her wedding-dress, and Gréjean has come to bless her nuptials with Raphaël. For the 'conditionnel passé', on which conversation had turned in the Kerlen salon during the previous day, has become the real past in Blanche's dream. In words and phrases that surge up from that conversation, Raphaël and his companions rejoice that the war which might have been has been conjured away as by a miracle; instead, it is their death and Blanche's engagement to Paul (who also figures in the dream) that belong to the 'conditionnel passé'. Blanche and Raphaël pronounce their marriage vows.

The vision changes. The domestic candle has turned into a baptismal 'cierge'. Around Blanche's bed are gathered the same ghostly crowd, this time to witness the christening of Blanche's and Raphaël's child. This new ceremony is accomplished; and now begins a sort of conflict between the two 'cauchemars'—the one during which, according to Raphaël, Blanche had stood before his portrait to contemplate the picture of the man she should have married, but whom her childhood wish had eliminated; and the nightmare through which, according to Paul, Blanche is passing even at that moment. Or rather, the waking reality gradually prevails over the hallucination of sleep. The child of Raphaël and Blanche, reverting to the 'might-have-been', becomes identified with the doll which, twelve years before, Marcel Neveu had given to the little girl; the doll whose eyes Blanche had kept closed. Mme Neveu appears among the group: 'Une poupée qui ferme les yeux est également faite pour les ouvrir! Les yeux clos, ça t'amuse? Si tu le mettais un peu debout, ton enfant... Allons, ne pleure pas...' The voices which formerly had been gentle and joyously affectionate take on inexorably accusing tones as Raphaël and his fellow-ghosts recede into the world of shadows. The baptismal candle is now a votive taper held in the hand of the seven-year-old

Blanche. 'Le cierge de la guerre!' cries the Baronne. 'De la guerre qui a tué mes fils, comme la tempête va tuer ton cierge.' In the final stages of the nightmare, only the figure of Paul remains. 'N'aie pas peur, petite Blanche ... C'est Paul qui est là. C'est de Paul que tu auras un enfant ...' He advances to embrace her. She retreats before him in horror—out on to the balcony ... And over it into the sea, as, 'souriant et muet', he presses towards her. The last wail of a siren is heard, and blackness falls.

In the last scene, the curtain rises again on Blanche's now empty room; the storm has subsided, morning has come. From the adjoining bedroom, which is the Baronne's, aunt and nephew, in happy mood, all unaware of the horrible discovery which awaits them, are heard calling to Blanche to wake up. Paul is heard drawing the curtains in his aunt's room. 'Il fait un temps splendide', he cries. 'Plus une trace d'écume sur la mer. (*Se retournant, sans doute, vers la baronne, il résume avec enthousiasme son impression*) ... Un soleil!'

In despair of achieving a satisfactory analysis of *Le Conditionnel passé*, a veritable model of simplicity in complexity, I have been driven to offer a summary of the plot. But neither analysis nor summary can give an adequate notion of the finished artistry that has gone to the making of this undoubted chef-d'œuvre. In all M. Bruyez's major plays there is a remarkably delicate intricacy of pattern. But this play has something truly symphonic in the inter-weaving of its themes and the recurrence of its motifs. The steady accumulation from act to act of suggestions and influences which bring Blanche's sense of guilt to a climax and strain her sanity to the breaking-point, the building-up of her weird and appalling night-mare from the ingredients furnished by incidents and conversations of the previous day, and the skill with which the author communi-cates to his audience the *frisson* of the supernatural: all this reveals an exquisite craftsmanship which I do not think M. Bruyez has surpassed elsewhere.

Judged from the positive point of view, *Le Conditionnel passé* is a penetrating study of an ingrown obsession which has never been 'rationalized' and so brings its victim to a tragic death. Viewed from a more imaginative angle, it is a subtle and disturbing meditation on the problem of individual responsibility, on the possible power which lies within each one of us to 'déclencher les destins' for good or ill. There are few of us who have not, at some moment in our lives, had the intuition of a mysterious connection between our acts and volitions and the general shape of things or trend of events. Is this impression a relic of primitive irrationalism or the dim perception of a reality more profound than the reality which is measurable by science and common sense? Can our puny acts do more than raise a local ripple on the vast waters of the universe? Or is it conceivable that in certain conjunctures this ripple may provoke a cataclysm? The admission of this even as a mere possibility does not make for bovine tranquillity.

Yet there is a brighter side to the problem. 'Nous sommes les artisans de ce que la Providence a permis', says Paul de Kerlen summing up the thought of Mgr Gréjean. But if we are free—and we must be free if responsibility comes into the question at all—we can be more than the passive instruments of Providence. We may frame our purposes and concert our actions in such wise that the natural determinism of cause and effect may be harnessed, so to speak, to high and ineffable ends. This happier and more comforting view of things is set forth in the last play of M. Bruyez that comes within my purview: his 'épopée mystique', *Jeanne et la Vie des Autres*.

I have written elsewhere[16] of this exceptionally attractive contribution to the repertory of plays on Joan of Arc. It has been many times performed—in Orleans, Paris and South America—was awarded the Prix Brieux by the Académie Française, and has recently been revived for the Joan of Arc festival in Paris, with Mlle Fanny Robiane taking the title-role, as she has always done, and repeating if not surpassing her previous triumphs.[17] When M. Bruyez composed his 'épopée mystique', he was venturing into very distinguished company, that of Charles Péguy and G. B. Shaw. And he has no need to stand cap in hand before them. His *Jeanne* is a real poem, new in its conception and arresting in the appeal it makes to the imagination. In selecting his material, the author decided to get out of the common rut, to avoid stock scenes and dialogue culled from the chronicles and documents, to make use of 'éléments inédits', and, at need, to supplement recorded facts with conjectured events relevant to the decisive moments in Joan's career, especially such events as might illustrate the impact on Joan of the private influences and interests around her. Hence the title: *Jeanne et la Vie des Autres.*

N'est-ce pas, enfin, par l'utilisation des éléments authentiques mais peu connus, comme par l'invention de ce que la chronique elle-même n'a point enregistré, que l'auteur d'une pièce historique parvient quelquefois quand il se meut dans certaine pénombre, à faire douter le spectateur le plus averti, d'un dénouement que chacun se flatte, cependant, de connaître avant que le rideau ne se lève?—La conclusion d'un drame historique n'étant ignorée de personne, allègue-t-on souvent, un tel ouvrage se voit ainsi privé, *a priori*, d'une des conditions essentielles de l'intérêt qu'il devrait présenter: la curiosité du spectateur soucieux, en principe, de savoir 'comment ça finira'. Quoi qu'il en soit, cette curiosité du public c'est à l'auteur, s'il est vraiment un écrivain dramatique, de la faire naître, de l'entretenir et, jusqu'à la dernière scène de son œuvre, de la sauvegarder.

Most dramatists (including Péguy) build up a first act round Joan's life at Domrémy before her departure for Chinon. M. Bruyez imagines a local tragedy at Domrémy, arising out of the anarchy and brutality of war, which electrifies Joan to a sense of the immediate urgency of her mission and gives a peremptory quality to the commands of the Saints with whom she communes in the village church. Most dramatists stage the scene at Chinon where Joan picks out the Dauphin mingled among his courtiers: M. Bruyez concentrates upon the private talk which followed between them, in order to show by what rational means the heroine instils courage and purpose into the dispirited prince. The coronation is also a favourite subject for dramatic pageantry. M. Bruyez relegates it to the wings, and devises a moving scene in which Joan prevails upon the newly anointed King to cede his crown to her and to receive it back as the gift of God. He passes next to an episode in the abortive assault on Paris, in order to show how Joan, wounded, feverish, abandoned, listening in vain for the encouragement of her Voices, nevertheless clings to her vision of a liberated France—and fights on. He by-passes the Trial Scenes, preferring to stage a colloquy between Joan and Bishop Cauchon in her prison cell, a day or two before her death, in order that she may reiterate. and justify, her conviction that her past triumphs were truly ordained of God. Other episodes in later tableaux of *Jeanne et la Vie des Autres* give the play a quite unique stamp. M. Bruyez evokes the consternation and bewilderment of the simple folk after the capture and disappearance of their saviour, a bewilderment intensified by the appearance in various provinces of adventuresses who usurp Joan's name and exploit her prestige. He fixes the limelight on Charles VII, who remains inactive and perplexed in his castle while Joan's enemies work their will on her at Rouen, and in the end is persuaded by his mother-in-law, Yolande of Anjou, that Joan's martyrdom is an essential part of her destiny. Finally he takes the spectator back to Domrémy, twenty-five years later, to end his play on the note of appeasement and reconciliation—the fruit of Joan's immolation.

This choice of *scènes inédites,* unfolded in a series of tableaux and appended interludes, is not prompted by the desire to be original at all costs. Of these scenes, some are quietly realistic, like that of the beginning, where Joan learns of the shame of Gertrude Cochart (terrified at the return of her wounded soldier-husband because she is with child through the assault of a roving English deserter), dominates the situation by the exertion of a new-found authority, and then gazes meditatively out on the symbolic glare of distant fires lighting up the horizon. Some scenes are vivid with local colour, especially the one (later expunged from the play) in which Joan arrives at the castle of Vaucouleurs and brings a breath of fresh air to the atmosphere of troubadour *galanterie* fostered by the frivolous Dame de Baudricourt. Many are solemn and tense, like the scene of the *transfert* in Reims cathedral, or Joan's colloquy with her sister Claude during the campaign outside Paris, or the debate with Cauchon in prison, or the discussion of reasons of state between Charles and Yolande at Meung-sur-Yèvre. But all are significant and symbolic, all fit into a pattern in conformity with that cohesion of artistry which is always M. Bruyez's evident preoccupation, so that from them may emerge the dominant idea which gives them unity.

What is that dominant idea? How far is the philosopher of *La Puissance des Mots, Le Triomphe du Silence* and *Le Passé conditionnel* still recognizable in the author of *Jeanne et la Vie des Autres*?

It will have been observed that in the above-mentioned plays (due allowance being made to the mythological framework of *Le Triomphe du Silence*), M. Bruyez never hoists his subject on to the plane of the supernatural. In so far as the supernatural has its place, it is there only as a potential emergence from the natural: it is as it were the spark struck from the flint and tinder of familiar and explicable events. So, in *La Puissance des Mots*, Gisèle Courtin, the woman Raymond Daryelles has striven to create artistically, is in common reality only the daughter of a woman in whose eyes Daryelles had long ago seen the dawning of his ideal. Inherited features may account for everything. So, in *Le Triomphe du Silence*, if Œdipe forces the Sphinx to deliver up her secret, it is not by magic, but by subtlety and ruse. So, in *Le Conditionnel passé*, it is only in Blanche's tortured imagination that those ghostly figures take shape to drive her to the chastisement which awaits her childish 'crime'. Now the story of Joan of Arc is already firmly grounded in the supernatural, crystallized in the Visions and Voices that inspire the Saint. No doubt it is permissible to surmise, if one feels so inclined, a psychological or psychophysiological mechanism by whose means these manifestations became apparent to the peasant-girl. But M. Bruyez remains totally uninterested in such surmises, and quite adamant in resisting the temptation to apply to Joan's case those methods of psycho-analysis of which in fact he has never been the dupe. He never questions the objective authenticity of the Voices, for he senses that this particular 'miracle' is only part and parcel of a larger and even more astounding 'miracle' —that of Joan's own personality, her marvellous achievement and its consequences. And this brings him face to face once more with the problem implicit in *Le Conditionnel passé*: does human responsibility play its part in the weaving of determined events?

He certainly finds, and builds his play on the belief, that the 'miracle' of Joan of Arc is explicable in terms of natural causation. The Cochart incident determines Joan to a further effort to extract from Baudricourt de Vaucouleurs an escort for her journey to Chinon. Her uncle Durand Laxart only consents to take Joan to Vaucouleurs a second time in the hope that a second rebuff will drive the nonsense out of her head. Baudricourt gives way because he is glad of the opportunity to send away three of his lieutenants, who, he suspects, are being too attentive to his flighty wife. Joan faces Charles at Chinon with no claims to magic powers or miraculous prescience; she is content to find her proof of divine guidance in the fact of obstacles surmounted, and the certainty of Charles's legitimacy (his doubts on that score are paralysing his will) in the arguments of common sense. At every turn we are confronted, as Bishop Cauchon vehemently urges in his final appeal to Joan, with happy coincidences and a lucky chain of events which as a skilful opportunist Joan has exploited to gain her ends.

It falls to Joan herself to counter this sceptical thesis with the argument that the apparently fortuitous concourse of events, which has led to results so favourable for France, confirms the fact of supernatural planning—

CAUCHON. Heureux enchaînement, qui vous a conduite où vous êtes!

JEANNE. L'objet de mon message, c'était la liberté du Royaume, non la mienne.

CAUCHON. Croyez-vous de bon que vous eussiez levé le siège d'Orléans, si lord Salisbury n'eût été tué?

JEANNE. Non, sans doute. Mais Dieu a permis qu'il le fût. — Semblablement, on pourrait alléguer que si Talbot n'eût été pris, à Patay, nous n'eussions point triomphé . . .

CAUCHON. Tu ne dépars pas de ton insolence . . .

JEANNE. . . . Autant d'événements explicables, en effet, à la faveur desquels j'ai pu conduire Charles à Reims, autant de miracles!

And finally, in a last-minute talk with the Monk who prepares her for death, Joan expresses in lapidary form the conclusion to which her conversation with the Bishop has led her. '*Plus une chose est dans l'ordre, plus un événement se justifie, plus La Providence y éclate!*'

The most cogent illustration of this truth M. Bruyez finds in the beneficent and timely support afforded by Yolande of Anjou, Queen of Sicily, first of all to Charles, as a minor and an outcast, and then to Joan herself. She it was who perhaps smoothed the way for Joan's expedition to Chinon, encouraged Charles to receive her, and presided over the jury of women appointed by the theologians to pronounce on the question of Joan's virginity, as well as undertaking the provision of arms and equipment for the attack on the English at Orleans. Later on, with no less firmness and decision than that with which she had supported the victorious Joan, she intervenes against her, and dissuades the vacillating Charles from taking steps to rescue Joan at Rouen. This inexorability on her part is deliberate, for she divines that, just as surely as Providence had engineered Joan's rise and triumph, it had designed her capture and martyrdom. There was no place, she argues, in court, castle or cottage, no possible return to commonplace, normal life for the woman who had saved France and restored its lawful dynasty. The far-seeing Yolande is, then, yet another instrument of a divine plan in which Bishop Cauchon can only detect 'une entreprise favorisée par certaines conjonctures de LA VIE DES AUTRES'.

What then of Joan herself? Is the Saint too a mere 'artisan de la Providence' swept along in a flood of events over which she has no control and for which she can claim no merit? M. Bruyez does not answer this question in so many words; but it is indeed a sufficient answer to picture Joan reverently and faithfully, as he has done (and as Mlle Robiane with such exquisite sympathy and artistry presents her to the audience), in the selflessness of her purpose, the ardour and eloquence of her radiant conviction, the inflexibility of her will when guidance seems to be withdrawn from her and her work seems to lie about her in ruins. If Blanche Darsenne represents the failure of a mind and will to take reality in hand and imprint a desired pattern on the stuff of her life and the lives of others, Joan of Arc represents the lucid mind, the unalterable will which are the more effective and productive because they are attuned to the higher resonances of the universe and in harmony with its most lofty designs. For this acuity of spiritual vision, and for other features as well—width of range, variety of colouring, and depth of poetic feeling—*Jeanne et la Vie des Autres* marks a new high level in M. Bruyez's dramatic attainment. 'Situer la personne mystique de Jeanne dans l'atmosphère de légende qui lui convient': this purpose, announced in a 'Notice' written for the Paris performance of 1939, he has amply fulfilled.

To what pitch will his inspiration soar hereafter? He has been working recently on another historical subject, culled from Livy:

the self-immolation of Regulus to the interests of Rome. If it is not impertinent to voice a hope, I could wish that he might more often feel inclined, in defiance of the scriptural adage, to pour his new wine into the stout old bottles of historical or mythological symbols—preferably the latter. Utilization of the ageless myths can give potency and permanency to ideas and divinations of metaphysic truth which otherwise may appear evanescent when clothed in the garb of actuality—for instance, if *Le Conditionnel passé* suffers from any disadvantage at all it is from being closely associated, by period and atmosphere, with the war of 1914 and its aftermath. And the use of such fictions would enable M. Bruyez to emerge from the contemporary *climat* in which his works have been produced, and to stand more definitely apart, not indeed from those who have influenced him—they are not easy to discern—but from those whom, apparently, he has influenced.

I say 'apparently', because influence is not always the right word to use with regard to affinities between his work and that of others. He evidently has influenced others: *La Puissance des Mots* gave rise, round about 1928, to quite a few plays on the same theme, though bearing different titles. He has certainly preceded others: the case of *La Machine infernale* has already been cited in this respect, and it is not difficult to perceive that Mme Simone de Beauvoir's *Le Sang des Autres* treats, albeit in a vastly different spirit, the theme latent in *Le Conditionnel passé*—that of human responsibility and solidarity. But this question of correspondences and foreshadowings is too complex to be solved by a single formula. M. Bruyez is possessed of an almost embarrassing kind of originality: he has been less the exploiter of current themes than the proponent of future ones. In 1913 he executed, and in 1920 gave to a review, a drawing entitled *Une Idée dans l'air*—a profile figuring, to quote his own definition, 'l'Idée préexistant au cerveau qui le concevra, ou, tout au moins, à la conscience que le dit cerveau en prendra un jour'.[18]

If there be such pre-existent ideas, one would say that M. Bruyez is particularly susceptible to them, that sometimes he anticipates their formation in the mind of others, but that sometimes his reception of them has been contemporaneous with that of others, or on occasions posterior, though still independent. Thus, the chief character in *Le Sceptique ébloui* shares with Pirandello's Baldovino[19] a certain cult of heroism, inspired in his case, it is true, by contempt for the common run of men, while in Baldovino it is due to a strange kind of histrionic dilettantism. In all other points there is a complete absence of similarity between the two plays. Such coincidences can be a source of chagrin to one of M. Bruyez's charmingly wayward temperament. He lives in the world of his own ideas, in a kind of detachment from current literary events. It is only recently[20] that he has become belatedly cognisant, through the film, of André Gide's *Symphonie pastorale*, and ruefully notes that he has had in his 'cartons', for a matter of fifteen years, an unfinished play which has one feature in common with the Gidian novel: investigation of the psychological and moral complications arising from recovery of sight in a blind person.

M. Bruyez has an alternative explanation to offer of these disconcerting 'short-circuits': telepathy, he indicates, may also play its part.

Je pense de plus en plus que les auteurs sont—étant simultanément, sur le plan spirituel, mâles et femelles—des postes alternativement émettants et récepteurs. Une idée est dans l'air peut-être avant d'avoir été pensée . . . mais peut-être aussi parce que, à des milliers de kilomètres, un poète l'a conçue . . . Nous touchons ici à ce qu'il y a de plus mystérieux dans la création de l'esprit. Et rien n'est plus normal qu'une œuvre née . . . du Saint-Esprit. Par son opération qui ne doit sembler miraculeuse qu'aux gens à qui n'est pas familière la transe de la création. Ce que l'on observe, d'ailleurs, sur le plan poétique est parfaitement vrai dans le domaine de la science. N'y a-t-il pas une véritable 'contagion des laboratoires' même entre ceux qui ne communiquent point?

But in whatever way these processes may work, and however universally available an 'idée dans l'air' may be, its appropriation by an individual writer is the more complete and indisputable the more resistant the material in which it is crystallized. That is why I presume to suggest for M. Bruyez further and more ambitious ventures into the ideal space-time of classical affabulation. But, do what he will in the future, it is not to be denied that he has produced up to the present an extremely interesting series of works. I look forward to the day when an intelligent publisher will deem it worth while to print a complete edition of them.

NOTES

(1) Preface to *Jeanne et la Vie des Autres* (Durassié et Cie, Paris, 1938), p. 9.

(2) Three acts, four tableaux; performed at the Théâtre Féminin by the Compagnie du Griffon in 1922.

(3) Two acts; performed in Nov. 1924 at the Théâtre Ésotérique.

(4) One act, 1924 (Atelier).

(5) One act, 1925 (Théâtre Albert-Premier).

(6) One act, Odéon, 25 Jan. 1926.

(7) Written 1926, performed 1928 at the Théâtre Antoine by the Cercle des Escholiers.

(8) Studio des Champs-Elysées, 1929. It had a run of over 300 performances.

(9) 1932 (Studio d'Art dramatique).

(10) 1937 (Gala de la Pièce en un Acte).

(11) Odéon, 1930.

(12) Studio d'Art dramatique, 1932: a first version, in one act only, of this play had been performed at the Théâtre de l'Œuvre in 1927.

(13) Published in 1929: Les Éditions du 'Journal du Peuple', Imprimerie Française (G. Dangon).

(14) Act I, scene vi.

(15) The persistent striking of a certain note on the piano incites him to an ever more and more precise visualization of his ideal woman as Clothilde looks on in anguish and Griseville in dismay.

(16) *Modern French Studies:* Oct. 1947. *St Joan of Arc in some recent French dramas.*

(17) Extremely well produced by M. Aldebert at the Palais de Chaillot, May 11th, 1947.

(18) I need scarcely refer again to *La Puissance des Mots* to show how strongly this conception has haunted M. Bruyez's imagination since those early days.

(19) In *Il piacere dell'onestà*, translated into French and performed at the Atelier in 1922, before M. Bruyez became associated with that theatre.

(20) These words were written in the summer of 1947.

BRÛLÉ DE PLUS DE FEUX...

R. C. KNIGHT

Lecturer in French in the University of Birmingham

Je souffre tous les maux que j'ai faits devant Troie.
Vaincu, chargé de fers, de regrets consumé,
Brûlé de plus de feux que je n'en allumai,
Tant de soins, tant de pleurs, tant d'ardeurs inquiètes . . .
Hélas! fus-je jamais si cruel que vous l'êtes?

For at least a century every student has been invited to censure these too famous lines from *Andromaque*. First, because their form is archaic, and seems to us forced and insincere; second, because their content is too modern—Pyrrhus is here at his furthest from the behaviour of a real Greek. Racine says he tried to make him the image of his father Achilles ('Horace nous recommande de dépeindre Achille farouche. . ., tel qu'il était, et tel qu'on dépeint [sc. ici] son fils'—Preface, 1668): but Achilles, we have all been taught, never felt a sentiment unknown to Homer and impossible, in its modern form, between the men and women of antiquity (cf., e.g., H.-J.-G. Patin, *Euripide*, 5e ed., 1879, t. I, p. 27).

Our century is able to be more lenient than the last, having grasped that the rule of *bienséance*, which is responsible for the change in Pyrrhus, did no more than ratify the law of the box-office, permitting the playwright to give the public at least a little of what it wanted. But we are not yet as lenient as the 'severe' Boileau:

> Peignez donc, j'y consens, des héros amoureux,
> Mais ne m'en formez pas des bergers doucereux;
> *Qu'Achille aime* autrement que Tircis et Philène.
>
> (*Art poétique*, III, 97–9)

The fact is that Boileau and all his age remembered a tradition we have forgotten, a tradition that was common knowledge from the Renaissance back to the twelfth century, and four centuries earlier still among the learned—to wit, that Achilles at Troy had played precisely this part of love-lorn swain, according to the written testimony of eye-witnesses, captains in the Greek and Trojan hosts.

The war history of Dares the Phrygian priest (named in Homer, *Iliad*, v, 9) and the siege diary of Dictys the comrade of Idomeneus of Crete are impudent and, to us, transparent forgeries. They are extant only in Latin versions compiled between the fourth and seventh centuries A.D.; though Dictys at least probably had a Greek original, equally spurious of course, now lost. But, so far as I can find, the earliest doubt of their complete authenticity was expressed by Vives in 1532, and it was not until 1702 that Perizonius conclusively proved them to be forgeries (the debate on Greek originals is hardly closed yet).

'Dares' is a very short, very bald narrative in execrable crabbed repetitive Latin. It covers the whole story of the Greeks and Troy from the Argonauts' landing which began the feud, to the dispersal of most of the Trojan survivors after the sack. Achilles's romance receives rather fuller attention than most of the other events, and runs as follows (ch. 27–34, 42–3).

On the anniversary of Hector's death, Achilles (who had killed him) went during a truce to the tomb outside Troy gates to watch a commemorative ceremony. Thither came Priam, Hecuba and their daughter Polyxena, whose beauty went to his heart: *figit animum, amare eam vehementer coepit. Tunc ardore impulsus, odiosam vitam in amore consumere coepit.* He sent to Hecuba, promising to withdraw with his Myrmidons from the siege if he might have Polyxena to wife; Priam, when consulted, would accept nothing less than a treaty of perpetual peace and the departure of the whole Greek host. Achilles obediently tried to persuade his comrades that the war was profitless and should be ended; he himself went to battle no longer (this is Dares's version of the 'Wrath of Achilles'), though the battle turned against the Greeks. At last, in a crisis, months later, Achilles allowed his troops to fight; they were so cut to pieces by Troilus (brother of Hector and Polyxena) that the next day Achilles joined the fray; seven days later he killed Troilus. During yet another truce Hecuba inspired Paris with a plan of vengeance. Achilles, summoned by a false message to conclude a separate peace at the temple of Thymbrean Apollo, outside the gates, was cut down fighting valiantly.

When Troy fell at last, the Greek fleet was storm-bound, and Calchas declared that the dead had not received satisfaction. Neoptolemus (Pyrrhus), son of Achilles, remembered that Polyxena, whose name had lured his father to his death, had not been found: dragged from hiding, she was slain by him on Achilles's tomb.

'Dares' is the main source of subsequent tradition.

'Dictys', in an ampler narrative, tells the story in his own way— these apocrypha make it a point of honour to differ on minor points. Achilles here sees Polyxena twice (III, 2, and 20–27)— first at a temple ceremony, but before Hector's death; later, when she comes to his tent with Andromache and her two infants, accompanying Priam who seeks to ransom Hector's corpse—an ambitious revision of Homer's great episode. After the others have failed to move Achilles, she clasps his knees and offers herself as his slave; he weeps, and raises her; after deliberations and moralizing speeches he grants the corpse, and gives her all the raiment from Priam's gifts. Priam begs Achilles to keep her ('in gratitude, or perhaps for safety should Troy fall'), but 'the youth replies that this must be settled at another time, in another place'—which are never found.

Achilles is less treacherous here than in Dares, and Polyxena more forward. A much more sensational version (Philostratus, second cent. A.D., *Her.* 19, 11, *Vit. Ap.* IV, 16) makes her escape from Troy after Achilles's death and kill herself on his tomb.

Allusions to one or another episode of this romance are quite frequent in compilers and scholiasts of the early Christian era. It is absent, of course, from Homer, who never mentions the name of Polyxena. But the sacrifice of Polyxena—demanded, usually, by Achilles's voice or his shade—has good classical authority, in Euripides (*Troades, Hecuba*), Ovid (*Metam.* XIII), and Seneca (*Troades*).

Some previous link is implied between Achilles and Polyxena, since the dead Achilles demanded her by name. Sooner or later a romantically minded poet was bound to turn it into a full-scale love-story—such things did exist in antiquity; it even seems that this one began as early as the eighth century B.C. in the *Cypria* (cf. R. Förster in *Hermes*, XVIII, pp. 475 ff.).

The triumphant flowering of this legend throughout the Middle Ages is strictly but an episode in our story, for the Renaissance went back to the original Dares text—but the text reached a public permeated by countless re-workings of the legend. These have been much studied, both for their own sake and in relation to Chaucer's and Shakespeare's *Troilus*. Suffice it to say that, with claims the mediaeval mind was neither disposed nor equipped to question, Dares and Dictys carried all before them. As contemporary records, free of all fables of divine intervention, they eclipsed the classical Trojan story, as it remained on record in Virgil, Ovid, and a Latin abridgement of Homer. Adapted by French chroniclers from the eleventh century, translated into French in the twelfth, they passed through an unbroken succession of re-adaptations and retranslations, in Latin, French and most of the other tongues of Europe, which actually overlapped the first printed edition of the originals.

The first and finest of the French translations—if 'translation' fittingly describes an expansion into 30,000 lines of verse—is the *Roman de Troie* by Benoît de Sainte-Maure[1] (dated 1155–60 by its latest editor). Benoît, whose busy fancy clothes Troy in a barbaric profusion of magical splendours, exploits to the full also the personal relations sketched in Dares, and travesties them in the new fashion of courtly love. As is well known, from Dares's twenty-word 'portrait' of an otherwise unmentioned Briseida, Benoît created the loves and betrayal of Troilus.

Achilles and Polyxena attract him equally: they are the most tragic of the couples. It is with Benoît of course that the new language of love-making enters our tradition—plaintive but submissive, as we see it in *Andromaque*. He uses the plain Dares version—a meeting in a public place (scarcely a meeting, for we do not even learn that the maid noticed her admirer); love preferred to loyalty and glory; negotiations in which she is not consulted; Achilles's promise kept, then broken; his death by treachery, her death as a debt to the dead. Long dilemma-monologues by Achilles emphasize the dramatic conflict of love and enmity which is to be so important in later developments:

> N'est el ma mortel enemie?
> Oïl, mais or sera m'amie.
> Veire, quar bien est a mon chois!
> Jo meïsmes me trich e bois [*trompe*],

Jo me deceif, mien esciënt,
Quar jo sai bien certainement
Qu'el me voudreit aveir ocis.
Trop laidement sui entrepris,
Qui amer vueil ço que me hait.

.   .   .   .   .   .

Ja n'avrai mal qu'el ne vousist
Que cent itanz m'en avenist.
Son frere Hector li ai ocis;
Si grant duel ai en son cuer mis,
Ja mais jor ne voudra mon bien:
Ço m'ocira sor tote rien.   (17657–65, 17673–8)

Polyxena, a discreet background figure, never speaks to him, nor even to his emissary, but she is grieved when he takes up arms again (21227), and when he dies ambushed

S'osast, qu'en mal ne fust retrait,
Merveillos duel en eüst fait.
Vers sa mere en fu mout iriee,
Que l'uevre aveit apareilliee.
Por li est morz, e si l'en peise.
Mais n'est pas fole ne borgeise;
Sage est, si ne vueut faire mie
Rien qu'om li tort a vilenie.
Por ço s'en tot, si fist que sage:
Grant mal l'en vousist son lignage.   (22447–56)

On Achilles's tomb she accepts her death with a last speech in which his name is not once breathed: but this is maidenly reserve.

Two successors of Benoît attained the honours of print. Guido de Colonna (1287), from whose Latin version a new proliferation takes rise, repeats the Polyxena episode without embellishments. Jacques Millet of Orleans turned (presumably) Guido into a mystery in four *journées* (1450, printed 1484) in which Achilles's monologues are cut down, but Polyxena's feelings and motives built up.

But it is time to pick up the tradition where it emerges renewed from the original Dares with the printed editions and revived scholarship of the Renaissance.

Dares and Dictys were first printed in 1470–5—earlier than any of the main-stream sources of the Trojan legend (Seneca's tragedies, 1474–84; Homer, 1488; Euripides, not quite complete, by 1503). A new French translation appeared before 1500, and three more, with innumerable Latin editions, in the course of the sixteenth century. The rediscovery of Homer could not shake their popularity until scholars had upset their *bona fides*. Anne Lefèvre edited them for the Dauphin in 1680: it is true that her prefaces brand them both as spurious. A Lyons poet, Borée, in 1627, still appeals to them as 'Historiens et soldats des deux partis' (*Achille*, argument).

Did Racine know them? No evidence exists. Such a gap in his classical baggage would be surprising. It is impossible that he should not have known of them. What we can show is that he must have known plays which directly or indirectly drew upon their accounts.

Three Renaissance tragedies, before Hardy, choose Trojan themes. All show knowledge of Homer, but all make some use of Dares. Garnier in his *Troade* (1579), and Montchrestien in *Hector* (1601–4), used different episodes; Nicolas Filleul, however, wrote an *Achille* (1563) where the hero is killed (off-stage) during his actual marriage: but Polyxena does not even appear on the stage; the romantic possibilities of the story were unrealized or rejected.

The Love-Interest is absent from the tragedy of the Renaissance. It will make an appearance with Alexandre Hardy, and flourish as the tastes of a regular paying public make themselves heard more loudly than the examples of Seneca and the Greeks.

In the argument of *La Mort d'Achille* (date unknown, printed 1632) Hardy boasts of his debt to Dares and Dictys. His first scene shows Achille, after his first sight of Polixène, dreaming (like Racine's Pyrrhus) of restoring Troy for love of his Trojan, and bewailing the enmity between them. There are no less than four council-scenes; the pair meet once, and Polixène, who hates the Greek, pretends love—an original touch—to lure him to his death, which takes place on the stage in the fourth (and last) act.

Here then, in a volume much used by succeeding dramatists, was a dramatic treatment, rather clumsily executed, of Dares's romance of Achilles, which was thus launched on its seventeenth-century career.[2]

Hardy's play was recast in the year of the *Cid* by a more competent hand, that of the court poet Benserade. The new *Mort d'Achille* owes much to Hardy, and to the sources Hardy had indicated:

> ... Les plus beaux gestes de celuy qui en est le Herôs sont escrits d'un style si merueilleux par le diuin Homere; quelques Autheurs, comme Dares Phrygius, & Dictys Cretensis, en parlent historiquement, & auec plus de vray-semblance, i'ay pris des vns & des autres ce que i'en ay iugé necessaire pour l'embellissement de la chose sans en alterer la verité.

Homer gives him the figure of Briseide hovering jealously in the background; Dictys, the scene of the ransom of Hector (I, 3)—minus, of course, Polixene's humiliating offer to remain as a slave.

The great *scène à faire*, the lovers' meeting after their quasi-betrothal, is a perfect period-piece (II, 4):

Vne chambre paroist, Achille aux pieds de Polixene qui luy presente son espée nuë.

ACHILLE

. . . .

Espargnez-vous mon sang? i'ay tant versé du vostre.

. . . .

Ouy ie vous faschay moins meurtrissant vostre frere,
Ie ne fus que hardy, mais ie suis temeraire.
Tous mes faits ne sont rien, ie m'esleue au dessus,
I'ay beaucoup fait, Madame, & i'ose encore plus,

. . . .

Ie peche contre vous sans remors, & sans blasme.

POLIXENE

Mais quel est ce peché?

ACHILLE

Ie vous ayme, Madame,
C'est ma temerité, ma gloire, mon forfait,
Et voilà ce que i'ose apres ce que i'ay fait:

. . . .

Qu'vn pere ait soupiré, qu'vne mere ait gemy,
Ie n'ay point pour cela cessé d'estre ennemy:
Mais vos yeux ont flechy mon courage farouche ...

Polixene is coy—in words that will have a later echo—but leaves him hope.

> Mais vous estes Achille, & ie suis Polixene,
>
> . . . .
>
> Et comment voulez-vous que de bon œil ie voye
> L'homicide d'Hector, & l'ennemy de Troye?
>
> . . . .
>
> Esperez, ie veux suiure au point où ie me vois,
> Ce que leurs Majestés me prescriront de lois,

which she does, when (IV, 1) she obediently stifles her new-born love.

Achille, we have seen, belittles the violence of his exploits in comparison with the outrage of his love. In an earlier scene (II, 2), addressing Priam, he compares suffering with suffering and finds his own greater:

> Mais souffrez que tout haut ie vous proteste icy,
> Que si vous endurez, Achille endure aussy.
> I'ignore qui de nous a plus sujet de craindre,
> Encor vous plaignez-vous, moy ie ne m'ose plaindre.

This is to be the theme of Pyrrhus in *Andromaque*. Here, too, prefiguring Pyrrhus, he offers his aid to Troy:

> I'acheueray pour vous ce qu'Hector proiettoit.

The authority of the *vraisemblable* Dares and the precedent of Hardy and Benserade established on the French stage the loves of the Greek warrior and the Trojan maid. The example becomes contagious. In 1640 Rotrou showed Achilles transfixed at first sight of a different mistress, Iphigenia (*Iphigénie en Aulide*). In the same year a different Greek sighs, in vain, for a different Trojan, in the other Trojan subject of the captive women, as used by Euripides, Seneca and Garnier. Sallebray's *Troade* introduces the death of Polyxena, without enlargement. Here the Greek lover is Agamemnon himself, and his beloved, naturally, Cassandra. He has first choice of captives, but his love is respectful. He makes his own the complaint of Benserade's Achille. Troy was burnt; and here (Professor H. Carrington Lancaster has quoted the essential line in his *History of French dramatic literature*, pt. II, p. 160, n. 12) is the flame-conceit complete and luxuriant at last.[3]

> . . . A peine de lauriers i'ay la teste couuerte,
> Que le feu de mon cœur les a presque seichés.
>
> . . . .
>
> Les trais que i'ay lancés retournent contre moy,
> Ie brûle par le feu que i'alumay dans Troye,
> Ie suis de mon vaincu le butin et la proye,
> Et ie ressens le mal dont i'ay causé l'effroy.
>
> Pardon rare beauté dont mon ame est charmée
>
> . . . .
>
> Ne voyés que d'vn œil ce lieu qui brûle encore,
> Et pour vous consoler du feu qui le deuore,
> Iettés l'autre aussi tost sur celuy de mon cœur.
>
> Si l'espace est moins grãd, la flame en est plus forte,
> C'est aux lieux resserés que le feu brûle mieux,
> Celuy que i'excitay va cesser à vos yeux,
> Mais le leur dans mon ame agit d'vne autre sorte:
> N'accusés point l'auteur de cet embrasement,
> Ce seroit m'enseigner la façon de me plaindre,
> Et par vn juste Echo vous pouriés me contraindre,
> A traiter vos beaux yeux iniurieusement.   (I, 2, *stances*)

Surely this passage rules out, as the source of *brûlé de plus de feux* . . ., the oft-quoted phrase of Heliodorus[4] where both the torment and the fire are of a different nature—the personage is no lover, but a father sacrificing his child; the flames burn on an altar.

Racine, who always seems to have looked up earlier contemporaries who had treated his subjects, had good reason to be interested in Sallebray; for the death of Astyanax occupies several scenes, and imitates the same Senecan passages which Racine has transplanted to *Andromaque*:

> Redouter un enfant!   (*Troade*, II, 4)
>
> Ils redoutent son fils.
>
> — Digne objet de leur crainte!
>   (*Andr.* 270)

Several close resemblances of words and situation confirm our supposition. Here is the 'coquetterie vertueuse' of Cassandre, pleading for her nephew Astyanax:

> Ie suis vôtre captiue, & le Ciel rigoureux
> En cela seulement rend mon destin heureux.   (*Troade* III, 3)

>   . . . Je me suis quelquefois consolée
> Qu'ici plutôt qu'ailleurs le sort m'eût exilée,
> Qu'heureux dans son malheur . . . etc.   (*Andr.* 933–5)

Here is Agamemnon refusing the death of Polixene to Pyrre, and deprecating the atrocities of the sack of Troy:

> Mais vouloir retenir le soldat quand la rage,
> La victoire, & la nuit secondent son courage,
> C'est prétendre arréter ces torrens furieux,
> Que l'on void entrainer des rochers auec eux;
> Il faut donc a present conseruer ce qui reste . . . (*Troade* III, 4)

> *La victoire et la nuit,* plus cruelles que nous . . .   (*Andr.* 211)

> Madame, je sais trop à quel excès de *rage*
> La vengeance d'Hélène emporta mon *courage* . . .
>   (*Andr.* 1341–2)

And Andromaque, when the murder is imminent of her husband's sister Polixene by Pyrre:

> Quel barbare Démon pour m'affliger encor,
> Méle le fils d'Achille à la veufue d'Hector?   (*Troade* IV, 2)

> De la fille d'Hélène à la veuve d'Hector.   (*Andr.* 1320)

> Elle est veuve d'Hector, et je suis fils d'Achille.   (*Andr.* 662)

This romanticized Troy does not end with *Andromaque.* I might describe, for instance, Thomas Corneille's *Mort d'Achille* (1673), where Achilles and his son are rivals for Polyxena, with Briseis to make a fourth; or even the *Hector* which Racine's Jesuit uncle Adrien Sconin published at Soissons in 1675; or Pradon's *Troade* (1679), where Ulysses and Pyrrhus love each other's captives. But my intention was simply to link Dares with the only French masterpiece (since Benoît) derived, however indirectly, from his story.

I do not wish to exaggerate the influence of the Dares tradition on Racine. Public demand—rationalized as *bienséance*—was assuredly sufficient by itself to compel some changes in any role such as Pyrrhus: witness Achilles in Rotrou, Hippolytus in Gilbert, Bidar, Pradon (and Racine).

But Pyrrhus is a graver case than Achilles or Hippolytus; for most of the really important elements of *Iphigénie* and *Phèdre* existed in the classical models, and the Love-Interest deforms but does not transform them. Whereas Euripides's harem-quarrel in his *Andromache* makes a radically unacceptable plot for any modern audience; and Racine's *Andromaque*, with a fundamentally different situation, could not exist at all without love in the modern manner.

For a more serious discrepancy, Pyrrhus can plead a more serious justification: he appeals to a long and living tradition which claims to be older than Euripides or Homer himself. It matters little whether Racine had read Dares and Dictys, nor, if so, how he judged them, nor whether he knew that their authenticity was contested (he may have owned the copy of Isaac Vossius's *De historicis Graecis* of 1624 which his son sold in 1755). Just as he has falsified Andromaque's situation to keep it true to certain memories of Homer and Virgil which her name called up ('J'ai cru en cela me conformer à l'idée que nous avons maintenant de cette princesse'), so he makes Pyrrhus conform to a picture of his father Achilles which had been accepted in France as long as letters had been cultivated there.

WORKS CONSULTED

Roscher, *Ausführliches Lexikon d. griechischen u. röm. Mythologie*, art. Polyxena.
Dictys Cretensis, Dares Phrygius, ed. Valpy, London, 1825 (containing extracts from Scaliger, Vossius, A. Lefèvre, Perizonius).
—— Ed. Meister, Leipzig, 1872.
Griffin, N. E., *Dares and Dictys*, Baltimore, 1907.
Joly, A., *Benoît de Sainte-More et le 'Roman de Troie'*, Paris, 1870.
Constans, L., ed., *Le 'Roman de Troie' par Benoît de Sainte-Maure*, Paris, 1912. T. VI, pp. 192 ff.
Barnicle, M. E., ed., *The Seege or Batayle of Troy* (Early English Text Society). London, 1927. Pp. 216 ff.
Catalogue des livres de Monsieur R[acine], 1755, Bibliothèque nationale, MSS. Δ 3333.

NOTES

(1) Nothing is known of Benoît. It has always been assumed that Sainte-Maure was a French town; but my colleague Dr F. J. Tritsch, Reader in Ancient History and Archaeology at Birmingham, makes the suggestive remark that it was the mediaeval name of the Greek isle of Leucas. Can the poet have had Greek connections, which might have given him access to the hypothetical fuller version (in Greek ?) of Dares which some scholars have thought he used?

(2) The unskilful *Achille* of Borée (Lyons, 1627) shows imagination in making Memnon Achille's rival: but it can have had little influence, and Racine probably never read it.

(3) In Hardy and Benserade Troy had not yet burnt. Something like the conceit had occurred in Garnier's *Troade*: after the rape of Helen, says the Chorus,

> La Grece repassa la mer acheminee
> Apportant le brandon
> Qui vient d'enflamber Troye, et l'ardeur obstinee
> Du feu de Cupidon. (1801–4)

The conceit could have arisen from any of several associations. The mother of Paris dreamed she gave birth to a firebrand. The 'flames' of love appear often in Greek romance, Latin erotic verse, and French romance. Seneca, who, without implying a previous love-story, speaks of Polyxena's sacrifice as a sort of posthumous bridal, associates the flames of Troy with the Hymeneal torch:

> Taedis quid opus est quidve solenni face?
> Quid igne? thalamis Troja praelucet novis. (*Tro.* 899–900)

(4) '[Hydaspes] made to lead [Chariclea] to the altar and the pyre: but his own heart burned with a fiercer fire' (*Aethiopica*, x, 17). Or, if we need an ancient source, why not equally well this passage from another Greek romance?—'I shall carry fire into my enemies' country: but Love has lit another kind of torch against me' (*Clitophon*, IV, 7).

AN ANGLO-FRENCH
COLLECTION OF BOOKS IN THE
ROYAL MALTA LIBRARY

BY

FRASER MACKENZIE

Professor of French in the University of Birmingham

VALLETTA has a public library (*Bibliotheca*) with material for much research work. The richness of its mediaeval collection is known, although there is a great deal to be studied in its documents of that period. One section of the library, in which no research has been done, includes a collection of Anglo-French works, principally of the eighteenth century, the books being brought together by a decree of Louis XV, who ordered that one copy of every book published in his reign by the French Royal Press should be sent to the Bibliotheca of Valletta. There is in these volumes a mass of information on the penetration of British thought into France and Western Europe.

One result of that order is noteworthy. A vast number of the original French translations of our seventeenth and eighteenth-century classics of literature, of philosophy, of science, of travel are within the walls of a stately Maltese edifice in the main street of Valletta. They are intact. It will surprise no students of Malta to know that they are in a great Reading Room, which is an architectural treasure dating from the time of the Knights of Saint John. Therein are handsome early editions of Milton, of Locke, of Addison, of Hume, of Sterne, of Captain Cook—sometimes in English, as is the first edition of the *Areopagitica*, or of the *Sentimental Journey*, more often in the first French translation.

The translation of the *Sentimental Journey* may be taken as a characteristic example of precise information to be gleaned in many of the books. In 1769 it was translated:

Voyage Sentimental par M. Laurence Sterne, sous le nom d'Yorick.
Traduit de l'anglois par M. Frenais. Amsterdam, 1769, 2 tomes.
(Malta catalogue number: Af. 9. 52.)

As the word 'sentimental' was unknown in French, the translator apologizes for using this word and comments: 'Le mot anglois n'a pu se rendre en françois par aucune expression qui pût y répondre, et on l'a laissé subsister. Peut-être trouvera-t-on en lisant qu'il méritoit de passer dans notre langue.'

There is the origin of one of the basic terms of the Continental Romantic Movement. French *sentimental* is an Anglicism. The word was coined by Sterne, who uses it as early as 1740 in a *Letter*, quoted by Austin Dobson (*Bookman's Budget*, p. 135).

Another example is that of the international use of the word 'nerves', as used pathologically in an expression such as 'fit of nerves'. It derives from the writing of a Saint Andrews doctor, Robert Whytt, the translation in 1767 having the title:

Traité des maladies nerveuses, hypocondriaques et hystériques. Traduction de l'Anglois de M. Robert Whytt.

The second edition of this translation is in Valletta (1776), and it contains a preface with a long explanation of the novel use of *nerfs*, *nerveux*: 'Il seroit à souhaiter qu'à l'exemple de M. Whytt, on ne nommât *symptômes*, *accès* ou *accidens nerveux*, & *attaques* ou *Maladies nerveuses* que les maux occasionnés chez des personnes d'une très grande délicatesse, & d'une sensibilité extraordinaire.'

The original English work is not included in the library. It appeared in 1765, under the title: 'Observations on the nature, cause and cure of those diseases which are commonly called nervous, hypochondriac or hysteric' (Edinburgh).

If we describe the Romantic Movement as the 'Advent of nerves into literature', or as 'the penetration of sentimentality into literature', it is certainly not devoid of interest to be able to trace to the very source the origin of the terms 'nerves', 'sentimental' and allied words.

Moreover the first edition (in 20 volumes dated 1776–82) of the French translation by Le Tourneur of all Shakespeare is in the library, and the French preface (p. cxxii) contains a striking example of an early use of the word *romantique*: 'Ou qu'il [Shakespeare] la fixe sur le paysage aérien et *romantique* des nuages . . . le mot anglois est plus heureux et plus énergique.'

Like *nerfs* and *sentimental*, the French word *romantique* is a loan-word from English usage. It was accepted by the French Academy in 1798.

The foregoing details demonstrate the interest of this study. We add a selection of analogous finds made in the spare moments of a round-the-world tour in the Royal Navy.

A challenging title in the Catalogue reads:

> Considerations fortuites de Joseph Hall. Paris, 1609 . . . de la Version de Monsieur Chevreau, M. Bobin. 24mo. 1 vol. (Af. 1. 54.)

Now the oldest translation known of any English literary work into French is of 1610: 'Les Caractères', after Bishop Hall. This was affirmed by Sidney Lee in a lecture published in the *Transactions of the Bibliographical Society* of 15 January 1906. I know of nobody who has been able to find an earlier date, although in 1932 Albert W. Osborn published in his *Sir Philip Sidney en France* a partial translation made probably between 1605 and 1612 of Sidney's *Arcadia*. It is in the Bodleian Library.

So the date 1609 in the Malta catalogue is unexpected. That may advance the study of English literature in its international aspect by only one year, and that is certainly minute. But it does happen to be one of the strange facts of our cultural history that our vast English literature was completely inaccessible to the foreigner in translation form, long after the death of Elizabeth. This does not of course include works written in Latin, like *Utopia*.

Bishop Hall is represented by two other French translations:

(a) Contemplations sur l'Histoire de l'Ancien et du Nouveau Testament . . . Nouvellement tirées de l'Anglois de M. Joseph Hall, par Theodore Jaquemot. Genève, 1628.

(b) Ample & Naifoe (*sic*) paraphrase sur le Cantique des Cantiques de Salomon. Composée par le tres reverend & illustre Seigneur Joseph Hall. 2e édition. Genève, 1632.

Thomas More is included in the Catalogue:

(a) L'Utopie . . . Traduction par Samuel Sorbière, 1643. Amsterdam.

(b) L'Utopie, 1715. Leiden de Mr Guendeville.

A French translation dates from 1674 of Thomas Mun's work:

> Traité du Commerce dans lequel tous les Marchands trouveront les moyens dont ils se peuvent legitimement servir pour s'enrichir. Traduit de l'Anglois de Thomas Mun. Par Monsieur L. V. Paris, 1674. (G. 4. 53.)

That is more than fifty years before Voltaire visited England and interested the French in our economic life. A second French edition was printed in 1700.

A point of linguistic interest is that the translator of Mun's *Treasure* does not use the words: *Importer* or *exporter*. He resorts to several periphrases: *faire porter dans les pays étrangers* (p. 34); *emporter hors du pays*; *apporter dans leurs marchandises*. Mun was moreover the great exponent of the policy of 'Balance of Trade', but the translator omits this expression. The French phrase appears later as a translation from English, the correct French requiring *Équilibre du Commerce*, instead of *Balance du Commerce*, which is the current expression.

One final example of a seventeenth-century work must suffice here, and we choose an anonymous treatise on military science:

> Pratique de la Guerre par le Sieur ... Gentilhomme Anglois, Commissaire general des Feux et Artifices de l'Artillerie de France, capitaine general des Sappes & Mines d'icelle & Ingenieur es armées du Roi. Paris, 1681.

The eighteenth century is represented very early by six handsome volumes of Clarendon. The title appears as:

> Hyde, Edward, First Earl of Clarendon.—Histoire de la Rebellion et des Guerres Civiles d'Angleterre depuis 1641, jusqu'au retablissement du Roi Charles II, par Edmond, Comte de Clarendon. The Hague, 1704–1709. 16mo, 6 tomes.

A linguistic study of this translation has long ago been made by Paul Barbier, who contributes an article to this volume. The translator of the eighteenth century is unable to find a French equivalent of the English political term 'Constitution'. He begs permission (vol. I, pp. 16, 19) to give to the traditional French word *Constitution* a new meaning and to apply it to political institutions. The international use of the word as a political term comes from

Westminster. It can be found in French as early as 1649 referring to England, but only in the plural (*Constitutions fondamentales du Royaume*). It occurs again in the French translation of Milton's *Eikonoklastes* (1652). The first use that I can find of the term used in the singular is in the French translation of Bishop Burnet's work: 'Histoire de la Réformation de l'Eglise d'Angleterre. Londres, 1683–5.' Here we read in the Preface: 'Mais la constitution de l'Angleterre est fort différente de celle des autres pays.' It can be found again in French translations of John Locke (1691) and in the writings of Boyle (1701), referring directly to England.

It is worthy of note that the English word 'Constitution' is found as early as 1647, although the *O.E.D.* gives it from 1689 only. The history of the term in England has been studied in the *Bulletin of the Institute of Historical Research* (June 1927). This conception of a Constitution is one of the outstanding contributions that Britain has made to the intellectual development of European society.

Addison and Steele are particularly well represented, and we give the titles of the four oldest editions:

(*a*) Steele, Richard.—La Crise ou Discours où l'on démontre par les Actes les plus Authentiques les Justes Causes de l'heureuse Revolution. Amsterdam, 1st ed. 1714. 1 volume.

(*b*) Steele, Richard.—Suplément de la Crise, ou Relation du Débat qu'il y eut entre les Commissaires Deputez de la Chambre Haute & ceux des Communes sur l'abdication du Roi James & la Vacance du Thrône en 1689. Amsterdam, 1714. 1e édition, 1 volume, 24mo.

(*c*) Steele, Richard.—Oeuvres diverses de Mr Steele sur les affaires de la Grande Bretagne, traduit de l'Anglois. Amsterdam, 1715. 1 volume.

(*d*) Steele, Richard.—Reflexions sur l'Importance de Dunkerque et sur l'Etat present de cette place . . . Avec une Carte du Nouveau Port à Mardick & le Plan des Anciens Ouvrages de Dunkerque, . . . traduit de l'Anglois. Amsterdam, 1715. 24mo.

Although there are several seventeenth-century editions of Locke's works in the original English, there are no translations before the eighteenth century. There is, however, a very considerable number of editions of French versions that appeared throughout the age of Louis XV. They form a valuable means of assessing the persistence of Locke's prestige throughout the age of the youth and of the maturity of the Philosophes. The catalogue includes:

(a) Abregé de l'essay de M. Locke sur l'entendement humain par le docteur John Wynn. London, 1720. (286 pp.)
(b) Abregé de l'Essay de Mr Locke sur l'Entendement Humain, traduit de l'Anglois par Mr Bosset. London, 1741. 4 tomes.
(c) Essai philosophique concernant l'Entendement Humain, 1742. 4e édition par Pierre Coste.

Parts of this work had appeared in French as early as 1688 (*Journal des Savants*), before the first English edition (1690). The complete work of Locke was translated into French, and published in 1700, by Pierre Coste; and, as we have noticed so often in this article, the translator was embarrassed by some of the English expressions. Locke had used 'Association of ideas', and Coste fumbles with: *Liaison des idées, Combinaison des idées*, only finally to accept *Association des idées*. Therein is the origin of the contemporary use of that phrase, although few, if any, French people of to-day realize that *Association des idées* is historically an Anglicism.

There are several editions of Locke's educational essays:

(a) De l'Education des Enfans, traduit de l'Anglais de M. Locke par M. Coste, 1721. Amsterdam.
(b) Another edition dated 1747, Paris.

There are also two Italian translations of 1751 and of 1792 (*Della Educazione dei Fanciulli*, Venice).

The original translation of this work appeared in 1695, and in the Preface there is what must be one of the oldest foreign attempts to define at length the English word 'gentleman'. This preface deserves study. There had been a brief remark on the conception of 'Gentleman', in a marginal note to the article 'Milton', in the *Dictionnaire* of Bayle (1691). There is, incidentally, a very old edition of Bayle's work in the Valletta Library.

Locke's works continue as:

(a) Histoire de la Navigation, son Commencement, son Progrès et ses Découvertes jusqu'à présent, traduit de l'anglois de John Locke. Paris, 1722. 16mo.

(*b*) Le Christianisme raisonnable tel qu'il nous est représenté dans l'Écriture Sainte. . . . Traduit de l'Anglois de M. Locke par M. Coste. 4e édition. 1740.

(*c*) Du Gouvernement Civil où l'on traite de l'origine, des fondemens, de la nature, du pouvoir et des fins des Societés politiques, traduit de l'Anglais de M. Locke. Bruxelles. 1754.

It is in this last work, which was first translated in 1691, that three important words of modern society: 'legislative', 'federative', 'executive', begin their currency as European terminology. Here, likewise, is the oldest use yet found of the political term, 'majority', which in its turn has been borrowed, as *majorité*, by the French language.

There are five works of Newton, of which we quote the three oldest:

(*a*) Newton, Isaac.—Traité d'optique sur les reflexions, refractions, inflexions et les couleurs de la lumière par Monsieur le Chevalier Isaac Newton . . . Seconde édition françoise, beaucoup plus correcte que la première. Paris, 1722.

This title contains the original use of the French word *réfraction*. The oldest use of a now current French word *Inertie* can be found on page 517.

(*b*) La Chronologie des Anciens. . . . Paris, 1728. [A second edition is dated 1743, Genève.]

The third work has a famous name as the translator:

(*c*) Newton, Isaac.—La Méthode des Fluxions et des Suites Infinies par M. le Chevalier Isaac Newton. . . . Traduction par M. de Buffon, 1740. Paris.

Defoe's works are not numerous. The oldest reference is:

Histoire du Diable. . . . Traduit de l'anglois. Amsterdam, 1729. 2 tomes, 16mo.

Then comes

La Vie et les Avantures Surprenantes de Robinson Crusoe, 1761. Paris, Dufour, 3 tomes, 16mo.

The first French translation goes back to 1721. It would be fascinating to think that older French editions might have been kept by fervent readers and so lost.

Two curious editions in Malta of Robinson Crusoe are a Latin translation of 1823, and another in Arabic (1835), this latter one published in Malta.

From 1730 onwards the translations are more numerous than ever. They reach the highest figure in the number of David Hume's works that are translated.

Meanwhile, Francis Bacon is represented by a single volume:

Essais du Chevalier Bacon, Chancelier d'Angleterre, 1734. Paris, 1 tome.

This is the same year as Voltaire's *Lettres Philosophiques* appeared in French.

The following year, Dryden is represented by:

Tout pour l'amour ou le Monde bien perdu. Tragedie traduicte de l'Anglois de Dryden. Paris, Didot, 1735, 16mo. Traduction de l'abbé Prévost.

The first translation of a great English poem (the late date may surprise our students of English literature) is of 1729. It is *Paradise Lost* of Milton. However, it is an early Italian translation that can be found in Malta:

Milton.—Il Paradiso perduto, 1730. Verona (1st Italian edition).

Although there are French editions of this work in Valletta, they are later:

Le Paradis Perdu. . . . Traduit de l'Anglois. 1743. [Another edition dates from 1755.]

Milton coined the word 'pandemonium', and the source of the French equivalent is to be found herein. It is worthy of note that when English thought is studied in its international ramifications, instead of from a purely national angle, Milton's works have a much longer history than those of Shakespeare. It may be rash to say that they have also exerted more social influence. An example of this may be quoted by the fact that recently one of the greatest French linguists, Ferdinand Brunot, admitted that we could not find the texts where the expressions 'gouvernement *arbitraire*' and 'gouvernement *représentatif*' are first used. Both terms penetrate into seventeenth-century French translations of Milton's 'pamphlets', and it is *pamphlet* which represents the first literary term that France borrowed from us. It is found in 1653, and still means in French a 'political' essay.

This article will have served its purpose, if it has merely shown that Malta might well become a source of interesting research for some of our students. Our jottings could easily be increased in volume to form a vast thesis. But we shall leave the reader here with the simple statement that students of the second half of the eighteenth century would be particularly rewarded by a visit to the Library. There are no language barriers, as English is spoken by all.

So we conclude by a final reference to Shakespeare in Malta. We have referred in the first part of this study to the Shakespeare section bearing the reference to Le Tourneur's translation (1776–82) of the complete works of Shakespeare. This weighty assemblage of 20 tomes represents the first entry of Shakespeariana in the Library. The oldest entry of an English work dates from 1805. So it appears that in Malta, Shakespeare was accessible to readers in French disguise, long before the original version. There is in this paradox a fascinating addition to the study of eighteenth-century France, namely, that the greatest British ideas have been in considerable measure spread with the help of French translations. In the eighteenth century, French books were widely read in the Courts of Stanislas, of Frederick and of Catherine. Our liberal culture became more cosmopolitan thanks to the 'universality' of the French language and of the translations into French of our works. Even to-day there are in Malta many translations of our greatest works, but not the original English texts.

It would be a considerable omission if we did not include a note of eulogy on the encyclopaedic interests of Hannibal P. Scicluna, the librarian-in-chief of the Valletta *Bibliotheca*. His aristocratic and scholarly personality filters through the entire staff of the Library. His knowledge of books is truly remarkable.

In the same way, there is his principal assistant, who converses most eruditely on multiple aspects of the Library, and of Maltese scholarship in general. She is unsparing in her assistance to the new arrival and the keen searcher.

THÉOPHILE GAUTIER ET LE
DANDYSME ESTHÉTIQUE

BY

J. M. MILNER

Lecturer in French in the University of Birmingham

'C'EST un livre de médecine et de pathologie. Tout médecin de l'âme, tout moraliste doit l'avoir sur une tablette du fond dans sa bibliothèque.' C'est ainsi que Sainte-Beuve définit *Mademoiselle de Maupin*.¹ L'éminent critique avait très bien compris le sens de ce livre tant décrié qui, pendant longtemps, valait à son auteur d'être considéré comme immoral et dépravé. En effet, avec une lucidité parfaite et une exactitude scientifique, Gautier, par le truchement de D'Albert, y analyse, détail par détail et phase par phase, le mal qui le ronge, ce mal que Sainte-Beuve appelle 'une forme dernière de la maladie de René'.² Page par page nous découvrons ses désirs et ses désespoirs, ses élans et ses chutes, ses attentes et ses déceptions, son activité fiévreuse et la lassitude profonde qui y succède, ses efforts frénétiques pour se rapprocher de quelqu'un ou de quelque chose et l'isolement moral où toujours il retombe—en un mot, tous les symptômes du mal du siècle, aboutissant au pessimisme et au nihilisme.

Mais ce qui nous intéresse et ce que nous allons essayer de noter, ce n'est pas tant ce mal en soi que la façon dont Gautier tente de réagir contre le mal, la façon dont il cherche à s'en guérir. Pour lui, le remède souverain sera la beauté, la beauté visible et matérielle. Il se plonge dans la contemplation des belles apparences, il se fait 'un bonheur de surface', comme il dit lui-même quelque part. Quant au reste, il refuse de s'en occuper. Baudelaire souligna cet aspect du livre lorsqu'il écrivit: 'Avec *Mademoiselle de Maupin* apparaissait dans la littérature le Dilettantisme.'³ Le dandysme esthétique y est déjà tout entier.

D'abord, tout ce qui n'est pas beauté et luxe ne l'intéresse pas le moins du monde. Le sort des hommes, le bonheur ou le malheur de ses semblables, tout cela le laisse parfaitement froid. 'Je me soucie assez peu que les paysans sachent lire ou non, et que les hommes mangent du pain ou broutent de l'herbe. . . .'[4] Mais Gautier ne s'est pas seulement débarrassé de tout sentiment fraternel envers les hommes, il n'est pas seulement indifférent à eux, il a même des velléités de sadisme. Il peut se réjouir du spectacle des souffrances humaines. 'Je verrais de sang-froid les scènes les plus atroces, et il y a dans les souffrances et dans les malheurs de l'humanité quelque chose qui ne me déplaît pas.—J'éprouve à voir quelque calamité tomber sur le monde le même sentiment de volupté âcre et amère que l'on éprouve quand on se venge enfin d'une vieille insulte.'[5] C'est que Gautier hait la société qu'il rend responsable de ses malheurs et de ses ennuis.

Le nihilisme de Gautier ne s'arrête pas à la seule perte du sentiment de sa responsabilité sociale et humaine, il entraîne la suppression totale du sens moral. Non seulement il ne cherche plus d'une façon active le bien mais il ne sait plus distinguer entre le bien et le mal. Le monde moral n'existe plus pour lui et les valeurs dites morales ne signifient absolument rien. A ses yeux il n'y a plus que ce qui lui plaît et ce qui lui déplaît; il n'a pas d'autre critérium: '. . . je suis trop corrompu et trop blasé pour croire à la beauté morale, et la poursuivre avec quelque suite.—J'ai perdu complètement la science du bien et du mal. . . . Ma conscience est une sourde et muette.'[6]

Se sentant infiniment éloigné des hommes et profondément sceptique quant à la vie intérieure, Gautier se tourne vers la seule réalité qu'il connaisse—le monde visible et palpable qui constitue son unique refuge contre l'anéantissement. Il est déjà 'l'homme pour qui le monde visible existe'. 'Aussi par une espèce de réaction instinctive, je me suis toujours désespérément cramponné à la matière, à la silhouette extérieure des choses, et j'ai donné dans l'art une très grande place à la plastique.'[7] On comprend qu'avec de tels sentiments Gautier rejette violemment le christianisme qui prêche le mépris de la matière et qui cherche à supprimer le corps au profit de l'âme. Lui est païen et il adore le corps. 'Je suis un homme des temps homériques; le monde où je vis n'est pas le mien, et je ne comprends rien à la société qui m'entoure. Le Christ n'est pas venu pour moi; je suis aussi païen qu'Alcibiade et Phidias.—Je n'ai jamais été cueillir sur le Golgotha les fleurs de la passion, et le fleuve profond qui coule du flanc du crucifié et fait une ceinture rouge au monde, ne m'a pas baigné de ses flots. . . .'[8]

Non, décidément, sa vertu n'est pas la vertu chrétienne. Tout est transposé sur le plan esthétique. La vertu, c'est la beauté; le vice, c'est la laideur. Pourvu que le corps soit beau, il se moque de ce que peut être l'âme. 'Ce qui est beau physiquement est bien, tout ce qui est laid est mal.—Je verrais une belle femme que je saurais avoir l'âme la plus scélérate du monde, qui serait adultère et empoisonneuse, j'avoue que cela me serait parfaitement égal et ne m'empêcherait nullement de m'y complaire, si je trouvais la forme de son nez convenable.'[9]

Son amour de la beauté est tel que la seule vue d'une chose laide suffit pour le rendre malheureux. 'C'est un véritable supplice pour moi que de voir de vilaines choses ou de vilaines personnes.'[10] Il serait d'accord pour supprimer implacablement tout ce qui offense les yeux et, en parlant des peintres qui s'amusent à repré-senter des êtres laids, il dit: '. . . loin de vouloir doubler ces figures laides ou ignobles, ces têtes insignifiantes ou vulgaires, je pencherais plutôt à les faire couper sur l'original.—La férocité de Caligula, détournée en ce sens, me semblerait presque louable.'[11] Et la laideur du genre humain le désespère: 'En vérité, je crois que l'homme, et par l'homme j'entends aussi la femme, est le plus vilain animal qui soit sur la terre.'[12]

Gautier s'adonne donc au culte exclusif de la beauté matérielle et innombrables sont les invocations où il célèbre sa puissance consola-trice. 'J'adore sur toutes choses la beauté de la forme; la beauté pour moi, c'est la divinité visible, c'est le bonheur palpable, c'est le ciel descendu sur la terre . . . ô beauté! le plus radieux diadème dont le hasard puisse couronner un front. . . . Je ne demande que la beauté, il est vrai; mais il me la faut si parfaite, que je ne la rencontrerai probablement jamais.'[13] Ou encore cette apostrophe, la plus connue de toutes: 'O beauté! nous ne sommes créés que pour t'aimer et t'adorer à genoux, si nous t'avons trouvée, pour te chercher éternellement à travers le monde, si ce bonheur ne nous a pas été donné. . . .'[14]

Dans *Mademoiselle de Maupin* il est beaucoup question de l'amour. Les trois personnages principaux ne parlent guère d'autre chose, et s'ils le font, c'est comme par distraction. C'est donc à propos des femmes et de l'amour qu'on peut observer le mieux chez D'Albert-Gautier cette attitude de dandysme esthétique. Or l'amour de la beauté, si cette beauté se trouve être celle d'un paysage, d'une bague, d'une statue ou d'un tableau, ne peut être autre qu'objectif et, en un certain sens, impersonnel. Mais si la beauté s'est incarnée dans une femme, l'amour de la beauté risque fort de se changer en tout autre chose—en l'amour tout court, où les considérations esthétiques tendent à être quelque peu submergées, du moins lorsqu'il s'agit de l'homme moyen. Mais même sous ce rapport, chez le dandy esthétique la volupté de regarder, de contempler le beau primera toute autre volupté. C'est vis-à-vis de la femme que le dandysme esthétique se signale le plus nettement.

Il est clair que la première qualité que le dandy esthétique requiert chez la femme, c'est la beauté, mais une beauté superlative et parfaite en tout point. A vrai dire, la beauté n'est pas la *première* qualité requise mais la *seule*. Une femme qui est belle a tout ce qu'il faut; la beauté lui tiendra lieu d'âme, d'esprit et d'instruction. 'Je n'ai jamais demandé aux femmes qu'une seule chose, c'est la beauté; je me passe très-volontiers d'esprit et d'âme. Pour moi, une femme qui est belle a toujours de l'esprit; elle a l'esprit d'être belle, et je ne sais pas lequel vaut celui-là. . . . Je préfère une jolie bouche à un joli mot, et une épaule bien modelée à une vertu. . . .'[15]

Quant au genre de beauté féminine qu'il préconise, ce n'est pas du tout la beauté romantique, la beauté pâle, languissante et frêle qui est plutôt esprit que corps; non, c'est une beauté bien en chair, '. . . il ne me plairait guère de rencontrer une arête où je cherche un contour',[16] une beauté voluptueuse et sensuelle, 'quelque chose de rouge et de scintillant dans le sourire. La lèvre inférieure un peu large, la prunelle nageant dans un flot d'humide radical, . . . la démarche onduleuse comme une couleuvre debout sur sa queue, les hanches étoffées et mouvantes, l'épaule large, le derrière du cou couvert de duvet . . . .'[17]

Mais si Gautier ne demande à la femme que la beauté, il faut, pour que sa joie soit complète, que cette beauté s'encadre de luxe et de toutes les richesses imaginables. Le luxe et la richesse sont deux éléments indispensables au bonheur du dandy esthétique. D'abord parce qu'ils rehaussent la beauté et ensuite parce que le luxe est en lui-même une source de beauté et parce que la richesse représente l'indépendance, la liberté de suivre ses caprices et le pouvoir de réaliser ses rêves. ('L'art, c'est la liberté, le luxe, l'efflorescence, c'est l'épanouissement de l'âme dans l'oisiveté', proclamait-il déjà en 1832 dans la préface d'*Albertus*.)

La femme idéale de Gautier ne portera donc que des robes de soie, de velours ou de riche brocart; à ses mains, dans ses cheveux et autour de son cou brilleront des diamants, des rubis et des perles. Elle mènera un train royal; elle aura des châteaux, des voitures, des laquais sans nombre. Il convoite une reine ou une impératrice, non pas en tant que reine ou impératrice, mais parce que seule une reine ou une impératrice peut s'entourer de toute la splendeur si nécessaire au contentement de Gautier. 'Aussi, dans mes rêveries, je me suis donné pour maîtresse bien des reines, bien des impératrices, bien des princesses, bien des sultanes, bien des courtisanes célèbres, mais jamais des bourgeoises ou des bergères. . . . Je trouve que la beauté est un diamant qui doit être monté et enchâssé dans l'or . . . il y a une harmonie entre la beauté et la richesse. L'une demande l'autre; un joli pied appelle un joli soulier, un joli soulier appelle des tapis et une voiture, et ce qui s'ensuit. Une belle femme avec de pauvres habits dans une vilaine maison est, selon moi, le spectacle le plus pénible qu'on puisse voir, et je ne saurais avoir d'amour pour elle. Il n'y a que les beaux et les riches qui puissent être amoureux sans être ridicules ou à plaindre.'[18]

La femme aimée sera donc riche, élégante et, surtout, belle— belle au delà de toute imagination, de toute possibilité. La beauté qu'il cherche est une beauté impossible; c'est une chimère. D'Albert a trop vécu dans les musées et dans les bibliothèques; c'est de là que lui vient cet idéal. Sa femme rêvée—elle n'est que belle et jamais autre chose—est une synthèse de toutes les femmes peintes ou sculptées qu'il a jamais vues. Raphaël, Rubens, Praxitèle, tous les artistes ont apporté leurs plus beaux trésors pour créer cette femme unique. A l'un D'Albert a pris une main, à l'autre des cheveux, à celui-ci un sein, à celui-là un pied. Mais il ne s'en est pas tenu là. Quittant les peintres et les sculpteurs, il est allé chercher les poètes pour leur demander une beauté encore plus rare, encore plus sub-tile, et à tout cela il a ajouté pour dernier ingrédient sa propre passion, son propre désir.

La beauté idéale, réalisée par les peintres, ne vous a même pas suffi, et vous êtes allé demander aux poètes des contours encore plus arrondis, des formes plus éthérées, des grâces plus divines, des recherches plus exquises; vous les avez priés de donner le souffle et la parole à votre fantôme, tout leur amour, toute leur rêverie, toute leur joie et leur tristesse...et vous avez ajouté, pour mettre le comble à l'impossible, votre passion à vous, votre esprit à vous, votre rêve et votre pensée. L'étoile a prêté son rayon, la fleur son parfum, la palette sa couleur, le poète son harmonie, le marbre sa forme, vous votre désir.[19]

Si, de temps en temps, il aime ou croit aimer une femme réelle et vivante, c'est parce qu'elle lui semble—bien qu'imparfaitement— se rapprocher de son idéal de peintre-poète. C'est qu'il regarde les femmes avec un œil d'artiste et non d'amoureux. Elles sont pour lui autant de tableaux plus ou moins bien faits; il apprécie leurs formes comme on critiquerait celles d'une statue. 'J'ai regardé l'amour à la lumière antique et comme un morceau de sculpture plus ou moins parfait. . . . J'ai pour les femmes le regard d'un sculpteur et non celui d'un amant.'[20]

Lorsque D'Albert peut enfin regarder les beautés dévoilées de Madelaine de Maupin, il reste longtemps en extase devant elle avant de se rappeler que c'est une femme qu'il contemple et non pas une statue, et alors seulement, 'le peintre satisfait, l'amant prit le dessus'.[21]

Bien entendu, le dandy esthétique ne se contente pas toujours de regarder les femmes qui lui plaisent. A défaut de la femme idéale, il consent à trouver son plaisir auprès de créatures moins belles. Sur ce chapitre, aussi, il est tout à fait égoïste; les femmes ne sont là que pour répondre à ses désirs: 'Je considère la femme, à la manière antique, comme une belle esclave destinée à nos plaisirs.'[22]

Si la beauté est la seule qualité que le dandy esthétique exige chez la femme, elle est aussi, par dessus toute autre, la qualité dont il voudrait se voir doué lui-même. Posséder la beauté en une femme qui est à vous, c'est très bien; mais être soi-même beau, est infiniment mieux—c'est la suprême félicité. Pour le dandy esthétique la beauté personnelle est la seule, l'indéniable marque de supériorité; elle le met tout en haut de la seule échelle de valeurs qu'il reconnaisse, —celle des valeurs esthétiques. Puisque la beauté est tout, mais absolument tout pour lui, être beau, c'est être roi, bien plus que roi,

—dieu! Aussi D'Albert rêve-t-il souvent d'être beau à l'égal des divinités antiques. 'La seule chose au monde que j'aie enviée avec quelque suite, c'est d'être beau.—Par beau j'entends aussi beau que Pâris ou Apollon.'[23] 'Bien des fois je me regarde, des heures entières, dans le miroir avec une fixité et une attention inimaginables, pour voir s'il n'est pas survenu quelque amélioration dans ma figure. ...'[24] Et il entre dans des fureurs terribles contre le destin qui l'a fait non pas laid mais médiocre: 'En vérité, si je tenais le hasard à la gorge, je crois que je l'étranglerais.—Parce qu'il a plu à une misérable parcelle de je ne sais quoi de tomber je ne sais où et de se coaguler bêtement en la gauche figure qu'on me voit, je serai éternellement malheureux!'[25] Toute sa vie, Gautier a prisé hautement la beauté personnelle. Lorsqu'on lui demandait quel don il aurait voulu posséder, il répondait invariablement: la beauté. Vers la fin de sa vie, vieux et enlaidi par la maladie, il aimait beaucoup à montrer à qui voulait les voir, de vieux portraits où on le voyait jeune et beau avec ses longs cheveux bouclés—ses fameux cheveux 'mérovingiens'.

En la beauté personnelle le dandy esthétique ne voit pas seulement un signe de supériorité mais aussi une vraie source de puissance. Tout comme une belle femme, un homme qui est beau, croit-il, peut se dispenser d'avoir d'autres qualités; comme elle, il domine et règne par sa seule beauté.

Être beau, c'est-à-dire avoir en soi un charme qui fait que tout vous sourit et vous accueille; qu'avant que vous ayez parlé tout le monde est déjà prévenu en votre faveur et disposé à être de votre avis; que vous n'avez qu'à passer par une rue, ou vous montrer à un balcon pour vous créer, dans la foule, des amis ou des maîtresses. N'avoir pas besoin d'être aimable pour être aimé, être dispensé de tous ces frais d'esprit et de complaisance auxquels la laideur vous oblige, et de ces mille qualités morales qu'il faut avoir pour suppléer la beauté du corps; quel don splendide et magnifique![26]

En plus de la beauté et comme faisant partie d'elle, notre dandy admire et désire la force. La force, c'est en quelque sorte la beauté de l'homme; elle en est du moins la base. Le rêve suprême, c'est de réunir ces deux qualités, vieux rêve grec de l'hermaphrodite qui a toujours un peu hanté notre auteur. 'Et celui qui joindrait à la beauté suprême la force suprême, qui, sous la peau d'Antinoüs, aurait les muscles d'Hercule, que pourrait-il désirer de plus?'[27]

Une dernière chose, et son bonheur est complet: 'le don de me transporter aussi vite que la pensée d'un endroit à un autre'.[28] 'La beauté de l'ange, la force du tigre et les ailes de l'aigle. . . . Un beau masque pour séduire et fasciner sa proie, des ailes pour fondre dessus et l'enlever, des ongles pour la déchirer. . . .'[29] Ces images sont significatives car elles révèlent aussi clairement que possible le sadisme inhérent au dandysme esthétique; la jouissance est égoïste et cruelle.

Le portrait du dandy esthétique se dessine donc fort nettement. Il est beau, jeune, fort et riche. Egoïste et pessimiste, il méprise l'humanité et ses lois sociales et morales. Il ne reconnaît qu'une valeur, ne cherche qu'une chose—la beauté, la beauté physique et matérielle. Surtout, il est féru d'art. Déçu par la médiocrité de l'existence, blessé par la laideur du monde qui l'entoure, il se réfugie chez les peintres et les sculpteurs pour leur demander à la fois une consolation et une raison d'être. De plus en plus, il regarde le monde en artiste et sa vision finit par en être faussée; dédaignant le naturel, il ne sait plus apprécier que l'artificiel—à une belle femme il préfère une belle statue. Tout païen qu'il est, il a, lui aussi, sa Trinité— la voici: 'Trois choses me plaisent: l'or, le marbre et la pourpre, éclat, solidité, couleur. Mes rêves sont faits de cela, et tous les palais que je bâtis à mes chimères sont construits de ces matériaux.'[30]

C'est donc dans un monde—ou un rêve—d'art, de beauté et de luxe que s'enferme le dandy esthétique, un monde d'où sont exclues toute laideur, toute imperfection et même toute idée qui n'est pas une idée esthétique. C'est un monde clos, irréel, irréalisable, quelque chose comme un paradis artificiel:

Voici comme je me représente le bonheur suprême:—c'est un grand bâtiment carré sans fenêtre au dehors; une grande cour entourée d'une colonnade de marbre blanc, au milieu une fontaine de cristal avec un jet de vif-argent à la manière arabe, des caisses d'orangers et de grenadiers posées alternativement; par là-dessus un ciel très-bleu et un soleil très-jaune;—de grands lévriers au museau de brochet dormiraient çà et là; de temps en temps des nègres pieds nus avec des cercles d'or aux jambes, de belles servantes blanches et sveltes, habillées de vêtements riches et capricieux, passeraient entre les arcades évidées, quelque corbeille au bras, ou quelque amphore sur la tête. Moi, je serais là, immobile, silencieux, sous un dais magnifique, entouré de piles de carreaux, un grand lion privé sous mon coude, la gorge nue d'une jeune esclave sous mon pied en manière d'escabeau, et fumant de l'opium dans une grande pipe de jade.[31]

On voit donc bien que déjà dans ce roman de *Mademoiselle de Maupin*, écrit en plein romantisme et qui n'est pas tant un roman qu'une allégorie, qu'une manière de parabole, se trouvent hautement proclamées et nettement formulées (abstraction faite d'une certaine 'truculence' romantique et d'un désir toujours évident d'épater le bourgeois) les idées maîtresses de l'esthétique de Théophile Gautier, c'est-à-dire la doctrine de *l'art pour l'art*. Dès 1835 sa voie est trouvée, sa profession de foi est faite. Désormais il n'a plus qu'à aller, à travers sa poésie, ses contes, ses romans, ses récits de voyage et même ces comptes-rendus quotidiens, cette basse cuisine littéraire de tous les jours qui lui soulevait tant le cœur, au pourchas de la beauté visible qui, sous toutes ses formes, seule le consolera de vivre. Il n'a plus qu'à s'acheminer, sa vie durant, avec une foi de pèlerin aussi touchante qu'admirable, vers ce pays fuyant et incertain où, pour reprendre les paroles de celui qui se targuait d'être le disciple du parfait magicien ès lettres françaises:

> . . . tout n'est qu'ordre et beauté,
> Luxe, calme et volupté.

NOTES

(1) *Nouveaux lundis*, t. VI, p. 282 (Paris, Michel Lévy, 1866).
(2) Ibid. p. 284.
(3) *L'Art romantique*, p. 155 (*Œuvres complètes*, t. I, Conard, 1925).
(4) *Mademoiselle de Maupin*, p. 283 (Bibliothèque Charpentier, 1899).
(5) Ibid. p. 197.　　(6) Ibid. p. 197.　　(7) Ibid. p. 272.
(8) Ibid. p. 211.　　(9) Ibid. p. 221.　　(10) Ibid. p. 148.
(11) Ibid. p. 149.　　(12) Ibid. p. 59.　　(13) Ibid. p. 146.
(14) Ibid. p. 208.　　(15) Ibid. p. 145.　　(16) Ibid. p. 52.
(17) Ibid. p. 53.　　(18) Ibid. p. 54.　　(19) Ibid. p. 65.
(20) Ibid. p. 212.　　(21) Ibid. p. 415.　　(22) Ibid. p. 216.
(23) Ibid. p. 149.　　(24) Ibid. p. 150.　　(25) Ibid. p. 150.
(26) Ibid. p. 152.　　(27) Ibid. p. 152.　　(28) Ibid. p. 152.
(29) Ibid. p. 152.　　(30) Ibid. p. 211.　　(31) Ibid. p. 222.

TEXTUAL PROBLEMS OF THE
LAI DE L'OMBRE

BY

JOHN ORR

Professor of French in the University of Edinburgh

BÉDIER's edition of the *Lai de l'Ombre*, published in 1913 for the Société des Anciens Textes Français, is a landmark in Old French studies, ushering in as it did a new method in the editing of Old French texts. His earlier edition, published twenty-three years before, had been constructed according to the then accepted method: by grouping the MSS. into families, and endeavouring to reproduce the original text by adhering to those readings upon which, in cases of conflict, two MSS. of different families were in agreement. The result, as Bédier himself says, was a composite text, something unreal, a so-called 'critical' edition, made still more unlike any version of the poem that actually existed by a strictly normalized and regularized system of spelling.

In 1913, the whole method is changed. Scathingly sceptical about all attempts to set up a convincing classification of all the MSS. of the text, that is to say, a classification that would automatically produce the original version, he confines himself to one, the readings of which he reproduces with the minimum number of corrections. It is recognized now by most scholars that this is the only truly 'scientific' method. But none the less it still leaves ample scope for scholarship and taste on the part of an editor, first in the choice of the manuscript he decides to follow, secondly in determining what is the minimum of correction required.

Bédier himself, despite his good intentions, departs from his model in no less than forty-five lines out of a total of 962—a not inconsiderable number for a MS. 'imprimé presque sans retouche'[1] —so that, in fact, as ten of these lines comprise three passages that are actually missing in the MS. he took as his 'basis', the final result can still with some justification be termed a composite text.

Having recently examined anew the MSS. of this delightful poem, with no higher ambition than to provide for university students a convenient edition of a work of great intrinsic merit and of historic interest to our discipline, I have encountered a number of problems that have remained unnoticed or unsolved. It is with pleasure that I here submit attempted solutions of some of these to the acknowledged acumen of the recipient of this volume.

A preliminary word of enlightenment[2] on the MSS. tradition will be not out of place. There are seven MSS., all of them in the Bibliothèque Nationale, Paris. Keeping to Bédier's sigla, they are as follows: *A* fonds français 837, *B* f. fr. 1593, *C* f. fr. 12603, *G* f. fr. 1553, *D* f. fr. 19152, *E* Nouvelles acquisitions fr. 1104, *F* f. fr. 14971. Despite Bédier's scepticism, they can be confidently characterized and grouped as follows. *A* and *B* speak with one voice, *B* with a less polished accent. *A*'s version was reproduced by Fr. Michel in his *Lais inédits* (Paris, 1836), and is the 'basis' of Bedier's 1913 edition. *C* and *G* go together. They speak with a strong Picard tang and are not averse to talking nonsense. *A B C G* have a number of lacunae in common: their relationship is certain. *D* and *F* have in common a lacuna of twelve lines, which can scarcely be fortuitous. Though they are frequently at variance, they show occasional agreement when disagreeing with the rest. *F* in particular has a great number of variant readings, some of them very attractive, so attractive that this MS. was used by Jubinal in his edition of the poem (Paris, 1846). Unfortunately, it lacks the prologue of fifty-two lines and has in places become illegible through damp. *E* is both complete—save for two lines (674 and 812) where the remarkably careful scribe has had a lapse—and, as Bédier himself admits, of quite excellent quality. Bédier even suggests that it may represent a version of the poem revised by the author himself.

It is this MS. which, after considerable reflection, I had already chosen to reproduce for the purpose indicated, before noticing that Bédier himself had, in 1928, announced his intention of publishing yet a third edition of the poem based upon it, an intention carried out somewhat perfunctorily the following year as an appendix to the *Romania* articles referred to above, published in book form. Adopting Bédier's method of minimum correction, I have been able to preserve its version in all but thirty-eight lines, including the two that are missing, and much of the retouching I have felt constrained to do is quite minute, and confined to one or two letters of a word. Now for the points at issue.

The final passage of the prologue (ll. 38–52) is one of particular interest and difficulty. It runs as follows in the competing MSS. *A* and *E*.

A	*E*
Et por ce l'ai je si empris	Et por ce ai cest lai empris
Que je vueil mon sens emploier	Que je voil mon sens desploier
40 A bien dire et a souploier	A bien dire et a souploier
A la hautece de l'Eslit.	A la hautesce de l'Eslit.
Mout par me torne a grant delit	Molt par me torne a grant delit
Quant ma volentez est eslite	Qant la volente m'est eslite
A fere ce qui me delite,	A fere ce que me delite,
45 Une aventure a metre en rime.	D'une aventure metre en rime.
L'en dit: Qui bien nage et bien rime,	On dit: Qui bien nage bien rime;
Qui de haute mer vient a rive,	Qui de haute mer vient a rive
Qui a port de bien dire arrive,	Fox est se a la mer estrive;
Plus l'en proisent et roi et conte.	Miex l'en prisent et roi et conte.
50 Or orrés par tens en monte (*sic*)	Or escoutez en icest conte
Que dirai, s'anuis ne m'encombre,	Que ferai, s'aucuns ne m'encombre,
En cest lai que je fais de l'Ombre.	Et dirai ci, du lay de l'Ombre.

It should be explained, first of all, that the *Eslit* referred to in l. 41 is believed to be Miles de Nanteuil, to whom Jehan Renart dedicated his *Roman de la Rose* (better known as *Guillaume de Dôle*), and who was *episcopus electus* to the diocese of Beauvais from 1217 until his consecration by the Pope, on his way home from the Holy Land, in 1222. Ll. 40 and 41, which Bédier says 'nous restent obscurs', thus seem fairly clear. The author wishes to show (*desploier*) or to apply (*emploier*) his wit in a good poem, and to yield (*souploier*, 'bow down') to the eminence of the Electus; which would seem to imply, from what follows, that the work was undertaken at the request of Miles himself.

Before turning to the textual problems, let us observe the metrical construction of the passage, which is interesting and peculiar. It will be seen that, whatever text we may ultimately adopt, ll. 41–52 are composed of four couplets with the same rhyming-vowel *i*, followed by two couplets with the rhyming vowel *õ*. In no other passage of the *Lai* is there such a succession of similar rhymes; and, as there is talk in our passage of 'good rhyming' (l. 46), we may conclude that the arrangement is not fortuitous, and that the author is making a special effort to round off his prologue handsomely. A recognition of this fact may help us, if not to solve, at least to account for some of the textual difficulties. To these we now turn.

All the MSS. other than *E* are in general agreement about l. 38. We can only say, at this stage, that both versions go back to a common original, and that the divergence arises from a misreading by one or more scribes of the group of letters *lai*. This situation is not quite the same with regard to l. 39, where again *E* is in a minority of one. For in an earlier passage (ll. 8–10) the author has said:

> Vilains est qui ses gas en fet
> Qant ma cortoisie s'aoevre
> A dire [*var*. faire] aucune plesant oevre
> Ou il n'a ramposne ne lait.

Here, in spite of the hint given by *C*, who writes *descuevre*, Bédier misconstrued *s'aoevre* as 's'emploie', whereas it is not from *s'aovrer* but from *s'aovrir* and means 'se manifeste'. *E*'s *desploier*, clearly, is both less banal than *emploier*, and more in accordance with what precedes. *E* would appear therefore to be one up, and his version of l. 38 rendered so much the more worthy of acceptance.

A more difficult problem is that raised by the innocuous looking l. 43. It will have been noticed that ll. 41–44 form a series of what have been called grammatical rhymes, composed of variations on similar etymological themes: *eslit, delit, eslite, delite*. This scheme, though not unknown elsewhere in Jehan Renart's works (there are three examples in *l'Escoufle*, but none in *Guillaume de Dôle*), may possibly occur in one other passage of the *Lai* (ll. 621–4), where four out of the seven MSS. give the sequence *aprist, prist, aprise, prise*, although not in complete agreement about l. 623; but, even if genuine, the sequence has not, there, the same sophisticated and deliberate quality of ll. 41–44. Let us now examine the variants of l. 43. They are as follows:

> *A:* Quant ma volentez est eslite
> *B:* Quant sa volanté m'a eslite
> *C:* Que ma volentes est eslite
> *G:* Que sa volentes est eslite
> *D:* Quant sa volonté m'a eslit
> *E:* Qant la volenté m'est eslite.

In view of the general agreement as to the rhyme-word *eslite*, and in view also of the special character of the whole passage, we are not justified in accepting an emendation suggested by Tobler :[3]

> Quant sa volontez m'a eslit
> A faire ce qui li delit,

a suggestion made (and approved by L.-A. Vigneras,[4] with the substitution of *me* for *li*) with a view to strengthening the interpretation of the *eslit* of l. 41 given above. *D* alone provides any justification for it; in *D*, however, l. 44 reads:

> A faire ce qui m'enbelit.

M. Vigneras comments that this line 'n'a pas grand sens', but in reality it is a perfect paraphrase of *A faire ce qui me delite* (*ABCG*). *D*'s version is, moreover, so completely intelligible as to offer no difficulty, and cannot possibly account for the divergence of the MSS. with regard to l. 43. It is obviously a recasting of a troublesome original.

It will be noticed that three MSS. belonging to different groups, *B*, *G*, and *D*, read *sa* volonte, while a fourth, *E*, reads *la*, which, palaeographically, is much the same. Can it possibly be that *B*, with what appears to be a barbarism, namely, a past participle agreeing, not with the preceding direct object *me*, but with the subject *volonté*, has preserved the correct and disturbing reading? The answer, I think, is yes.

In his study of the language of *l'Escoufle*,[5] Mussafia pointed out some remarkable cases of agreement of the past participle, some of which, e.g. l. 4668: *Cil qui m'erent venue querre*, it would be extremely difficult to emend, and others, more similar to that in *B*'s version of l. 43, which, though easily emended, apparently caused no tremor in a thirteenth-century scribe; e.g.: *Mout ot biaus bras et beles gemmes* [jambes] *Teus com li ot* faite *nature* (ll. 2986–7), and *Comment est ce que j'ai trovée Celi ou tout a* esprouvée *Nature quanqu'el a de sens?* In a note to his article, Mussafia alludes to a remark of Stimming's in a review[6] of Jeanroy and Teulié's edition of the fifteenth-century Provençal *Mystère de l'Ascension* (Toulouse, 1895) with reference to a passage in that text which runs as follows: '*la poisansa del demoni, La qual lo premier home Avia* subjugada.'

Stimming asserted that such cases of agreement occasionally occur in French texts, and quotes as examples, inter alia, *Cleomadès*, ll. 12898–9: *Sachiez bien que trestout l'anui Qu'ele a eüe et tout le mal*, and *Quatre Livres des Rois*, p. 361: *e vint devant le rei pur lui mustrer cume ot* parlee *la pucele de Israel*.[7] Such passages can, of course, be easily emended; but, on the evidence, it seems safe to conclude that Jehan Renart, with his extremely cavalier attitude towards syntax, has here ventured on a construction which shocked the scribes, but which he may well have considered 'une élégance de plus'. Only so, I think, can we account for such a variety of versions of what, in other respects, is a very simple line.

Still, it would be a bold editor who would introduce B's version into his 'critical' text. Prudence and correct method alike bid him abide by his chosen MS. And if this is *E*, a satisfactory rendering can, at a pinch, be given: 'Quand la bonne volonté que j'ai de rimer une aventure a été choisie pour faire une tâche qui m'enchante.'[8]

More difficult even, and more interesting are the problems raised by ll. 46–49.

Bédier accepts *A*'s version without change. The important variants other than those of *E* are as follows: l. 46: *CDG*, like *E*, omit *et*; *D*, *rive* for *rime*; l. 48: *C*, *Et au pont*; *G*, *Et au port*. Let us take *A*'s version first. Gaston Paris, in his review of Bédier's first edition, found it embarrassing and suggested that it should be modified as follows:

> On dit que bien nage et bien rime
> Qui de haute mer vient a rive;
> Qui a port de bien dire arrive
> Plus l'en proisent et roi et conte.

To this Bédier replies: 'Mieux vaut, à mon sens, conserver la leçon de *A*, en admettant une sorte de chiasme ou de croisement: On dit: Qui navigue bien (développé dans le vers *Qui de haute mer vient a rive*) est plus estimé des rois et des comtes; et pareillement, qui rime bien (développé dans le vers *Qui a port de bien dire arrive*) est plus estimé des rois et des comtes.'

This seems to me strained and quite unconvincing, and implies a somewhat excessive interest on the part of kings and counts in good navigation. That they are, or should be interested in good poesy, is of course, in a poet's eyes, quite natural. I would suggest that all the scribes, and Bédier himself, have been thrown off the track by the word *rime* in l. 46.

If *rime* means 'rhymes', not even the ingenuity of a Bédier can make acceptable sense of the passage. But if it is a nautical term—something akin to the verb *nagier* ('to navigate')—the passage reads naturally and becomes clear. Now Godefroy has three examples of *rimer*, which he translates by 'ramer', 'naviguer', and in one of them it is coupled with the word *nagier* as in our text:

> Si s'en entrent el bac endui
> Et si *nagierent* tant et *riment*
> Que a l'autre rive s'en vinrent. *Perceval,* 9738

The word is, however, not a variant of *ramer*, as Bloch states (*Dict. Étym.*, s.v. RAMER), but a quasi-synonym of *nagier* and means, originally, 'to steer', or 'to set a course'. Cf. the following from *Aiol* (*S.A.T.*), ll. 9301 ff.

> Des or naga Teris, molt eslonge Makaire;
> Tout contreval le rive *se conduist* et *se nage*;
> Onques ne tresfinerent tant qu'il vinrent a avene.

The word *arrimer* is well known as a nautical term, meaning 'to stow', 'to trim'. But it has also an earlier meaning of 'to plot a course on a map'; cf. Cotgrave, s.v. ARRUMÉ, carte arrumée, *a sea-card, wherein all the quarter winds, or travers, boords, are delineated*; and ARRUMER, *to delineate or set out in a sea-card all the Rums of winds*. But, it will be objected, *arrumer* is not *arrimer* and *arrimer* is not *rimer*. To this, remembering O.F. *rimeur*, a variant of *rumeur*, we would reply:

1. Cotgrave has an early ARRUMER: *to ranke, sort, range, dispose, put in order, set in array* (i.e. Mod. *arrimer*).

2. Godefroy, s.v. ARINER: 'arranger, disposer, mettre en ordre' (i.e. Mod. *arrimer*) gives us such variants as *arinner, arimer, arrimer, arruner, arisner*.

3. Cotgrave has an entry: RIM DE VENT: *a puffe of wind*; or as Rum; another, RUM: *the hole, or hold of a ship*; *also as* Rumb;

and a third, RUMB: *A roomb or point of the compasse; a line drawn directly from wind to wind in a compasse, Travers-boord on Sea-card.* Voguer de rumb en rumb: *To saile by travers.* Voguer par divers rumbs: *Upon divers boords or changes of winds.*

4. Godefroy, VII, 199c has an entry RIN, 'rumb', with alternative forms *rim, ryn, rym.*

From the above it seems certain that *rime* in l. 46 comes from *rim* an alternative form of *rum*, 'rhumb', that it is a nautical term and means, roughly, as we have said, 'to steer', or 'to keep a course'.

In l. 46, therefore, omitting with *CDGE* the word *et*, we have what appears to be a 'dicton' (introduced in the customary manner by *On dit*) the point of which seems to be a pun on the two meanings of the word *rime*; a pun analogous to that which ends the *Lai*: *Contez, vous qui savez de nombre!*⁹ Both elements of the adage are then developed, in *ABCDG*'s version, in the following lines. But what of *E*'s *Fox est se a la mer estrive*, which competes with *Qui* (or *Et*) *au port de bien dire arrive* for l. 48, and which, though it makes such admirable sense after *Qui de haute mer vient a rive*, seems quite out of place in the remaining context? I find it difficult to believe that either this line or its competitor is the invention of a scribe. But if both are by the author, then both *ABCDG*'s version and that of *E* are corrupt.

The only solution I can see is that in the original there was a series of identical rimes, either of four (a suggestion of my colleague Miss Legge's), as occurs once elsewhere in the *Lai*, six times in *l'Escoufle*, and eight times in *Guillaume de Dôle*, or of three, instances of which are common in Anglo-Norman texts, but are extremely rare in continental works.¹⁰

One point which speaks strongly in favour of a three-rime series is that it is more likely to have been 'corrected' independently by different scribes. I therefore suggest the following as possibly the version of the original:

> On dit: Qui bien nage, bien rime.
> Qui de haute mer vient a rive,
> Fox est se a la mer estrive.
> Qui a port de bien dire arrive,
> Plus l'en prisent et roi et conte.

This I translate as follows: '"Steer well, *rhyme* well" they say: He who comes safe to shore from the high seas is a fool if he chides the waves. He who reaches the haven of good poesy wins greater praise from the discerning.'

D's *rive*, l. 46, is obviously an error, because it is unlikely that in this particular passage the author would have allowed himself the imperfect rhyme, *rime: rive*, although similar rhymes are frequent in his other works. But it does actually give us a succession of three identical rimes, and this may be some confirmation of our conjecture. As for the nautical term *rimer*, that this is not merely an alternative form of *ramer* is well shown by a passage from Eustache Deschamps's ballade *Contre la mauvaise mer* (*S.A.T.* vol. I, pp. 80 f.). After having said (str. 2):

> Et chascuns d'eux [des dieux de la mer] de
> *sejorner* me presse.
> Mon navire font par leur force *encrer*;
> *Mouvoir ne puis*...,

he says in the Envoy:

> Dieux Mars, j'atten printemps de douçor plain,
> Que l'en pourra paisiblement *rymer*;
> Lors y fait bon, en yver n'y fait sain:
> Contre les vens ne puet nulz de la mer.

Here *rymer* should clearly be translated by 'voguer' and not by 'ramer' as in the footnote to the text.

NOTES

(1) Bédier, in *Romania*, LIV (1928), 177.

(2) I deliberately refrain from giving details, as these are easily accessible in the Introduction to Bédier's edition. See also *Romania*, LIV (1928), 161 ff., 321 ff.

(3) *Archiv*, LXXXV (1890), 355.

(4) *Modern Philology*, XXX (1933), 358.

(5) *Wien. Akad. Sitz. Ber., Phil.-Hist. Cl.* vol. CXXXV (1896), Abh. XIV, pp. 19–21.

(6) *Zeitschr.* XX (1896), 546.

(7) The other examples quoted by Stimming I have not been able to identify; they are Henri de Valenciennes, § 609, and Froissart, XI, 448 u.ö. He goes so

far as to add that similar cases of agreement are to be found in Ronsard, Pascal, Boileau, Molière and other authors.

(8) That thirteenth-century scribes were not always shocked by such agreement is seen in the variants to l. 844, where the knight, speaking of his lady, says, (*CG*) *Qui de s'amor m'a conjuree*, or (*D*) *Qui si forment m'a conjuree*.

(9) A similar pun on *rimer* is to be found in the *Roman de la Violete*, 6334 ff.:

> Gyrbers de Mosteruel define
> De la Violete son conte;
> N'en velt plus faire lonc aconte;
> Tant a rimé k'il est a rive.

There is other evidence that Gerbert de Montreuil knew the *Lai de l'Ombre* almost by heart. His familiarity with the other works of Jean Renart is well known.

(10) A case occurs in *Le Roman du Comte de Poitiers* (ed. Malmerg, Lund, 1940), ll. 1201–3:

> Mais molt malvaisement li vait,
> Car li faus sairemens c'ot fait
> L'a le jor houni entresait.

I owe the knowledge of this text to Miss Legge. The editor makes (p. 106) a queer commentary on the passage.

GOETHE'S AUTOBIOGRAPHY AND
ROUSSEAU'S *CONFESSIONS*

BY

ROY PASCAL

Professor of German in the University of Birmingham

ROUSSEAU'S writings were one of the major sources of the German culture of the Goethe period. His proclamation of the rights of the individual, and particularly of the emotive and irrational side of man, deeply affected almost all Goethe's contemporaries, and Goethe himself in his early manhood. Evidence of a direct influence of Rousseau's social ideas is to be found in *Götz von Berlichingen*; *Werther* is linked with *La Nouvelle Héloïse*; and Goethe's little pamphlet, *Letter of a Parish Priest* ... expresses ideas similar to those in the *Profession de Foi du Vicaire Savoyard*— it is easy to add to the list. Many of Goethe's young friends took Rousseau's mode of life, his withdrawal from polite society, as a model, as Goethe noted in his autobiography when writing of Klinger;[1] Goethe's own 'Gartenhaus' in the Weimar park had something of a 'Hermitage' about it.

The relationship of the older Goethe to Rousseau is much more obscure and problematical. Like most of his friends, he read the first six books of the *Confessions*, when they appeared in 1782, with profound interest and admiration. But the book appeared at a time when he himself was going through a period of transformation, when he was consciously wrestling with some of what one may call the Rousseauian elements in his nature. In spite of the few comments of his old age appreciative of Rousseau,[2] Goethe became cool, even hostile. In his autobiography, *Dichtung und Wahrheit*, most of which was written between 1811 and 1814, he even seems deliberately to suppress acknowledgment of Rousseau's contribution to his own growth.

In comparing the two autobiographies, both of which have had so great an influence on autobiographical writing, one is of course not comparing the two men directly, but rather their own views on

147   10-2

themselves; and in this paper I am searching primarily for the significant differences between the two writers, differences which enable us to perceive more clearly the specific characteristics of each.

Rousseau's autobiography is a confession, a confession of faith as well as a confession of sin. After describing his deceitfulness over the theft of the ribbon (*Confessions*, Partie I, Livre I) Rousseau writes: 'Ce poids est donc resté jusqu'à ce jour sans allègement sur ma conscience; et je puis dire que le désir de m'en délivrer en quelque sorte a beaucoup contribué à la résolution que j'ai prise d'écrire mes confessions.' But the book also asserts the joys and values of personal life, of natural innocence, of rural retreats. In its Second Part it becomes, against Rousseau's own avowed intention, more and more of a self-justification and an accusation against others. The term 'confessions' scarcely applies here; and in the degree to which Rousseau appears to himself as an innocent victim the book loses in autobiographical value. But I intend in this paper to ignore the problems arising from the persecution of Rousseau, and to concern myself with that part of the *Confessions* where the author most vigorously and clearly achieves his original intention.

A much more subtle purpose is evident in Goethe's approach to his task. The very title has mystery and ambiguity in it. 'Wahrheit', 'truth', is clear enough; but there is also 'Dichtung', and 'Dichtung' can mean 'poetry', or 'invention', or 'fiction'. He invents and re-arranges, not of course with the intention of deceiving, but in order to give a deeper truth than can be revealed by the fortuitous associations of real life. As his old friend Fritz Jacobi, who knew at first hand many of the events and persons of the autobiography, put it: 'the truth of this work of poetical fiction is often truer than truth itself'. Thus Goethe skilfully introduces important experiences with *motifs* which, even if not true, mark their significance. The Sesenheim love affair is introduced by the re-telling of the story of the *Vicar of Wakefield*, which he actually read later, in order to illustrate the significance of this rural innocence for him, and to shed over the whole a poetic charm which softens the harshness of its ending. Goethe's relations with his father appear much more serene and fruitful than we should expect after reading the contemporary documents. Such a method, in which the actual past

is merged with retrospective valuation of the past, is highly interesting, and artistically engaging; but it holds great dangers of mis-
representation. We rarely if ever feel the force of spontaneous
memory; and are aware that we are presented with a carefully
pondered interpretation of Goethe's youth.

Goethe says in *Dichtung und Wahrheit* that all his poetical works
are 'fragments of a great confession' (Teil II, Buch 7), and for a
time he thought of giving the title 'Confessions' to his autobiography. But, surprising as it may seem, *Dichtung und Wahrheit*
is one of the least 'confessional' of all his major works. Written
when he was over sixty years of age, it is a serene and vigorous
reflection on his development, free equally of remorse and nostalgia.
It has the lucid self-detachment of a man not compelled to write
by emotive or moral pressure, who is indicating to us how he came
to achievement. His mood is comparable with that which nature
and time induced in his own *Faust*, when he put the catastrophe
of Part I resolutely behind him:

> Soften the heavy blow to the heart;
> Remove the rankling arrows of reproach,
> From horror cleanse his inner part.

The immediate occasion for his composing his autobiography
accounts for this mood. A new edition of his complete works had
appeared in 1806–8, in which Goethe had arranged them not
chronologically, but according to associations of theme or form.
His admirers sought to distinguish between the productions of the
various periods, and, in response to their interest, Goethe began to
arrange the past in his mind. The task developed as he proceeded,
and in the introduction to *Dichtung und Wahrheit* he defines his
purpose in its full form:

As I endeavoured to describe in right order the inner stirrings, the
external influences, the stages through which theory and practice had
carried me, I was thrown out of my narrow private life into the wide
world. The figures of a hundred important personalities who had
exerted a near or distant influence on me emerged into prominence;
indeed I had to pay particular attention to the immense movements
of the general political world which had had the greatest effect on me as
on the whole mass of my contemporaries. For this seems to be the chief

ROY PASCAL

task of biography, to depict a man in the circumstances of his times, and to show to what extent the whole stood in his way, to what extent it favoured him, how he shaped out of it an outlook on the world and on mankind, and, if he is an artist, poet, or writer, how he in turn reflects it . . . so that one may well say that each man, were he born a mere ten years earlier or later, would have become a quite different person, as far as his own inner development[3] and his effect on the outer world are concerned.[4]

Thus Goethe portrays his life as an evolution, a product of the interaction of his own innate character and external circumstance. His ultimate concern is the elucidation of himself as a poet, the unfolding of a poetical temperament, the genesis of his poetical works: he once says his object is 'to fill in the gaps of an author's life' (Teil III, Buch 12). But the development of a poet is for him not a mere aesthetic or spiritual process, it springs from the development of his whole personality, and Goethe's method is remarkably consistent and exhaustive. He shows his innate characteristics, his early tendency to dramatize, his love of masquerade and disguise, of games and make-believe; his warm response to friendship and love; his intellectual and practical interests. We see the formative influence of the domestic circle, grandparents, father, mother and sister, and of the family friends; of his own childhood friends and then, later, of kindred spirits like Herder and Merck. The help he received from great writers of the past, such as Shakespeare and Spinoza, is lovingly and gratefully described. His contemporaries appear, not only as writers, but with engaging clarity as men. Local, national, and world events and circumstances are given a due place, the rebuilding of the paternal house, the Frankfurt municipality, Frederick the Great and the Seven Years' War, as invigorating stimuli; but also account is taken of circumstances which put hindrances in his way. It is the pettiness of the 'tedious, un-inspired, burgher life', and the fragmentation of German political life, that provoke the 'surly arrogance' of his generation.

At times Goethe seems even too conscientious a biographer, and enters into matters which are interesting only to the serious student of German literature. His grasp of his purpose often took him into realms which have little direct attraction. He shrewdly enlarges on the tedious business of the law courts at Wetzlar, and on the idle make-believe of the bored young lawyers there, in order to make understandable the emotive outburst which found artistic expression in *Werther*. But he himself felt the strain of such expositions, and he ushers in the account of his meeting with Lotte Buff (the original of Werther's Lotte) with the words: 'As the author comes to this stage of his task, for the first time his heart grows light' (Teil III, Buch 12). And even then, his account is laconic, helped out by a quotation from *La Nouvelle Héloïse*. He tells us little of the rapture and anguish which this experience brought him. It would be vain to expect him, he writes, to recall the vital energies of his experience. In any case, *Werther* is there, and that suffices.

Rousseau's method is the very contrary. Life has brought him only disenchantment; the more he knows of men, the less profit he has learned to expect from intercourse with them. He sees his inner self threatened and overshadowed by the external world, and enfeebled by the process of growing old and infirm.[5] He evokes the past only when it is brightly lit, when it evokes nostalgia, indignation, or remorse. Thus his prose frequently has an ardour, a brilliance, a seduction which hardly any pages of Goethe's often somewhat pedantically phrased autobiography achieve—except perhaps the latter's description of his visits to Sesenheim, which is much more of a poetic reconstruction than a historical account.

Rousseau defined his purpose in his famous opening words:

Je veux montrer à mes semblables un homme dans toute la vérité de la nature, et cet homme, ce sera moi. Moi seul. Je sens mon cœur, et je connais les hommes. Je ne suis fait comme aucun de ceux que j'ai vus; j'ose croire n'être fait comme aucun de ceux qui existent . . .. Je me suis montré tel que je fus; méprisable et vil quand je l'ai été; bon, généreux, sublime, quand je l'ai été.

He sees himself as a unique being in two senses: on the one hand, fundamentally different from all others, on the other, detached from all others, existing *per se*. Thus the social environment, other personalities, are pale, scarcely sketched, except where they arouse or reflect his impulses to the good or the bad, the ideal or the sordid. With the deepest insight into his own temperament, and a frankness which has not been equalled, he is incapable of recording the outside social world; though rural nature is all the more vivid, since in nature he could commune with himself, be 'himself'. Mme Basile in her shop, the maid whom he accuses of having stolen the ribbon, are vivid in that moment when they cross his path; Mme de Warens is described with a depth and delicacy of appreciation which makes later expositions of her 'true' character seem clumsy and ridiculous.[6] Nothing is more alive than the early association with Thérèse in Paris. But how vague is Rousseau's world in general, whether it be Geneva, Paris, or the villages in or near which he lived! One could never guess from the *Confessions* what specific importance Voltaire or Diderot had for Rousseau, even less what sort of people they were. Not that Rousseau tried to suppress acknowledgment of his debt to them; they simply did not seem to affect his essential self. Even the persons who provided in later life an outlet for his emotions, or a setting for his existence, Mme d'Houdetot, or M. and Mme de Luxembourg, are shadowy. They do not contribute to his development, but merely allow him to be what he felt he essentially was. When he wrote to Malesherbes: 'J'ai pris en mépris mon siècle et mes contemporains',[7] he was uttering a principle which is evident in the whole conception of his autobiography, in his repudiation of any educative formative influence in his environment and his concentration on his naked personality.

So contrasting an approach in Rousseau and Goethe indicates a deep difference in their appreciation of the interplay of necessity and will. Rousseau emphasizes like Goethe the importance of his innate characteristics, and of his early upbringing. But his early taste for novels, and the indulgence of his imagination by his father, induce a 'romantic taste' which prevents him from ever coming to grips with the outer world. He describes himself as, from his childhood, a prey to his own temperament, and his main virtue, in his maturity, has been 'cet indomptable esprit de liberté',[8] which has inspired him to protect his character against the intrigues of the world. Social circumstance thus becomes indifferent; and it is symptomatic that he believes that, but for an accident, he might well have settled down as an artisan, a gardener, or botanist. Goethe, on the other hand, tends to emphasize—even to over-emphasize— the necessity governing his development. The artistic arrangement of *Dichtung und Wahrheit* brings out the operation of an invisible law, which in Goethe's novel, *Wilhelm Meisters Lehrjahre*, finds symbolic form in the secret society which guides the hero's destinies. More than once he indicates in his autobiography his sense of an impelling necessity governing the development of each individual personality:

> Few biographies are able to show a clear, quiet, constant progress of the individual. Our life, like the whole in which we are contained, is inextricably woven of freedom and necessity. Our willing is an announcement of what we shall do under any circumstances. But these circumstances seize us in their own peculiar way. The 'what' lies in us, the 'how' rarely depends on us, we may not ask after the 'why', and therefore we are always rightly directed to the 'because'.[9]

Differently from Rousseau Goethe affirmed the rightness and goodness of this influence of circumstance on the individual, even where it leads to disaster. *Dichtung und Wahrheit* closes, as with a final chord, with a quotation from his tragedy *Egmont* which affirms the fate which drives men along, even though it may be to their disaster. His religious feeling, as he defines it in his autobiography, is an interpretation of this trust in the world—'faith is a great feeling of security for the present and the future, and this security arises from the trust in a superlatively great, omnipotent and inscrutable Being' (Teil III, Buch 14). This faith of Goethe's arises from his whole experience, in the world of man as of nature. Rousseau's God, on the other hand, is revealed only in nature and the inner stirrings of the heart; elsewhere, and above all in the social world, He is obscured or absent.

The trust in the ultimate goodness of the world is a marked characteristic of the Goethe of *Dichtung und Wahrheit*, an engaging, open, active 'good lad' (as he calls himself in the poem 'An Belinden'), who everywhere finds food for his intellectual and practical interests and his spiritual profit. The real crisis in Goethe's life occurred only at Weimar, i.e. after the events described at the close of the autobiography; and so we do not see the inner struggles and maturing of those vital years between 1775 and 1786. But no doubt Goethe would have described them too as a period of organic and gradual assimilation and unfolding. In Rousseau, on the contrary, we see on the one hand the undefined, uneducable 'romantic'; and, as an abrupt contrast, and introduced by an abrupt revelation (on the road to Vincennes), the heroic Rousseau.[10] Rousseau remains true to himself in a more simple sense than Goethe, but at the same time he turns himself into a myth, 'le citoyen'. In justifying his abandonment of his children he asks whether it is possible that he, so open to virtue, so generous, could be depraved; and answers: 'Jamais un seul instant de sa vie Jean-Jacques n'a pu être un homme sans sentiment, sans entrailles, un père dénaturé' (Partie II, Livre 8). A little earlier he had checked a very natural inquisitive eagerness on his part by asking himself: 'Jean-Jacques se laisserait-il subjuguer par l'intérêt et la curiosité?' (Livre 7). The two personalities of Rousseau are strangely contrasted, the one simple, unassuming, sentimental, affectionate; the other lapidary, pretentious, heroic, to which he appeals for strength when other guidance fails. This self-dramatization through which Rousseau created a myth of himself, a process for which Spitteler found a name in his *Imago*, is indicative of Rousseau's uncertainty of self, the lack of maturity of his character, the inadequacy of his conception of what constitutes the truth of a man. Goethe defined this weakness very profoundly when he wrote, in one of his aphorisms: 'A man is not only what he possesses as his innate characteristics, but also what he acquires.'[11]

No doubt the fortunate circumstances of Goethe's life, his financial independence, contributed greatly to his affirmation of the interplay of self and environment. To them we may attribute, too, his accommodation with existing social and political institutions. Though right to the end of his life Goethe remained a profoundly disturbing influence in the moral sphere, his political thought and behaviour were traditionalist and barren. His description in his autobiography of the revolutionary turmoil of his youth is one of the least satisfactory parts of the book. He passes over it with an unsympathetic irony, and attributes the unrest of his generation merely to the quietude of a peaceful period which produced no great cause to canalize the energies of youth. His distaste for the enthusiasm for freedom is evident in his reference to its 'infinitely unhappy results' (the French Revolution), and he mentions the 'disgust of social life', which Rousseau and Diderot had disseminated, as 'a quiet introduction to those monstrous convulsions of the world, in which all existing institutions seemed to be over-whelmed' (Teil III, Buch 2). The fragmentation of Germany and the pettiness of burgher life appear as misfortunes, but they did not lead Goethe, in his life or his autobiography, to suggest political reforms. In *Dichtung und Wahrheit* they are described partly to elucidate his own spiritual development, and partly to offset the advantages of the small state, to which he draws attention first in his account of the writings of Justus Möser, the practical states-man, and then in his description of his meeting with the Duke of Weimar, to whose invitation to live in Weimar Goethe responds at the end of the book. Praise of the potentialities of the small semi-patriarchal state is the only positive political doctrine of the autobiography.

In one sense Goethe may not, in this, be so different from Rousseau. Rousseau found himself very happy with great lords as long as he knew them merely as landed gentry, and in the *Contrat Social* he stresses the advantages the small state presents.[12] His own political theory arose from his intimate contact with French intellectual life, and his experience of a great state; and though he would have been dissatisfied in any Swiss Canton or petty German state of the time, his discontent might well in such circum-stances never have found expression in political theories.

In the *Confessions*, Rousseau says very little about his theories of state, of history, and of education. Just as Goethe felt it not to be necessary to conjure up again the experiences embodied in his poetical works, so Rousseau seems to assume that we know all about his great theoretical works, and only writes about their sources. It is interesting however to note that he lays stress above all on the personal and emotive sources, rather than on the ratiocinative and intellectual processes involved. His childhood experiences of Geneva, his personal relations with the French ambassador in Venice, the visit to the peasant who hides his good food for fear of the tax-collector, and the intrigues in fashionable society at Paris: these are the decisive stimuli of his social thought. He gives us the picture of an essentially emotional man, devoted to simplicity and truth, whose political thought is a generalization of his own private experiences. We see little of the rational labour which was necessary before he could complete his theories; we see little of the effort of the will which shook him out of the confines of personal experience and forced him to generalize, to consider the whole of humanity. Rousseau might well have painted a much rosier picture of himself, and have shown us the process by which he turned his subjective love of justice and liberty into a cogent theory of society. In fact he prefers to appear virtuous only through the spontaneity of his heart and the frankness of his reflections on himself.

The 'freedom' which appears in the *Confessions* is then less of a political or social principle than a personal, psychological one. One might quote the phrase he uses in his disarming letter to Malesherbes: 'L'espèce de devoir qu'il me faut, n'est pas tant de faire ce que je veux, que de ne pas faire ce que je ne veux pas.'[13] This is the sort of freedom which Goethe would not recognize. His own life, which he conceived as an education, brought the lesson that he must learn to 'purify' himself, to find new values whose worth he learnt from other persons, such as Frau von Stein, and from social necessity itself. That Goethe was aware that education of this kind may easily slip into acceptance of arbitrary and unworthy conventional values is evident from his play *Torquato Tasso*, in which the tensions between social life and the poet are portrayed; but in the autobiography these tensions are minimized, and the style of the writing consistently suggests accommodation. It is perennially refreshing to observe Rousseau's determined resistance to social and moral proprieties. He himself has revealed many of the unheroic sources of this characteristic, and later writers can add pathological or physiological determinants, the symptoms of which are plain enough. But this determination not to become enmeshed in prevailing social and moral manners is one of Rousseau's greatest gifts to posterity.

It is not true that Goethe was a conformist. To the end of his life he continued to startle and outrage the orthodox. But he combines this challenge with a stiff formalism of social manners, and often with a conformism of doctrine, which make it seem that he claims eccentricity as a personal right, as the right of an intellectual and poetic genius: a combination which Thomas Mann has subtly revealed in his study, *Lotte in Weimar*. Rousseau, on the other hand, establishes his non-conformity as a right which belongs

GOETHE AND ROUSSEAU

to him as a simple individual, and therefore as the right of anyone who feels as he did. For that reason anyone in any generation who is oppressed can find sustenance in him.

This non-conformism of Rousseau reaches deep into accepted conventions, and nowhere more deeply than into the chaos of irrational instinct, particularly of sexual life, over which usually a prudent veil is drawn. His frank descriptions of his youthful exhibitionism, and of the advances of homosexuals, have often been dismissed as shameless effrontery. It is however clear enough that, still disgusted and horrified by some of these phenomena, he felt impelled to put them before his readers as significant aspects of human behaviour. Goethe's autobiography is singularly lacking in evidence of normal or abnormal sex life, except in the sublimated form of love. Only one passage has, to my knowledge, given occasion to psycho-analytical treatment—the passage where he describes the delight he once took, as a child, in breaking all the crockery, which Freud analysed as a typical result of a repression.[14] There can be no doubt that Goethe went through the sexual experiences common to youngsters, and probably they were more lively in his case than in most. It belongs to the whole intention of his autobiography that he suppresses this side of experience.[15]

While one feels, in reading the *Confessions*, that here a soul is laid bare, one is sometimes persuaded to forget that one is reading, not of a simple and harmless private person, but of Rousseau, a challenging political and social philosopher. In *Dichtung und Wahrheit*, on the other hand, Goethe is deliberately showing us the formation of a poet, not a simple or normal person at all; and it is necessary, in judging the work as a whole, to examine a little closer what is involved in his being a poet.

Goethe wrote about Rousseau's *Pygmalion*, for which he had in his youth the liveliest admiration:

This queer production oscillates between nature and art, with the false intention of dissolving the latter in the former. We see an artist, who has created something perfect and yet does not find satisfaction in having projected his idea outside himself into a work of art and having given it a higher life; no, it has to be dragged down to him into his earthly life. He desires to destroy the highest achievement of spirit and deed by the most vulgar act of sensuality (Teil III, Buch 2).

157

There is a good deal of truth in this sharp criticism; certainly it illustrates Goethe's view of the meaning and function of poetry. Over and over again in *Dichtung und Wahrheit* he stresses the peculiar function of poetry in liberating him from the earthly pressures which gave rise to his works. Poetry meant for him the tendency 'to turn whatever delighted or tormented me, or busied me in any other way, into an image, a poem, and thus to settle with myself, both in so far as I corrected my notions of external things, and in so far as I thus found inner quiet' (Teil II, Buch 7). Thus of *Werther* he wrote: 'By this composition I rescued myself from the tempestuous element, in which I had been tossed to and fro in the most violent fashion' (Teil III, Buch 13). The farces and pranks of his youth served the same end; by turning the sources of his vexation into a fantastic guise, into an extravaganza, he was able to get rid of bitterness and rancour. He did not, like Rousseau, bear in him for years remorse for unworthy deeds, to be relieved only by a direct confession; he found remission of sins immediately, through poetry. In discussing the importance of *Werther*, he writes the significant words: 'I felt, as after a general confession, cheerful and free again, and fully entitled to take up a new life' (*ibid.*). This is the theme of his later work, *Tasso*:

> And when man in his agony is dumb,
> A God has granted me to say, how I suffer.

For this reason Goethe expresses, in the autobiography, his surprise and vexation that his contemporaries misunderstood his works, saw them as didactic statements, as direct calls to action. They argued about *Werther* as if it were a treatise on suicide, and Nicolai actually wrote a sequel showing how Werther could have settled down if the characters had all acted a little more reasonably. Goethe's answer was, '*Werther* just had to be'; the practical question, how we are to behave, is something quite different from the poetical release of the strains of life.

The imagination of Rousseau served quite a different purpose. He faithfully describes his own tendency to prefer the world of his imagination to the real world, and traces the influences—for instance the novel-reading of his childhood—which deepened the abyss between imagination and life. His poetical work, particularly

La Nouvelle Héloïse, arose out of his estrangement from mankind, and strengthens that estrangement.

> L'impossibilité d'atteindre aux êtres réels me jeta dans le pays des chimères; et ne voyant rien d'existant qui fût digne de mon délire, je le nourris dans un monde idéal que mon imagination créatrice eut bientôt peuplé d'êtres selon mon cœur. Jamais cette ressource ne vint plus à propos et ne se trouva plus féconde. Dans mes continuelles extases, je m'enivrais à torrents des plus délicieux sentiments qui jamais soient entrés dans un cœur d'homme. Oubliant tout à fait la race humaine, je me fis une société de créatures parfaites, aussi célestes par leurs vertus que par leurs beautés, d'amis sûrs, tendres, fidèles, tels que je n'en trouvai jamais ici-bas. ... Quand, prêt à partir pour le monde enchanté, je voyais arriver de malheureux mortels qui venaient me retenir sur la terre, je ne pouvais modérer ni cacher mon dépit; et, n'étant plus maître de moi, je leur faisais un accueil si brusque, qu'il pouvait porter le nom de brutal. (Partie II, Livre 9.)

Rousseau makes the point again in his letters to Malesherbes:

> Sentant que je ne trouverais au milieu d'eux [mes contemporains] une situation qui pût contenter mon cœur, je l'ai peu à peu détaché de la société des hommes, et je m'en suis fait une autre dans mon imagination.[16]

It is characteristic of Rousseau's imagination that, because of this conflict between his inner and the outer world, he has to lead his *Héloïse* to a moral solution; and he himself emphasized that the final book, that in which the characters come to terms with the moral world, was the most important. They have to overcome their natural disposition; and the novel itself turns into a moral lesson. Goethe's major works, of his youth as of his old age, leave us in the throes of a deep problem. By expressing the inner stresses in artistic form he has achieved his poetical goal; there is for him a fundamental falsehood in treating his creations as models of behaviour, as persons of normal life.

The worlds of imagination and normal society are, then, for both writers two opposed worlds, but opposed in a totally different way. The world of Rousseau's imagination was a refuge, it left him with a nostalgic yearning which unfitted him for normal life; it is an expression of that conflict between the individual and society which found its most valuable formulation in his theoretical works on state and society. Goethe's imaginative world is a sphere to which the criteria of normal life do not apply; but it continually arises from and reflects the normal world, and its function is cathartic in the true sense in that it releases him emotively and enables him to play his part in the normal world.

The distinction between the two worlds grew clearer for Goethe as he grew older; it was much clearer to the Goethe of *Dichtung und Wahrheit* than to the Goethe of *Werther*. His 'classicism' was to a large extent the process of his appreciating this distinction. But, if he was to avoid the pitfall of an aestheticism in which art is completely divorced from life, he had to cleanse his imagination from purely individual, subjective obsessions (such as Werther had), and to keep himself broadly facing the real world. His friend Merck had noted this danger early in his life. As he said to Goethe: 'Your undeviating trend is, to give reality a poetic form; the others (their contemporaries) seek to realize what is usually taken to be poetic and imaginative, and the result is nothing but stupid stuff.'[17] This theme is represented most clearly in Goethe's *Faust*, for it is the alliance with Helen, with classical beauty, that leads Faust to turn his efforts to earthly achievement. Goethe defined this whole trend in his later life as classicism, and the following remark might be considered to be not only an estimate of his own character as a poet, but also a criticism of Rousseau's imagination: 'As long as the poet expresses merely his subjective feelings, he does not really deserve the name; but as soon as he can assimilate the world and express it, he is a poet. . . . People are always talking about the study of the Ancients. But what does this mean but: Turn to the real world and seek to express it.'[18]

Both these writers were charged in their own day with excessive egoism, and it is true that both were deeply concerned with working out the problems which arose from their own emotive experience. Both however could rightly claim to be contributing to universal problems. It is fascinating to observe how different was the temperamental material with which they had to work, and how different were their solutions. Rousseau's disordered imagination made it impossible for him to find a *modus vivendi* with his contemporaries, or a poetical expression which would reconcile him with social life; Goethe's imagination continually restored him to balance and enabled him to make fruitful contributions to social life. It is characteristic that Goethe's plan of education stresses to a remarkable degree the formal constituents of behaviour.[19] But, on the other hand, while Goethe carefully weaned himself of the nebulous but noble enthusiasms of his youth, Rousseau to the end of his life preserved 'les divins élans qu'il n'appartient qu'au plus pur amour du juste et du beau de produire dans mon cœur' (Partie II, Livre 7). 'Enivré de la vertu' (Partie II, Livre 9), he sought solutions in the sphere of social and political relations, and his scheme of education (in *Émile*) leads above all to the awakening of the moral conscience, of enthusiasm for the virtues. Opposed as these two great writers are, they seem to be rather complementary than antagonistic. It is fruitful to compare them, for their contrast brings out in sharp relief the specific character of the achievement of each.

NOTES

(1) *Dichtung und Wahrheit*, Teil III, Buch 14.

(2) The most important are collected in Bertram Barnes, *Goethe's Knowledge of French Literature*. Oxford, 1937.

(3) Goethe uses his favourite term 'Bildung', which means the education and shaping of the personality.

(4) *Dichtung und Wahrheit*, Vorwort.

(5) It is characteristic that illness is for Rousseau a painful and burdensome disturbance of his life; while Goethe describes his major illnesses as a healthy reaction of his body to spiritual crises, and a means of getting rid of disorders. See M. Sommerfeld, 'J.-J. Rousseaus *Bekenntnisse* und Goethes *Dichtung und Wahrheit*', in *Goethe in Umwelt und Folgezeit*. Leiden, 1935.

(6) For example, R. B. Mowat's in *J.-J. Rousseau*, 1938.

(7) Lettre à Malesherbes, 12 janvier 1762.

(8) Lettre à Malesherbes, 4 janvier 1762.

(9) *Dichtung und Wahrheit*, Teil III, Buch 11.

(10) His description of this inner revolution (Partie II, Livre 9) shows clearly his consciousness of the contrast between his two selves, and of his ineradicable trend to rush to extremes: 'Si la révolution n'eût fait que me rendre à moi-même et s'arrêter là, tout était bien; mais malheureusement elle alla plus loin, et m'emporta rapidement à l'autre extrême. Dès lors mon âme en branle n'a plus fait que passer par la ligne du repos, et ses oscillations toujours renouvelées ne lui ont jamais permis d'y rester.'

(11) Goethe, *Maximen und Reflexionen*, VII.

(12) *Du Contrat Social*, Livre II, Chap. II. Cf. 'Plus l'État s'agrandit, plus la liberté diminue', Livre III, Chap. I.

ROY PASCAL

(13) 4 janvier 1762.
(14) S. Freud, *Collected Papers*, 1925, vol. IV.
(15) Goethe's distaste for self-analysis found expression in his strong criticism of the Delphic 'Know thyself', which he considered to be a maxim for preventing action and constructive thought (*Sprüche in Reimen*, and *Maximen und Reflexionen*, VI).
(16) Lettre à Malesherbes, 12 janvier 1762.
(17) Goethe reports this opinion in *Dichtung und Wahrheit*, Teil IV, Buch 18.
(18) *Gespräche mit Eckermann*, 29 January 1926.
(19) In the 'Pädagogische Provinz', *Wilhelm Meisters Wanderjahre*.

UNE AMITIÉ ENTRE HONNÊTES GENS, LE COMTE ROGER DE BUSSY-RABUTIN, 'LIBERTIN', ET LE PÈRE RENÉ RAPIN, JÉSUITE

BY

ELFRIEDA PICHLER

formerly Assistant Lecturer in French in the University of Sheffield*

'J'AI un livre à vous envoyer', écrivit Mme de Scudéry, la belle-sœur de l'illustre Sappho, à son ami, le comte de Bussy-Rabutin, 'de la part du Père Rapin, que vous ne connaissez point. C'est une des premières têtes d'entre eux [les jésuites] et qui a beaucoup de crédit.' Ce fut donc le premier contact entre deux esprits si profondément différents, à tous points de vue: carrière, mœurs, position sociale, mais qui se sont rencontrés, par la suite, sur un plan commun, la littérature. C'est un bel exemple d'une parfaite amitié entre honnêtes gens, entre beaux esprits dans le sens où le dix-septième siècle l'entendait. Dans cette même lettre du 27 juin 1671, Mme de Scudéry fait à son ami l'éloge du Père Rapin.

Il a une physionomie [dit-elle] qui découvre une partie de sa bonté et de sa douceur. Dans ses manières et dans son procédé il n'y a rien d'affecté, comme ont la plupart de ceux qui portent un habit de religieux. . . . Il est non seulement moralement bon, il a une grande piété. . . . Il aime mieux prier pour les pécheurs que de s'amuser à leur faire des remontrances, quand il voit qu'elles ne serviraient qu'à leur aigrir l'esprit.

Le P. Rapin, 'un des plus savants hommes de son siècle', dit encore Mme de Scudéry, désire soumettre à la critique du comte de Bussy-Rabutin son livre des *Comparaisons de Cicéron et de Démosthène* qu'il vient de terminer et lui annonce en même temps un autre travail, la *Comparaison d'Aristote et de Platon*. Dans sa première lettre (24 juillet 1671) le P. Rapin fait allusion à ses *Comparaisons* tout en expliquant son intention de dégager de

---

* Now Mrs Dubois, lecturer in French in the University of Durham (King's College, Newcastle).

163   11-2

cet ouvrage 'une philosophie, une rhétorique et une poétique historique'.

La réponse du comte fut rapide; le 18 août 1671 il écrivait au Père que sa lettre l'avait gagné; il ajoutait: 'Je vous déclare que l'ouvrage m'a charmé. Je n'ai jamais rien vu de si net ni de si bien prouvé, de façons de parler si naturelles ni une justesse si finement cachée.'

Afin de mieux comprendre cette amitié si inattendue et qui devait durer 16 ans, rappelons brièvement les étapes essentielles de leur vie avant leur rencontre.

Né en 1618, parent de Sainte Chantal et cousin de Mme de Sévigné, Roger de Bussy-Rabutin avait eu une carrière militaire des plus brillantes, tour à tour au service du Grand Condé et de Turenne mais gardant toujours une absolue loyauté envers le roi. Ce fut une carrière mouvementée, entremêlée d'affaires galantes et de duels qui lui valurent un premier séjour à la Bastille. Puis il fut exilé de la cour, à la suite d'une fâcheuse affaire de débauche durant la Semaine Sainte de 1659. Les bruits qui couraient sur cette histoire en augmentèrent encore le scandale. De retour à la cour l'année suivante, Bussy, alors au sommet de sa carrière militaire, se mit à rédiger son *Histore amoureuse des Gaules*, livre clandestin dédié à sa maîtresse Mme de Montglas, et qui fut un peu plus tard porté à la connaissance du roi, par la jalousie d'une femme. Le scandale n'éclata que quelques années plus tard, après son élection à l'Académie Française, en 1665. Des accusations justes mêlées à des calomnies décidèrent le roi à enfermer à la Bastille un serviteur aussi fidèle et loyal que le comte de Bussy-Rabutin. Ce second séjour en prison qui le fit gémir et qui finit par le rendre malade, fut suivi d'un exil prolongé, loin de la cour. Bussy-Rabutin se retira dans ses terres de Bourgogne, à Bussy et à Chaseu, où il mena une vie triste et d'où il envoya de fréquentes plaintes au roi et à ceux de son entourage qu'il jugeait influents. Dans la lettre du 13 novembre 1671, il explique au P. Rapin comment il passe son temps en exil: 'à embellir sa maison et à entretenir un commerce agréable avec ses bons amis'. En effet, six volumes de correspondance (édition Lalanne) rassemblent ce commerce avec ses amis, correspondance des plus intéressantes et agréables à lire, à la fois par sa documentation sur l'époque, sa verve et son esprit. Cinq années d'exil s'étaient écoulées lorsque Bussy-Rabutin fit la connaissance de ce jésuite, homme de lettres et 'mondain' pour lequel il éprouva un vif sentiment d'amitié. Né en 1620,[1] Tourangeau de famille bourgeoise, René Rapin était entré à la Compagnie de Jésus à l'âge de 18 ans. Très jeune il fut nommé professeur de rhétorique et pendant les neuf ans de cette charge il se distingua par son érudition et son bon sens. Son jugement littéraire commença bientôt à lui faire une réputation considérable d'homme de lettres. Résidant au collège de Clermont à Paris, il se lia avec les plus grands esprits de son siècle, connut les dames de la haute société, Mme de Sablé, Mme de Longueville, Mme de Sévigné et combien d'autres. Il était le familier, le membre respecté et écouté de cette 'académie' de Lamoignon, qui, à Paris et à Bâville, réunissait les plus beaux esprits, M. Despréaux, Baillet, Gui Patin, Racine, Bossuet, et l'ami et le confrère du P. Rapin, le P. Dominique Bouhours.

Plusieurs poésies d'occasion, mais surtout ses *Eclogae sacrae* publiées en 1659, révélèrent son génie de poète latin. Mais l'inspiration virgilienne s'épanouit surtout dans son chef-d'œuvre qui le fit connaître presque immédiatement hors des frontières de la France, les *Hortorum libri IV* publiés en 1665. S'inspirant de ces lignes de Virgile:

> Forsitan et pingues hortos quae cura colendi
> Ornaret, canerem, biferique rosaria Paesti. . . .
> Verum hace ipse equidem spatiis exclusus iniquis
> Praetereo, atque aliis post commemoranda relinquo.
>
> (*Georgica* IV)

il s'était proposé de réaliser un projet du poète latin et de faire une description poétique et toute pastorale des fleurs, des arbres, des eaux et des bois. Sa première œuvre de critique date de 1667; c'est un discours académique sur Homère et Virgile.

L'année même de leur rencontre le P. Rapin avait commencé son œuvre en prose par la *Comparaison de Cicéron et de Démosthène* déjà mentionnée et suivie de la *Comparaison de Platon et d'Aristote*. Ses travaux le menaient bientôt aux idées générales, à la critique littéraire à proprement parler, à ses *Réflexions*, notamment celles sur la *Poétique* d'Aristote, publiées la même année que l'*Art*

ELFRIEDA PICHLER

Poétique de M. Despréaux, son compagnon et ami au salon de M. le Premier Président. A partir de 1671 on peut suivre cette correspondance entre Bussy-Rabutin et le P. Rapin, correspondance très régulière, interrompue seulement par les quelques séjours assez brefs d'ailleurs, que Bussy-Rabutin faisait à Paris lorsque le roi lui en accordait la grâce et que les affaires l'y attiraient (1677, 1679–80, 1682).

Au début, cette correspondance est limitée presque entièrement à la littérature, soutenue, il est vrai, par un sentiment d'admiration, de respect et d'amitié entre les deux hommes. Mais dès la seconde année de leur relation le P. Rapin s'inquiète de la vie spirituelle de son ami; et il a de quoi se faire des soucis. La lettre du 17 février 1672 annonce à Bussy-Rabutin la publication d'un livre de dévotion pour le carême; celle du 19 mars est jointe à un exemplaire de *L'Esprit du Christianisme*, dédié à l'abbesse de Fontevrault, sœur de Mme de Montespan et amie du P. Rapin. *L'Esprit du Christianisme* est un de ces livres dévots que le P. Rapin passait pour produire à peu près tous les six mois, les faisant alterner avec ses œuvres littéraires—telle était au moins l'idée que se faisaient de lui ses contemporains.

La sollicitude du prêtre va continuer et on en verra maints exemples dans les lettres. Jamais le P. Rapin ne montre la moindre indiscrétion à l'égard de son ami, mais par sa persévérance et sa prière, sans doute prépara-t-il la conversion définitive et sincère de Bussy-Rabutin. Il est vrai qu'on a beaucoup glosé sur ses débauches, tout n'était pas exact mais une grande partie l'était. Néanmoins Bussy-Rabutin ne fut jamais un athée. Un souvenir trop vague de la foi, surtout beaucoup d'orgueil, un tempérament vif et très enclin à l'aventure galante le séparaient de la pratique religieuse. La contemplation de ses malheurs et l'amitié des deux Pères jésuites, Rapin et Bouhours, finirent par l'ouvrir à la grâce. Le *Discours à ses enfants sur les Illustres Malheureux*, écrit peu de temps avant sa mort (en 1693), le montre pieux, tourné vers Dieu, attendant la justice du ciel.

A l'époque où il commença à connaître le P. Rapin ce n'était guère qu'un début de vie spirituelle et encore un début très hésitant.

Nous suivons à travers les lettres le développement de l'œuvre littéraire du P. Rapin. Ayant terminé ses *Comparaisons* il en avait tiré des idées générales qu'il appelle *Réflexions*. Le 13 août 1672 une discussion épistolaire fort intéressante au point de vue littéraire s'engage entre les deux hommes à propos d'un questionnaire que le P. Rapin envoie à son ami. La première question est de savoir si la langue française est capable du grand genre, c'est-à-dire du poème épique tel que l'a connu l'antiquité. Beaucoup trop de soi-disant poètes de l'époque du P. Rapin se contentent des petits genres, des sonnets et madrigaux, et croient mériter le titre de poète. La réponse de Bussy se réduit à une anticipation du fameux jugement que le Français n'a pas la tête épique. Les *Moïse*, les *Pucelle*, les *S. Louis* ne peuvent rivaliser avec les grandes œuvres épiques des Grecs et des Latins.

De l'épopée nous passons au théâtre. Le P. Rapin condamne la comédie moderne, il ose à peine nommer son illustre contemporain, auteur dramatique, car dit-il, 'Molière est de nos amis'. Le P. Rapin accuse Molière d'exagérer, de grossir les sentiments, les caractères, de faire un Tartuffe plus hypocrite qu'il ne l'est en réalité. Il lui reproche également de mêler trop de badinage d'amour et de tendresse aux pièces sérieuses. Rapin est en effet un avocat entêté de la pureté des genres. Mais Bussy-Rabutin fait preuve d'un jugement plus sûr; il trouve tout simplement Molière admirable. Le P. Rapin modifia son jugement à la publication des *Femmes Savantes* dont il recommanda la lecture à Mlle de Bussy.

D'autres débats s'ajoutent à celui-là, ils portent tous sur des questions de règles, de genres et de comparaisons de la littérature française avec celle de l'antiquité. Une parenté d'idées et de goût entre le P. Rapin et M. Despréaux, son ami et rival chez M. de Lamoignon, est manifeste. Les deux familiers de l'hôtel Lamoignon, tant à Paris qu'à Bâville, avaient l'occasion d'échanger fréquemment leurs idées d'où il résultait probablement une certaine rivalité. Aussi est-il curieux de noter que l'année 1674 vit la publication de l'*Art Poétique* de Boileau et aussi celle des *Réflexions sur l'Art Poétique d'Aristote* du P. Rapin. Chose plus curieuse encore— l'œuvre du P. Rapin eut un succès immédiat, éclatant; des traductions anglaises et italiennes furent publiées rapidement et les répercussions de son succès littéraire se manifestèrent même en Allemagne. Sa réputation surpassa—un bref moment—celle de Boileau. Mais il fut très vite oublié en faveur de son ami.

La correspondance du comte de Bussy-Rabutin et du P. Rapin ne se limite pas à la littérature. Tous les deux témoignent un vif intérêt aux événements de la cour; le P. Rapin rapporte des détails sur les dernières médisances de la cour. Il semble être très bien informé sur les vicissitudes de la position de Mme de Montespan auprès du roi (lettres du 24 juin 1677, du 12 juillet de la même année). On parle aussi d'un autre personnage de la famille royale, la grande nouvelle qui intéresse tout le monde, c'est que le Grand Condé s'est retiré de la vie publique. 'Que dites-vous', écrivit le P. Rapin le 11 mars 1676, 'sur la destinée de M. le Prince qui est allé se renfermer à Chantilly pour y vivre de lait de vache dont il se porte bien?' La nouvelle a dû profondément toucher Bussy, à la fois par son ancien attachement au Grand Condé et par une certaine similitude dans leurs infortunes. Le P. Rapin avec une compréhension psychologique aiguë s'en doutait. 'Quoi qu'il en soit,' ajouta-t-il, 'un homme détrompé comme vous doit avoir bien du plaisir de voir de sa solitude l'agitation des passions des hommes sur le théâtre du monde.'

Serait-il possible que l'amitié de Bussy-Rabutin n'eût pas été désintéressée? Après tout le P. Rapin était non seulement en relation avec les gens les plus influents de son temps mais il appartenait aussi à un ordre qui avait gagné beaucoup d'ascendant durant ce siècle et qui jouait un rôle important à la cour. Or, précisément, Bussy-Rabutin recherchait un appui auprès du roi. Le confesseur de Sa Majesté n'était-il pas un confrère du P. Rapin? Aussi, à travers la correspondance, est-il souvent question de remettre de la part du comte telle lettre, telle demande aux bons soins du P. de La Chaise. Loin de vouloir accuser Bussy-Rabutin d'un égoïsme trop marqué il faudrait se rappeler ici que la sollicitude de l'exilé se portait en grande partie sur l'avenir de ses enfants. Et s'il quête des faveurs auprès du roi pour lui-même, il en réclame autant sinon plus pour sa famille.

L'ami de M. le Premier Président relate souvent ses voyages à Bâville et ses séjours dans ce charmant petit château Louis XIII, entouré d'un parc magnifique où murmure la fontaine inspiratrice de la lyre du P. Rapin ('Ad Fontem Polycrenen') et de son ami Boileau. Aussi la mort du Premier Président de Lamoignon fit-elle pousser des lamentations douloureuses aux deux correspondants.

Le P. Rapin a sincèrement pleuré son ami et protecteur et il était inconsolable, mande Mme de Scudéry, quoique le Premier Président lui eût laissé 'une pension de cent écus et mille éloges dans son testament'. Le P. Rapin se mit aussitôt à rédiger un article à la mémoire de son ancien protecteur et demanda à Bussy de l'y aider. Mais très affligé de la perte de son ami le P. Rapin se rendit malade. Alors Bussy lui fit une réflexion qui éclaire les conceptions littéraires de son siècle. 'Vous voulez bien, mon Révérend Père,' écrivit Bussy le 16 février 1678, 'que je vous fasse une petite correction en vous disant qu'au lieu de travailler à écrire la vie de notre cher ami aussitôt après sa mort, il fallait songer à tout autre chose, parce que cette perte était encore si fraîche, notre douleur ne nous laissait pas la liberté d'esprit qu'il faut avoir pour ces ouvrages et c'est assurément celui [sic] qui vous a fait malade.' On entrevoit à travers ces lignes l'idée de l'esprit créateur qui s'élève au-dessus de la passion et du sentiment afin de pouvoir les exprimer plus tard sous une forme poétique ou éloquente, mais désintéressée. Conception très chère à l'esprit classique qui tendait vers une liberté de création poétique, un détachement du *hic et nunc* du sentiment et de la passion.

Préparant sa dernière œuvre, un petit traité de psychologie morale, *Le Grand et le Sublime*, le P. Rapin recourt à son ami Bussy pour lui demander l'aide de ses connaissances personnelles. Il s'agit dans ce traité de Turenne et du Grand Condé; or Bussy les avait connus tous deux.

Le P. Rapin remet à son ami avec autant d'empressement, sinon avec plus de zèle, ses livres de dévotion. On a déjà vu qu'il avait offert à Bussy un premier livre (*L'Esprit du Christianisme*) pour le carême de l'année 1672. A cet ouvrage il ne joint que des observations générales sur l'intention de son écrit. 'Vous trouverez dans ce livre', écrivit-il le 19 mars 1672, 'de nouvelles découvertes dans le cœur humain que j'ai tâché un peu de connaître dans les réflexions que je fais sur les actions des hommes. En même temps ce livre expose une morale bien pure et bien chrétienne.'

Quelques années plus tard (1675) le P. Rapin ayant écrit un autre livre de dévotion, *L'Importance du Salut*, l'envoya pour Pâques à son ami, mais cette fois avec une recommandation de prêtre qui a charge d'âmes. 'Voici Pâques qui s'approche,' écrivit-il le 27 mars, 'souvenez-vous, Monsieur, de votre devoir de chrétien. C'est par là qu'il faut commencer par attirer sa bénédiction.' Cette remarque est d'autant plus opportune que Bussy-Rabutin se trouve au milieu d'une véritable campagne de demandes, de supplications pour regagner la faveur du roi. Les paroles du P. Rapin ont-elles eu du succès auprès de son ami? Bussy a lu le livre du P. Rapin, il l'a trouvé admirable et qu'en pense-t-il? 'Cela me fait voir la faiblesse de la nature humaine', écrivit-il dans sa lettre du 9 avril, 'qu'on soit convaincu de la raison et qu'on ne la suive pas: j'appelle ne pas la suivre, de n'avoir que de faibles désirs.' Les deux livres ont-ils déjà porté fruit dans la vie du comte? Le P. Rapin semble bien le penser. 'J'ai été bien édifié, Monsieur, de votre résignation aux ordres de la providence de Dieu sur vous' (3 juillet 1675). Ce progrès ne suffit pas au Père; il veut aller plus loin. Dans la même lettre il écrit: 'J'espère vous voir un de ces jours dévot . . .' et, continue-t-il, 'il n'y a que la morale chrétienne qui donne de la joie dans la disgrâce et du plaisir dans les afflictions; toutes les autres morales sont bien froides sur le chapitre de la consolation dans les grandes souffrances.'

Une année s'écoule, c'est à nouveau le carême (1676) et le P. Rapin se met à faire des réflexions d'ordre spirituel à son ami. L'occasion en est la retraite à Chantilly du Grand Condé. Penser aux agitations et aux passions humaines 'c'est de quoi faire le philosophe; mais ce n'est pas assez de quoi faire le chrétien. Pensez-y, Monsieur, car voici la bonne fête. Nous sommes de ces amis qui pensent à tout, mais qui étendent leur vue par delà toutes les bornes du temps et qui vont penser à l'autre vie: car tout bien considéré, il n'y a que cela de réel et de solide.'

Mais les réflexions du P. Rapin ne sont pas seulement propres au temps du carême. De plus en plus il profite de toutes les occasions pour ramener son ami sur le chemin de la foi. Déjà Bussy se croit si imprégné de l'esprit religieux, tel qu'il l'a reçu de son ami jésuite, qu'il rédige à son tour des sermons. Il conseille à sa cousine Mme de Sévigné (14 mai 1677) de se préoccuper davantage des affaires de l'autre vie que des vicissitudes de celle-ci. L'influence que le P. Rapin et le P. Bouhours avaient exercée sur Bussy commençait à se faire connaître, car Bussy ajoute à sa lettre à Mme de Sévigné: 'Je ne doute pas que quand vous lirez cette lettre à la belle Maguelonne, elle ne se récrie que cela sent le P. Rapin et le P. Bouhours à pleine gorge.'

Le P. Rapin commence à se rassurer sur la vie chrétienne de son ami. Il lui écrit durant le carême de 1679: 'Vous faites vos dévotions plus tranquillement, car vous n'avez plus de combats à donner, tout est soumis dans votre cœur, et je ne doute pas que vous ne soyez le reste de vos jours un bon chrétien.'

Les vrais fruits de cette conversion, le P. Rapin ne devait pas les voir en ce monde. Le mémoire que Bussy-Rabutin adressa vers la fin de sa vie à ses enfants montre en effet une compréhension plus approfondie de la foi, une soumission de la volonté humaine à celle de Dieu. Néanmoins l'ancien libertin montre encore parfois son orgueil et sa vanité; peu importe, il avait compris la Vérité. Le P. Bouhours acheva la tâche commencée par son illustre confrère.

Cette brève étude d'une amitié inattendue entre deux hommes essentiellement différents montre l'épanouissement d'une humanité et d'un humanisme caractéristiques du XVIIe siècle. A travers ces deux personnages on aperçoit les diverses tendances de ce siècle complexe. La vie brillante et souvent scandaleuse éblouit, les questions littéraires semblent préoccuper tout le monde et pourtant c'est aussi un siècle de profonde dévotion, un siècle de saints. Les deux personnages n'y occupent guère qu'une place secondaire, il est vrai. Mais cela n'empêche pas de voir en eux ce raisonnement 'raisonnable', cette préciosité délicate et agréable, mais aussi le fond très chrétien, la foi solide de ce jésuite qui apparemment ne fait que fréquenter les salons et qui ne semble avoir d'autres préoccupations que la littérature. N'était-ce pas la mission du P. Rapin comme du P. Bouhours et d'autres, de répandre les sentiments chrétiens, l'esprit de l'évangile dans les milieux où l'on y pensait le moins?

Vrai fils de St Ignace, le P. Rapin a mis en valeur l'esprit même de sa Compagnie; se servir de toute chose, de toute pensée, de toute relation sur le plan mondain et terrestre pour les intégrer à la Vérité, 'ad maiorem Dei gloriam'.

NOTE

(1) E. Chambert, 'La Famille de René Rapin', dans *Bulletin trimestriel de la Société archéologique de Touraine*, 1921–23, 2e série, Tome 6.

VARIANT READINGS TO THREE
ANGLO-NORMAN POEMS

BY

MILDRED K. POPE

Emeritus Professor of the University of Manchester

THE study of the variants of the *Romance of Horn* combined with the perusal of the article that Miss Brereton contributed to the volume of *Studies* presented to me suggested to me the possibility that a comparison of Anglo-Norman Texts with the readings of some of their variant MSS. might contribute to our understanding of the development of Anglo-Norman. With this in view, I am proposing to study in this article the vocabulary and syntax of the three poems: *The Voyage of St Brendan* (*Brendan*),[1] the *Seinte Resureccion* (*Resureccion*)[2] and the *Romance of Horn* (*Horn*), written, the first *c.* 1121, the other two in the latter half of the twelfth century. All three are extant in versions of later date. *Brendan* was revised in the thirteenth century by a Picard poet, whose work is contained in a MS. (*E*) comprised in a volume 'completed in the year 1267 or 1268'.[3] The *Resureccion* was worked over by an Anglo-Norman by the beginning of the thirteenth century, the extant fragment of the original drama is contained in a fourteenth-century Anglo-Norman MS. (*P. fr.* 902) of the Bibliothèque Nationale, a rather longer fragment of the remaniement in a MS. (*C*) written at Canterbury 'shortly after 1275'.[4] *Horn* was re-cast in the thirteenth century: the greater portion of the original poem is extant in a Cambridge University MS. of the thirteenth century (*C*); fragments of the remaniement are contained in four Anglo-Norman MSS., three of the same century: of the two containing the main part, *O*, the earlier, in the Douce Collection at the Bodleian, comprises lines 1–2391 and ll. 4596 to the end; *H*, the later, No. 527 in the Harleian Collection of the British Museum, contains ll. 1455–4233.[5]

In the perspicacious account that Professor Waters gave of the main differences between the readings of his text of the *Brendan* and MS. *E* (Introd., pp. xix–xxii) he adduced two main types of modification: avoidance of Anglo-Normanisms and modernization: 'Anglo-Norman rimes and forms have been avoided . . . the vocabulary, grammar, phraseology and metre have been modernized.' Despite the fact that Anglo-Norman features in words and constructions have been occasionally eliminated (see below) and morphological forms, become archaic (e.g. *ert, erent, estreit, estrat*), occasionally replaced by more modern, the difference in the treatment of the two categories here indicated appears to me to be substantially correct and suggests what is, I think, in accordance with fact, viz. that Anglo-Norman in its earliest stage diverged more rapidly in pronunciation and flexional forms from Continental French than in vocabulary and syntax.

Among the many substitutions of words made by the reviser the only terms eliminated that appear to belong to insular speech are the three words of English origin: *bat, haspes, raps* and the unexplained adverb *senes*. The bulk of the changes in vocabulary are evidently intended to make the text more readily intelligible and to bring it up to date. They include not only the elimination of the not inconsiderable number of words peculiar to Benedeit's poem (cf. Introd., pp. clxxxiii–clxxxv), but also the avoidance or replacement of others that were of relatively frequent use in the twelfth, but fell into disfavour in the thirteenth century, e.g. *altel* (*alter*), *aprisment* (*aprochent*), *blef, concreit* (*chargent*), *detriers* (*derriers*), *enfertet* (*enfermeté*), *enteins, faitre* (*maistre*), *ila* (*iluec*), *mesters* ('domestic offices', *soliers*), *prement* (*grievent*), *nepurtant* (*nepurquant*), *tamez, toluns!* (*tornes de ci!*). The shift of meaning of the verb *choisir* is indicated by the replacement of its past participle, used in its original meaning, by *veu* in l. 1674. The replacement of the adverb *denz* by *enz* in l. 801 is less surprising than its use by Benedeit, for it is a word of very rare occurrence in twelfth-century French, attested with some frequency only in the Tours MS. of the *Chronique des Ducs de Normandie*.[6]

The syntax is very considerably modified. Like other thirteenth-century writers the Picard reviser makes use of a French of a more conversational type.[7] Word-order is not infrequently modified, especially the initial position of the verb, cf. ll. 110, 151, 203, 271, etc., and 203, 204, 238, 308, etc.; connecting words are occasionally introduced, e.g. *car* 99, 393; *e* 155; *si* 113, 161; *qui* 492, and subject pronouns frequently, e.g. *il* 111, 122, 158, 174, 234, etc., (imp.) 303, 411; *je* 296; rather more frequent use is made of the definite article, cf. ll. 289, 300, 488, 515, etc., of the negative expletive *pas*, e.g. 215, 419; and the imperfect indicative is sometimes preferred to the past definite, e.g. *descendoit* 172, *avoient* 240, *purveoit* 300, *voloit* 325.

The only clear examples of Anglo-Norman constructions modified are the use of the definite article to denote measure in l. 760 *Cire ne oile le plus n'en vait*, MS. *E, de plus* and the weakened use of *prendre* in l. 48 *Dunt Deu prier prent plus suvent*, MS. *E, Dont il prioit Deu p. s.*[8] Two or three other constructions replaced are found more frequently in Later Anglo-Norman than in Continental French. Their presence both in the *Brendan* and in insular usage is probably due to the influence of Latin syntax, which is notably strong with Benedeit and in Anglo-Norman literature, so much of which is clerkly. The conjunction *cum* is usually replaced by *quant*, cf. ll. 228, 241, 309, etc.; the use of the subjunctive in indirect question is eliminated in 668 *l'abes ad quis Quels leus ço soit* . . ., MS. *E, est; nul* employed without intensifying negative in 738 *Mais de terre unt nul asens* is allotted one in MS. *E, de terre n'unt* . . .; the use of a simple infinitive dependent on the verbs *defendre* and *metre talent* is modified: *Prendre si tost jol vus defent*, 649, MS. *E, Del p. que jol* . . ., *Mist m'en talent prendre* . . . 311, MS. *E, Mist li t. de p.*

In the vocabulary of the remaniement of the *Resureccion* the only trace of the influence of insular speech seems to be in the replacement of the adverb *celeement* by *priveement*, an adverb derived from a stock that took firm root in our language. Modernization is rather more frequently attested: several words and locutions of the later twelfth century are introduced, such as the locutions *jadis* and *tel i ad* and the clerkly words and locutions *devoluper, vostre persone* and *aver devociun: avalee* is explicated by the addition of the adverb *dever val, C* 125.

In the construction Anglo-Norman influence is slightly more apparent. The use of the subjunctive in the if-clause of doubtful condition, which occurs once in *P* 299, and in *C* 367, replaces the indicative employed in *P* 299: it is a construction in which English and Latin influence combined to influence French. In the part added by the remanieur use is made in l. 327 of the neuter demonstrative pronoun *cest*, a use far more frequent in Anglo-Norman than on the Continent, and of the neuter pronoun *ço* as an adjective (*De ço sarcu*), an instance that is so surprisingly early that it is due in all probability to the scribe. Modernization plays again a more important part: *celui* used as a possessive is replaced by the substantive *Jesu* in *C* 108; *il* (impersonal) is introduced in l. 5 (*Purveeᴣ ke il eit . . .*); the reflexive pronoun is employed in the perfect of *sei apercever* in *C* 490 (*ke s'est aparceuᴣ*), but is absent in the past anterior of *sei traire* in *P* 24 (*U Jesu fut al hostel trait*); more frequent recourse is had to the imperfect indicative, cf. Introd., pp. lxiii–lxiv; the older type of conditional clause formed by inversion *Encusé m'eussent en Romanie . . .* is replaced by the modern type introduced by *se*; *Se il m'encusasent en R. . . . C* 75.

All these latter changes are in accord with the normal development of Continental French and bear witness to the fact that insular speech at the time of the remanieur was keeping step with the usage of the Continent.

The manuscripts of *Horn* utilized here are, as stated above, all three Anglo-Norman and of the thirteenth century. The differences between them are twofold: (1) the Cambridge MS. (*C*), on which by common agreement the text must be based, contains evidently a version of the poem which is original or nearly so; (2) it is the work of a careful and intelligent scribe, fully conversant with the French language. The Oxford MS. (*O*) and the London MS. (*H*), both fragmentary, represent a somewhat later and rather careless version, based possibly on oral tradition and completely destructive of metrical idiosyncrasies, which are for the most part preserved in *C*; both are the work of scribes who are very imperfectly acquainted with the French language, the scribe of *O* being more careful than the scribe of *H* but also more stupid; both muddle many lines and not infrequently content themselves with meaningless words or sheer nonsense. They write, for instance, *O: culurs* for *colier*, *abatist* for *esbahist*, *al noel* for *anuel*, *purchaleer* for *purchacier*, *menus* for *menors*; *H: acoilt* for *coitie*, *frai vestir* for *fervestu*, *si grant* for *siglant*. The scribe of *O* makes Rimel take hold of Herland by his moustache (*gernun*), instead of by the lappet of his tunic (*gerun*); the scribe of *H* represents Queen Gudborc and her daughters *spurring* up the steps to the Hall (*poignant*) instead of *ascending* (*poiant*), to instance one absurdity from each.

The vocabulary of the romance resembles that of *Brendan* in that the author possesses a very full command of all the resources of the French language of his day: he makes free use of the various processes of word-formation and employs at will clerkly and popular words and technical terms of many kinds, legal, military, architectural, sporting, musical. In the version preserved in *O* and *H* this vocabulary is not only modernized to some extent, it is also very considerably impoverished.

Words, significations and locutions that have fallen out of use are avoided or replaced, e.g. *blaʒon* (shield), *cointe* (discreet), *detries* (*derière*), *endart* (in vain), *errant* (speedily), *geste* (race), *giens* (negative expletive), *iste* (*d'iste vie*), *maigne* (replaced by *meisme*), *maor*, *message* (messenger), *multes*, *nobile* (three-syllabled), *sudeement* (*O*, *suddeinement*), *tresparmi*, *uelment* (equally), *verté*; *le jor* is replaced by *cel jor*, *tuʒ dis* by *tuʒ jors*, *merveilles* by *a merveille*, *argent muneié* by *muneie d'argent*, *bien i mustrent lur cors* by *Bien i sentent lur cops*.

A few words and locutions that belong to the thirteenth century rather than the twelfth are introduced: the locution *servir nostre nobilité* in *OH* 2351; the collective use of *chevalerie* in *H* 2472, replacing *e cunte e chevalier* of *C*; the word *kere* (chair) and the locution *cuillir la nape*, these two last indicative of changed social customs. In *C* 806, Rimenhild bids Herland seat himself upon the rush-strewn floor (*la jonchiere*), but in *O* a chair is substituted for this lowly seat—*serreʒ la sur une kere*—the only mention of a chair in the poem; in *H* 2471 the clause *la nape fu cuillie* is substituted for the one employed in this line in *C* and in 4581 *les tables funt oster*.

Restriction of vocabulary is illustrated both in the elimination of some of the technical words employed by Thomas and of a considerable number of those that are of a relatively rare use or are employed by him in a somewhat unusual manner. Of legal terms may be cited: *chasement, escundire, faider, faide, forsjugier, pledé*; military and sporting: *aguait, destendre, doblun* (shield-lining), *fortelesce, jet, paleter, poigneur*; architectural: *umbrelenc*; general: *ajornal* (dawn), *aruteement* (rapidly), *bugle* (buffalo horn), *cuitus* (hasty), *deduiement, empeindre, envoluʒ* (ingulfed), *esmoluʒ, estutie*, *fóltage, sei leecier, pavementé, putel* (pit), *resun* (sound), *soavet, trebuʒ* (leggings), *veil* (sail); *aluer* (bestow), *bailler* (touch the harp, replaced in *H* 2838 by *manier*), *dampneʒ,* replaced in *H* 3189 by *damageʒ, guenchir* (fail, replaced in *H* by *revelir*) and further the locutions *a aïr, faire dolur, a genoillons, de rechief, si devient, sanʒ nul retenement* (completely).

In some substitutions we may discern a definite tendency towards the employment of words that have taken root in English or belong to stock that has done so. Examples are: *broillant* for *ardant, cunversant* for *manant, cunquerre* for *mater, cunter* for *deviser* (relate), *esguabement* for *esguarement, escreppe* for *trebuʒ, grant* for *cungie, granter* for *otrier, mariners* for *marinaus, preisier* for *loer, sauver* for *garir* and *tenser, targer* for *durer.* The only word of English origin introduced is *welcumeʒ* in *O* 800, but the work of both scribes, more particularly that of *H,* is characterized by the instability of prefixes that is so common in Anglo-Norman MSS., prefixes being freely suppressed as well as exchanged, e.g. *coillie* for *acoillie, ferant (auferant), hans (ahans), liement (aliement), sterman (esturman), voeʒ (avoeʒ),* etc.

In the face of this Anglo-Normanizing tendency it is a little surprising to find occasionally the replacement of a word that has taken root in English. Thus *grocier* (grumble), which gives English 'grudge', is twice replaced by *parler* (900, 1797), *traverser (un covent)* by *pesceer* or *fruisser, refuser* (reject) by *refoler, eskipre* (sailors) by *nageur.* The explanation may be that the replacing words are more general in significance than the words replaced.

The modifications observable in construction are largely in accordance with those noted above in the remaniement of *Brendan.* They, too, result in considerable measure from the use of a more conversational form of language, facilitated for both remanieurs by a disregard of the trammels imposed on the original poet by the strict observance of the metre adopted by him:

(1) There are numerous changes of word-order [9] and the concision of the original is impaired by the frequent introduction of tool-words—subject pronouns, articles, negative expletives, e.g.: *jo(e), O* 676, 1188, 2261, *H* 1486, 3220, etc.; *tu, H* 3971; *il, O* 189a, 710, 789, etc.; *H* 2241, 2315, etc.; (imp.) *O* 828, 845, 1212, *OH* 1646; *ele, H* 2528, 4188; *vus, H* 2324; *il* (pl.), *O* 102, *H* 1577a; *ki (qui),*

O 158, 220, etc., *H* 1574, 1620, etc.; *ke* (after negative), *O* 1134, *O* 1715, *H* 1574; *ke, ki* or *qui, H* 2847; *nuls, O* 720, 1460; def. art. *le, H* 2277, 2792, 2875, 2900, 2908, 3188, etc.; *li* (sg.), *H* 2197, 2313; *la, OH* 1872, 3114; *li* (pl.), 2921, 3092; (indef. art.) 448, 1488; *pas, H* 1485, 2724, 3282, 3347.

(2) The older paratactical construction employed with some frequency by Thomas is modified at times by the introduction of conjunctions—*mes, si* and frequently *ke*, e.g.: *meis, H* 2520, 3385, *si* (whether) *H* 3670, *cum si* for *cum, OH* 1762; *ke* (introducing noun clause), *O* 612, 821, *OH* 1802, *H* 1801, 2463, 3496, etc.; (consecutive) *H* 2404, 3200, 3340, 3484; (modal) *H* 3886. The causal conjunction *kar*, of which Thomas made considerable use, is introduced in *H* in ll. 2028, 2474, 2798, but occasionally omitted in *O*, e.g. in 649, 663, 828, 852. In 3924 the old construction with *si* and the future to express until (*Ja ne fineront mais si seront arivez*) is replaced in *H* by the more modern conjunctional type *Ja ne finerent mes trekerent arivez*.

In the syntax of the verb various points of difference are observable. Some of these are due to the normal development of Old French syntactical usage; others which are more frequent in Anglo-Norman than on the Continent are probably to some extent induced by the influence of Middle English syntax.

Of changes of the first type I will cite:

(1) In ll. 1976-77 the clause construction used in *C, Ainz me larraie traire le quoer . . . Ke serement face*, is replaced in *OH* by the infinitive *Ke fere. . . .*

(2) In descriptions, the imperfect indicative, more particularly of the verbs *estre* and *avoir* (frequently *ere*, more rarely *esteit* and *aveit*), is substituted for the preterite, e.g. *O* 106, 262, 793, etc.; *H* 1533, 1771, 1999, 2555, etc.

(3) The imperfect subjunctive employed in the apodosis in *C* 2834 (*Ki dunc l'esgardast . . .*) *li poüst remembrer* is replaced by the conditional in *H, li pureit remembrer*, but it may be noted that in the protasis of a conditional clause an imperfect subjunctive *eüst* is substituted in *H* for the more modern imperfect indicative of *C* 3696.

The influence of English speech may be responsible for the introduction of the future in the protasis of a conditional clause in *O* 1210 *Si vus apres . . . parleret* (*C, parlez*), but sporadic examples of such use occur at all periods of the French language.[10] The replacement of *porent* by *porunt H* 1685, *purrunt H* 2845, 3434 is graphical rather than syntactical. In the protasis of clauses of potential condition there is, as in the remaniement of the *Resureccion*, some extension of the use of the subjunctive, cf. *O* 581, *e si il seit mortal* (*C, est*), *OH* 1478 *Si seit ki . . .* (*C, est*), *H* 2599.

More frequently the move is in the other direction, for it is the indicative that occasionally replaces the subjunctive in both adjective and noun clauses, a tendency observable in Anglo-Norman and characteristic of Middle English, where it is increased by the disappearance of much of the typical flexion of the subjunctive:[11]

(1) In adjective clauses dependent on a negative or indefinite antecedent the subjunctive used in *C* is replaced by the indicative in *O* 393, 556, 1170, 1173; *H* 1861 *a*, e.g. 393 *Kar mestre n'out de rien qu'il n'oüst tut passé* (*O, n'ot*).

(2) In three noun clauses the subjunctive of *C* is replaced by the indicative in *H*: 3129–30 *ni ad plus atendu Qu'il grant cop ne ferist* (*H, feri*); 3291–92 *ke nul n'en seit vantant Ke les puisse tenser . . .* (*H, puet*); 3567–68 *ne poet el avenir Ke . . . n'estoece hum murir* (*H, estuet*). A close parallel to this last construction is seen in the A.N. poem *La Vie Seint Edmund le Rei: A l'encontrer ne puet guandir D'Hubbe, que il n'estuet morir* (ll. 2079–89).[12]

The study of these three poems and their variants provides evidently a basis of fact too narrow to enable one to draw any very wide or sweeping general conclusions, but it does suggest two points of some interest. There is in the first place much more similarity in the way the two thirteenth-century remanieurs treated their texts than one might have expected. The Picard reviser had evidently little more scruple about modifying the metre and language of his predecessor than had the Anglo-Norman and he, like him, also failed at times to understand the older poem and perpetrated rather surprising blunders. He substitutes, for instance, *Ne vus ramez* (row) for *Ne vus tamez* (fear not), *mal en a* for *enmalat* (stowed away), *N'entres* for *N'enteins* (not even). More important, however, is the evidence afforded that up to the time of the remanieur of *Horn*, i.e. well into the thirteenth century, insular French was a form of the language that was developing steadily along the lines of Continental French, albeit progressively more and more influenced by English speech habits, and this does at least put entirely out of court Professor Prior's suggestion that 'Anglo-Norman was a purely artificial language forced upon an English population for political purposes by the Conqueror'.[13] No purely artificial form of speech could have shown such continuous organic development.

NOTES

(1) *The Anglo-Norman Voyage of St Brendan*, by Benedeit, ed. by E. G. R. Waters, Oxford, 1928.

(2) *La Seinte Resureccion*, ed. by T. A. Jenkins, J. M. Manly, M. K. Pope and J. G. Wright. Anglo-Norman Texts, IV, Oxford, 1943.

(3) Op. cit. Introd., p. xviii.

(4) Op. cit. Introd., p. x.

(5) Rudolf Brede, *Ueber die Handschriften der Chanson de Horn*. Marburg, 1882.

(6) C. Fahlin, *Etude sur le MS. de Tours de la Chronique des Ducs de Normandie*, par Benoit. Uppsala, 1937, pp. 127–8.

(7) Cf. L. Foulet, *Petite Syntaxe de l'Ancien Français*, pp. 326–9, 346–57. The disregard of the metrical idiosyncrasies of the *Brendan* facilitated these modifications.

(8) Cf. also l. 307.

(9) Foulet, *Petite Syntaxe de l'Ancien Français*, pp. 326–9, 346–57.

(10) Cf J. Haas, *Französische Syntax*, § 454 (note).

(11) The replacement of the older forms of the third person singular of the subjunctive employed in *C* by analogical ones is probably also morphological rather than syntactical. Examples are: *C, ameint, deint, jeut, turt; O, ameinet* 996, *deigne* 848; *H, jue* 2770; *torne* 2967.

(12) Cf. Kjellman's *Introduction* to this poem, p. cvi.

(13) *Cambridge Anglo-Norman Texts*, Introd. pp. xv–xvi.

GRAMMAR, GRIMOIRE, GLAMOUR, GOMEREL

BY

T. B. W. REID

*Professor of Romance Philology in the
University of Manchester*

THE derivation from Latin *grammatica* of French *grimoire* and
English *gramary* and *glamour* is now generally accepted;[1] the
possibility of tracing Scots and dialectal English *gomerel* 'fool,
simpleton' back to Latin *grammaticus* may well have been suggested
before now. This note is therefore concerned only to fill in the
details and to discuss certain minor points which remain obscure.
Any lack of novelty in the subject-matter may perhaps be excused
by its appropriateness to a volume in honour of a scholar who
has made distinguished contributions to French grammar, both
descriptive and historical, to Middle Scots and to Franco-Scottish
lexicography.

The semi-learned phonetic evolution of Latin *grammatica* to
Old French *gramárie*, *gramaire* is paralleled by that of several other
words such as *dalmatica > daumaire*, *medicum > mire*, **fidicum >
firie*, etc. Alongside the normal form of Later Old French and
Middle French *gramere* (usually written *gramaire*, *grammaire*),
there occurs from the thirteenth century to the sixteenth century
a form with labialized vowel *gramwere* (written *gramoire*), as in
armoire, *aboi*, *émoi*, etc. (Old French *armaire*, *abai*, *esmai*).
The word was adopted by Middle English in the two forms
gramer(e) (later written *grammar* on the analogy of *scholar*, etc.)
and *gramary (-ie)*, *gramery* or *gramory* (on the analogy of words
borrowed through Old French from Latin forms in -*arium*, -*erium*,
-*orium*).

The most striking feature in the history of these words is undoubtedly the semantic development by which they acquired
senses relating to magic. For the French word, the etymologists
nearly all explain this development by assuming some such sequence

181

as 'grammar (the body of principles governing the correct use of the Latin language)', hence 'something incomprehensible to the unlettered', hence 'a mysterious book, a book containing magic spells'.[2] But this explanation does not account for the historical facts either in French or in English. The true sense-sequence is briefly indicated by the *O.E.D.*, s.v. *gramarye* (cf. also the article *grammar*): '1. Grammar, learning in general. 2. Occult learning, magic, necromancy.' The fact is that in Old French from an early date the word *gramaire* was applied not only to the first of the seven arts, the grammatical study of the Latin language, but also by extension to the Latin language itself,[3] and in particular to the works in classical or post-classical Latin which were studied in the Universities, as opposed to ecclesiastical or utilitarian writings in the ordinary Latin of the day. Philippe de Thaon, for example, refers to the source of his *Bestiaire* (a Latin version of the *Physiologus*) as *un livre de gramaire* (ed. Walberg, 4; cf. 1774 etc.) and speaks of a *lapidaire* as being *estrait de gramaire* (ibid. 3008); and Benoît de Sainte-Maure alleges that Cornelius Nepos, teaching at Athens, came upon Dares Phrygius's account of the Trojan War when he 'quereit en un aumaire Por traire livres de gramaire' (*Roman de Troie*, 87 f.). Old French *gramaire*, and consequently its English derivatives, thus came to signify not only the language which was the key to all higher learning, but that learning itself. But 'et ipsa scientia potestas est'; and at a time when few doubted the reality of magic, the uninitiated not unnaturally came to credit those who had studied 'grammar' with the possession of supernatural powers.[4] Our words therefore acquired the sense of 'necromancy, magic art': 'un pin Dont les branches furent d'or fin Tresgetees par artimaire, Par nigromance e par gramaire' (*Roman de Troie*, 6265 ff.); 'les pierres Que Amphyon . . . Assembla ci par artimaire Et par la force de gramaire Et par le chant de sa viele' (*Roman de Thèbes*, App. II, 9323 ff.); 'My mother was a westerne woman, And learned in gramarye' (*King Estmere*, 143 f., in Percy's *Reliques*).

From this stage the French and English words diverge both in meaning and in form. In English, *gramer*[5] and *gramery* in the vulgar sense of 'occult power' and then especially 'power of casting a spell, of deceiving the spectator's eyes', and 'the spell or deceit itself', lived on in popular speech in Scotland, and, having freed themselves from all connection with *grammar* in the linguistic sense, no longer resisted the natural phonetic tendency to dissimilate to *glamer* and *glamery*. Since the eighteenth century these words have been introduced into literary English in the forms *glamour* (on the analogy of abstract nouns in *-our*) and *glamoury*. The first, popularized chiefly by Scott (who also revived *gramarye*), has achieved in our own day an enormous vogue, which has had the effect of widening and blurring its meaning, so that it now signifies merely 'romantically attractive quality' in general; it has also given rise to a number of derivatives such as *glamorous, glamourful, glamourize*, etc.

In French, the sense of *gramaire* or *gramoire* became specialized in a rather different direction; from 'magic power' generally it passed to 'magician's spell or book of spells (for raising the devil, etc.)': 'Le grameire, se dient, lut Un clerc, qui sot molt de latin; L'Anemi tantost s'aparut' (*Martin Hapart*, 144 ff., Montaiglon et Raynaud, *R.G.F.* II, 176). The form *gramoire* survives in this meaning in the modern dialect of Bas-Maine (Dottin, *Glossaire des parlers du Bas-Maine*, 1899, p. 236). This sense-development is usually accompanied by a change in gender which may well be due (as suggested by the *Dictionnaire général*) to the influence of *livre*.[6] But the form of the word which ultimately prevailed in this sense was *grimaire* or more usually *grimoire*, which first occurs in an Anglo-Norman fabliau, probably of the thirteenth century: 'Devaunt nostre sire en pleinere cour Sunt meint jogleur e meint lechour; Molt bien sevent de tricherie, D'enchauntementz e genglerie, E font parroistre par lur grymoire Voir come mençonge, mençonge come voire' (*Le Roi d'Angleterre et le jongleur d'Ely*, 9 ff., *R.G.F.* II, 242). In Modern French *grimoire*, masc. (occasionally fem. in the sixteenth and seventeenth centuries), has survived in the sense of 'book of spells' (used either historically or jocularly), and hence on the one hand 'incomprehensible speech, gibberish', and on the other 'illegible document, scrawl'.

To account for the altered vowel in the first syllable of *grimoire* a whole series of possible sources of contamination have been successively proposed and rejected by the etymologists. It is perhaps time to consider returning to one of the earliest suggestions, that of Diez:[7] Germanic *grima* 'mask', 'ghost, bogey', 'witch' (for the association of senses cf. Lat. *larva*, Mod. Prov. *masco*). The difficulty here is to establish any relationship between a Germanic word which is attested only in Old Norse and Anglo-Saxon, and a French form which first appears late in the thirteenth century (it is hardly likely that *grimoire* arose in Anglo-Norman and then passed into Continental French). The connecting link, however, appears to be supplied by a group of French words which have hitherto usually been associated with Germanic *grĭm* adj. 'angry',[8] or assumed to have been borrowed by French at a date posterior to the appearance of *grimoire*. If we may assume that *grīma* existed in Frankish as well as in the cognate languages, its direct descendant in French may be the *grime* in 'Venez avant, ma dame grime' (Gautier le Long, *La Veuve* 422, *R.G.F.* II, 211), which Godefroy translates 'chagrine, irritée', but which might conceivably signify 'old witch'. In any case, some such Old French word must surely be postulated as the simplex for the derivatives *grimace* and Old French *grimuche*. *Grimace* is indeed generally considered to come ultimately from Germanic *grīma*, but by an indirect route through Spanish *grimazo*, 'distorted figure in a picture', also 'panic', a derivative of Spanish *grima* 'horror', representing a Gothic **grīma* of meaning similar to that of the Old Norse and Anglo-Saxon words.[9] There are, however, certain difficulties about this hypothesis (notably the rarity of Spanish *grimazo*, and the difference in gender, and to some extent in meaning, between the French and Spanish words); and there seems to be no valid ground for considering *grimace* as anything but a genuine French derivation[10] from an Old French *grime*. The early examples[11] (dating from the end of the fourteenth and the fifteenth centuries) show the word in the following senses: (1) 'a distortion of the features expressing hatred, derision etc.'; (2) 'a repulsive or terrifying person or creature' (a meaning which seems to have been overlooked by the lexicographers); (3) (rather later) 'a grotesque carved head as ornament'. All these senses could easily have arisen from *chiere grimace*, *femme grimace*, *figure grimace* etc., with *grimace* originally an adjective signifying 'characteristic of or resembling a witch or bogey'.[12] If the form *grimesse* in 'Johanna dicta la Grimesse' (Orléans, 1291; Godefroy IV, 359) represents a dialectal variant of *grimace* in sense 2 (it is true that the phonetic development suggests

Lorraine rather than the Orléanais), it would take the word back another century or so. Finally, *grimuche* appears about 1200 in the *Jeu de Saint Nicolas* of Jean Bodel (v. 505); Jeanroy translates it 'magot, figure grotesque', but since it is used by a pagan king in reference to an image of St Nicholas, which is also called a 'cornu mahommet', it may well mean something like 'fetish, witch's image'. Altogether, it seems not unreasonable to suppose that this group of words, attested from the beginning of the thirteenth century, with the stem *grim-* and the basic meaning of 'witch-like, repulsive, terrifying', may have been responsible for the alteration of *gramoire* to *grimoire*.[13]

This alteration may have been due, not to an unconscious con-tamination, but (as Bloch suggests) to a deliberate deformation. In any case, there is reason to believe that in the Middle French period some speakers at least remained conscious of the identity of *grimoire* and *grammaire*. This is suggested, for example, by the comment of Guillemette upon Pathelin's boast that he is the cleverest man in the district except the mayor: 'Aussi a il leu le grimaire Et aprins a clerc longue piece' (*Maistre Pierre Pathelin*, 18 f.). For the more educated, therefore, there probably subsisted a jocular or contemptuous association between *grammaire* 'the study of Latin' and *grimoire* 'magic book (as imagined by the vulgar)'. It is perhaps to this association that we owe the whole group of words that appear in the sixteenth century (at first chiefly in the works of anti-scholastic writers like Rabelais) with the stem *grim-* and with more or less depreciatory meanings relating to elementary Latin studies: *grimaud* 'pedant' or 'beginner in Latin', *grimelin* 'grammar-school boy', *grimaude* or *grimauderie* 'grammar-school', *grimeliner* 'to study the rudiments of Latin', also *grimouche* 'a paltrie Pedant, meane grammarian' (Cotgrave), *grimelet* 'as Grimouche; or, a smatterer in matters of learning' (Cotgrave).

Let us turn now to the representatives of Lat. *grammaticus* 'grammarian'. This developed phonetically in exactly the same way as *grammatica*, giving Old French *gramaire*, *gramere* 'gram-marian, teacher or student of Latin', which again was borrowed by Middle English in the two forms *grammer* and *gramery*.[14] The French word then seems to have given rise to a diminutive **gramerel* 'beginner in Latin, grammar-school boy'.[15] This was altered to *gromerel,* perhaps by contamination with the word which appears in Middle English as *grome* and in Middle French in the diminutive forms *gromet* (O. Prov. *gormet*) and *grometel*.[16] Finally, by a dissimilation similar to that which produced *glamour*, **gromerel* became *glomerel.* The only recorded instance of this word in French occurs in the thirteenth-century *Bataille des sept arts* of Henri d'Andeli: the logicians of the University of Paris insult the classical philologists of the University of Orléans by calling the authors they study *autoriaus* and the clerks themselves *glomeriaus* 'mere beginners in Latin, grammar-school boys' (ed. L. J. Paetow, *Memoirs of the University of California*, IV, 1 (1914), 6 ff.). Old French *glomerel* was, however, Latinized as *glomerellus*, in which form, together with the corresponding abstract noun *glomeria*, it appears from 1276 on in the records of the University of Cambridge, and a little later in those of Merton College, Oxford, Bury St Edmunds and Salisbury.[17] The Anglicized forms *glomerel* and *glomery* do not seem to be attested before the sixteenth century, but were no doubt in use much earlier. The glomerels were apparently schoolboys who were prepared by a Master of Glomery for the preliminary degree of Master in Grammar before proceeding to University studies proper.

If the English word *glomerel* passed into general use in the sense of '(mere) schoolboy, tyro', becoming dissociated from the technical term *glomery*, a dissimilation to *gomerel* would be very natural.[18] It seems at least possible that this is the origin of the dialectal English word *gomerel* 'fool, simpleton',[19] attested by the *English Dialect Dictionary* for Scotland, Ireland, N. England, the Midlands and E. Anglia. The complicated relationship between this and other words of similar meaning in *gom-, gaum-, gon-* etc.[20] must, however, be left for the Anglicists to disentangle.

NOTES

(1) Braune rejects *grammatica* as the source of *grimoire* (*Z.R.P.* XXXIX, 370), and Meyer-Lübke hesitates (*R.E.W.* 3rd ed. (1935), 3837).
(2) So the *Dictionnaire général*, Schuchardt (*Z.R.P.* XXXI, 8), Gamillscheg (*F.E.W.*), Bloch (*Dict. étym.*), all in connection with Fr. *grimoire*. Dauzat (*Dict. étym.*) says simply '*grimoire*, var. labialisé de *grammaire*, spécialisé dans un sens péjoratif'.

(3) Cf. Med. Lat. *grammatice* 'in Latin': 'Ungarice, Turce, Grammaticeque loquens' (Du Cange).

(4) Cf. 'Il ot un livre paré de toz latins Ou li art sont et li sonje descrit' (*Mort Aymeri*, 382 f.). It is well known that certain mediaeval schools and Universities, such as Toledo and Orléans, had a reputation for occult studies; and it may be that the Old French use of the word *arʒ* in the sense of 'magic arts' (*arʒ de Toulete*, etc.) derives directly from *arʒ* (*liberaus*) in the University sense.

(5) The form *gramer* does not seem to be actually attested in this sense in mediaeval literature.

(6) According to P. Barbier, *Miscellanea Lexicographica*, XVI, 12 (*Proceedings of the Leeds Philosophical and Literary Society, Literary and Historical Section*, vol. IV, part IV, p. 267), Old French probably had an adj. *gramaire*; but the expression *livre gramaire* does not seem to be attested.

(7) *Etymologisches Wörterbuch der romanischen Sprachen* (1853), p. 651, as modified in the second edition (1861–2), II, 320 f.—W. von Wartburg, whose *Französisches Etymologisches Wörterbuch* has reached the word *grammatica* since this article was originally written, admits as the probable cause of the change of vowel 'die Sippe von *grīma* (afr. *grimouart* "moue dédaigneuse" u.a.)'.

(8) Meyer-Lübke (*R.E.W.* 3867) suggests that some of the words he derives from *grīm* may have been influenced in form and sense by *grīma*. A similar contamination may perhaps have been responsible for dial. Eng. *grim* '1. A death's head, as sculpture or represented. 2. A ghost; a skeleton', and *church-grim* 'A hobgoblin, bogey' (J. Wright, *English Dialect Dictionary*).

(9) So Meyer-Lübke, Gamillscheg, Bloch and Dauzat; the first two, however, hesitate between *grīm* and *grīma* as the source of Sp. *grima*.

(10) By means of the suffix -*aʒ*, -*ace* (Lat. -*aceum*, -*acea*), which was throughout Old and Middle French a more active formative element than has generally been recognized. It was attached chiefly to noun stems, and furnished adjectives with the general sense of 'characterized by', 'consisting of', 'resembling' (there is usually no pejorative nuance). Adjectives of this character easily acquire substantival value; in most cases the derivative in -*aʒ* or -*ace* is in fact attested only in substantival function, but the noun it originally determined can often be identified. Examples dating from the twelfth and thirteenth centuries are *paonaʒ*, -*ace* adj. (rare in the masc.) and *paonace* sb.f. (sc. *escarlate*); *favaʒ*, *pesaʒ* and *veçaʒ* sbs.m. (sc. *estrain*); *borraʒ*, *chanevaʒ* and *fusaʒ* sbs.m. (sc. *drap*, cf. Old French *drap linge*, *drap lange*); *paillace* sb.f. (sc. *coute*?); *becaʒ* sb.m., *becace* sb.f.

(11) We may disregard *grimache* in 'Eustause de Hersta voit mult bin la grimache' (J. des Preis, *Geste de Liége*, II, 1643), which is often cited as the earliest occurrence of *grimace*, and on which some hypotheses have been founded; it is of uncertain interpretation, and is in any case not proved to be earlier than fourteenth-century examples.

(12) Is it a mere coincidence that in a *fatras* of Jehan Regnier (1432–33; *Fortunes et Adversiteʒ*, ed. E. Droz, 1100) *grimasse* in sense 2 is used in reference to a woman (or perhaps a snail) riding on a broomstick and associated with a he-goat?

(13) The influence of the same words may perhaps be seen also in *grimaud* 'devil', 'sorcerer', 'Huguenot', which appears to be the proper name Grimaud, jocularly or euphemistically given connotative value through a chance phonetic

association; since the common noun is not attested until 1561, it is difficult to admit with Barbier (*Misc. Lex.* XVI, 8) that the proper name acquired the sense of 'devil' at an early date through association with derivatives of Germanic *krimm-* 'to scratch, claw', and was itself responsible for the alteration of *gramoire* to *grimoire*.

Evidence of a sense-association between *grimoire* and *grimace* is perhaps provided by a passage in Chastellain (III, 177; Godefroy, IX, 726): 'Entre gens de tous divers degres, il y a des grimoires et des doleances tous les jours de droit et de tort', where *grimoire*, though translated by Godefroy 'chose indé-chiffrable, embrouillée', can hardly mean anything but 'grimace, sign of displeasure'.

(14) Not in the *O.E.D.*, but attested as surnames from the thirteenth century on (C. W. Bardsley, *Dictionary of English and Welsh Surnames*).

(15) Cf. Med. Lat. *grammaticellus* 'grammaticus parum eruditus', 969 (Du Cange); *grammaticella* 'beginner, ignoramus', 1271 (Baxter and Johnson, *Mediaeval Latin Word List*).

(16) The relation between the English and French words is debatable, but the primary sense appears to have been 'boy'; cf. *O.E.D.* s.vv. *groom* and *grummet* and the French dictionaries s.v. *gourmet*.

(17) A. F. Leach, *The Schools of Mediaeval England*, 1915, pp. 157, 171 f.

(18) Such a dissimilation is in fact attested for the Old French word: in the poem of Henri d'Andeli, one of the two MSS. (B.N. 19152) has *gomereax* for *glomeriaus*.

(19) The history of *dunce* (originally 'Duns-man, scholastic') shows a some-what similar vulgarization of a depreciatory term of academic origin.

(20) For example, the form *gaumeril* (attested by the *E.D.D.* for Scotland, Yorks, Lancs, Derbys and Warwicks) seems to be due to a contamination with *gaum* (widespread in dialects and probably of Celtic origin, cf. Irish *gam*, *gamal* etc.).

A NOTE ON
TAINE'S CONCEPTION OF THE
ENGLISH MIND

BY

F. C. ROE

Professor of French in the University of Aberdeen

TAINE, in his early thirties, reproached his friend Édouard de Suckau because, in an article on Germany, Suckau had not been systematic enough, had not led up to 'quelque grosse idée générale sur la différence de la France et de l'Allemagne' (*Corres.* II, 181). Taine's stricture revealed his own preoccupation. The year before, in 1858, he himself, after a brief journey in Germany, had set down a number of general ideas about German character and psychology (*Corres.* II, 175). Indeed, even before leaving France, he had, as he listened to the music of Bach, Schumann and Mendelssohn, made a very striking pronouncement: 'L'animal, là-bas, rêve et sent, et pénètre les ensembles, au lieu de causer, préciser, juger, découper comme ici' (*Corres.* II, 165).

This is a fundamental judgment, and of outstanding interest, for here we have, expressed for the first time, Taine's view on the comparative psychology of the German and French 'races'. On this foundation he built up, not only all that he wrote about Germany, but all that he wrote about Great Britain. This is the view that he develops so trenchantly in the *Introduction à l'Histoire de la littérature anglaise*. For Taine, the ultimate difference between the Frenchman on the one hand, and the English or German on the other, lies in their divergent ways of 'representing objects':

Selon que la représentation est nette, et comme découpée à l'emporte-pièce, ou bien confuse et mal délimitée, selon qu'elle concentre en soi un grand ou un petit nombre de caractères de l'objet, selon qu'elle est violente et accompagnée d'impulsions, ou tranquille et entourée de calme, toutes les opérations et tout le train courant de la machine humaine sont transformés (t. I, xix).

Both the generalization inspired by German music and the passage in the *Introduction* really amount to a distinction between the mental processes of the French—logical, precise, but incomplete or superficial—and the mental processes of the Englishman or German—intuitive, confused by emotion or sentiment, but penetrating to the heart of things.

Modern psychology would no doubt look askance at so sweeping a judgment. Can the whole character and mind of a nation be summed up, and its whole history be deduced from one psychological—or perhaps even physiological—cause? Is it true that for each nation there is a 'faculté maîtresse', the key to all its thought and action? Can we be really sure that all Frenchmen conceive objects, of whatever kind, in a clear-cut, sharply-defined manner, whereas an Englishman or a German sees all objects dimly, but, by intuition, penetrates more deeply into reality? And is it true that the Englishman, as Taine implies, differs from the German only in so far as his mind, in addition to the 'violent imagination' of the German, possesses a 'positive and practical' element? Such generalizations about national character are very tempting to make, impossible to substantiate. Taine makes his task infinitely harder by attempting to embrace, in a single formula, the German barbarian of Tacitus and the prim, top-hatted, chapel-going Victorian.

Whence did Taine acquire his ideas as to the essential differences between national minds? It would seem that he deduced them originally from his extremely wide reading of French, German and English literary works, and that German music, including that of Mendelssohn, helped to confirm him in his views. He satisfied himself—perhaps rather too easily—that his views were sound by rapid personal inspections in Germany and England and made fuller observations of his own country which he published in *Notes sur Paris* and *Carnets de voyage*.

Certain pages of Mme de Staël may well have suggested to Taine his ideas on national psychology. The account of Germany and the Germans in *De l'Allemagne*, 'une œuvre directrice de l'opinion' in France for generations, stressed the imaginative power of the northern German by reference to the climate: 'Les brouillards et les frimas semblent l'élément naturel des hommes d'une imagination forte et profonde.' 'Il faut en convenir, les climats tempérés sont plus propres à la société qu'à la poésie.' 'Ce sont les délices du midi ou les rigueurs du nord qui ébranlent fortement l'imagination. Soit qu'on lutte contre la nature, soit qu'on s'enivre de ses dons, la puissance de la création n'en est pas moins forte, et réveille en nous le sentiment des beaux-arts ou l'instinct des mystères de l'âme.' These quotations, all from Liv. 1er, ch. v, which bring out so strongly the imaginative powers of the Germans, remind one, by the importance accorded to climate, of Taine's famous evocation of the 'Anglo-Saxon', the tall, blue-eyed, phlegmatic barbarian in his muddy hut, who, all day and for days on end, listens to the rain pattering on the leaves of the oaks: 'Quelles rêveries peut-il avoir quand il contemple ses boues et son ciel terni?' (*Hist. litt. ang.* I, p. 6). 'Alourdies et figées, ses idées ne savent pas s'étaler aisément, abondamment, avec une suite naturelle et une régularité involontaire. Mais cet esprit exclu du sentiment du beau n'en est que plus propre au sentiment du vrai' (ibid. p. 70).

Taine's vision of the Englishman—whether Anglo-Saxon or Victorian—seems to be based, to some extent, on Mme de Staël's analysis of the German. His typical Frenchman bears a striking resemblance to Voltaire as defined by Carlyle in 1829:

The clear, quick vision, and the methodic arrangement which springs from it, are looked upon as particularly French qualities; and Voltaire, at all times, manifests them in a more than French degree. Let him but cast his eye over any subject, in a moment he sees, though indeed only to a short depth, yet with instinctive decision, where the main bearings of that short depth lie; what is, or appears to be, its logical adherence; how causes connect themselves with effects; how the whole is to be seized and in lucid sequence represented to his or other minds. (Carlyle, *Collected Works*, 1857, vol. 2, p. 164.)

What can we deduce from these points of resemblance? Since Taine was obviously well acquainted with the works of Mme de Staël and with those of Carlyle, shall we conclude that he simply adopted her view of the German and Carlyle's view of the Frenchman? That would be unwise as well as unfair. All we can safely deduce is that Taine's views on national psychology reflected the received notions of the time. He was prone to adopt rather too readily current opinions which fitted his own pattern of thought and to extend unduly the scope of the notion he adopted. Just as, in *Les Origines*, he was tempted to identify *l'esprit français* and *l'esprit classique*, he followed Mme de Staël in identifying German and English, accepting her suggestion that 'les mêmes traits de caractère se retrouvent constamment parmi les divers principes d'origine germanique' (*De l'Allemagne*, Observations générales). He assumed that the mind of Voltaire might safely be taken as the type of the French mind. At times he seemed to have more faith in his own system than in his own mind. For, in spite of the errors of his system, he occasionally hits upon the truth through that very intuition which he spent so much pains in proving to be German.

PASCAL AND BRUNSCHVICG

BY

DENIS SAURAT

*Professor of French Language and Literature
in the University of London
(King's College)*

MOST students of Pascal have lived for forty years or so on Brunschvicg's edition of the *Pensées*. Now M. Z. Tourneur (Vrin, 1942) publishes at last a true reproduction of the manuscripts of the *Pensées* as they exist in the Bibliothèque Nationale, recueil 9202. And this at once puts Brunschvicg out of date—in all sincerity, goodwill and intelligence, Brunschvicg has given us an erroneous picture of Pascal. It looks as though Brunschvicg had been unable to understand Pascal. From the eighteenth century onwards the editions of Pascal have been many, all have been necessary to the reputation of Pascal, but all have been erroneous. It should now be time to get on to a real edition of Pascal which can only be a reproduction of the manuscripts such as they exist without any attempt at classifications which inevitably substitute the mind of the editor for Pascal's mind. M. Tourneur writes, in a modest note at the end of the volume, on Brunschvicg's edition: 'there are obvious errors and definite misunderstandings but above all Brunschvicg deliberately betrays Pascal's scheme of thought. I do not believe that our understanding of the texts has been helped much and in many cases it has been hindered, through arbitrary classifications, even if we could eliminate the mistakes in details, and the facility thus offered to the reader is a delusion.'

M. Tourneur goes no further. But if we look at the texts we find that his moderation is unjustified and that we have been betrayed by Brunschvicg to an unforgivable extent. The living centre of Pascal is *Le Mystère de Jésus*. Brunschvicg puts this essential passage in the middle of his book where it is lost in a mass of apparently classified matter which is really irrelevant. Tourneur puts it where it should be chronologically, at the beginning of the book, since it is the key to the whole of Pascal. Brunschvicg has allowed himself to displace essential passages, and from a reading of the manuscript a greater Pascal than we knew of appears, a greater Pascal that the reader of Brunschvicg cannot know about. Between No. 554 and No. 555 of Brunschvicg's arrangement come, chronologically, some twelve *pensées* of the highest importance which Brunschvicg has put elsewhere. I will quote one only which formed an essential part of the texts contemporary with the *Mystère de Jésus*:

> Il n'y a rien de si périlleux que ce qui plaît à Dieu et aux hommes, car les états qui plaisent à Dieu et aux hommes ont une chose qui plaît à Dieu et une autre qui plaît aux hommes. Comme la grandeur de Ste.-Thérèse, ce qui plaît à Dieu est sa profonde humilité dans ses révélations; ce qui plaît aux hommes sont ses lumières. Et aussi on se tue d'imiter ses discours pensant imiter son état.

Brunschvicg had no right to displace this, which is a profound and fruitful observation. But he goes further and commits worse crimes. He takes away from the *Mystère de Jésus* sequence everything that relates to Nature and thus does away with one of the most wonderful elements of Pascal, a sort of Christian mystic pantheism. *Le Mystère de Jésus* is not only the relationship of Jesus to the human heart, it is also the relationship of Jesus to Nature. Brunschvicg suppresses all that side and scatters the texts about Nature which are parallel with the *Mystère de Jésus* to the four winds of his fantastic arrangement, or rather, disarrangement. Thus he truly betrays Pascal and us on one of the most essential points in Pascal's philosophy. He stops, p. 578, at: 'Ne t'inquiète donc pas', and passes on to another imagined section. This is no longer Pascal. For the manuscript goes on with two pages, 27 and 28 in Tourneur, on Nature, which are a consequence of the beginning of the *Mystère* and culminate in this fundamental statement (p. 27, Tourneur): 'la Nature—elle est toute le corps de Jésus-Christ en son patois mais il ne peut dire qu'elle est tout le corps de J-C.'

This means, if we look at the *Mystère* in its entirety, that Nature is a part of the physical aspect of Christ but *en son patois*: a *patois* is a deformation of a true language, Nature is partly a corruption of godhead, but yet the whole of Nature is in the body of Christ—but the body of Christ is much more than the whole of Nature.

This is a great theory, far more splendid than anything that Pascal has said elsewhere on the subject. Brunschvicg's index gives no clue to the whereabouts of this passage at all, but even though he has put it elsewhere in the book he remains unforgivable for having taken it away from the *Mystère de Jésus* where it is a culminating point of a whole series of passages on Nature.

It is obvious that Brunschvicg only understood half Pascal's ideas. Pascal describes in the part kept by Brunschvicg the union of Jesus and of the human heart. But he describes also the union of Jesus and of Nature. Pascal is not only a human mystic seeing God in Man, he is a cosmic mystic also and sees God in Nature— not only a cosmic pantheist but a cosmic *mystic*. In the two cases of the human heart and of Nature the reproduction of the image of God is deformed: hence the humility of Ste.-Thérèse (and this passage also should have been left with the *Mystère de Jésus*). Hence also the erratic element in Nature (Tourneur, p. 27, also displaced in Brunschvicg): 'Tout peut nous être mortel, même les choses faites pour nous servir, comme dans la nature.' It is, indeed, essential to keep in mind the fact that all these texts, the *Mystère* and the passages on nature here referred to, belong to the period *before* Pascal had thought of his 'Apology' and therefore, to be understood, must not be scattered throughout the fragments of the 'Apology', but considered separately.

It is therefore strictly exact, to quote Tourneur, that Brunschvicg 'trahit délibérément le dessein de Pascal'.

From now on, every serious student of Pascal will have to ignore Brunschvicg and begin by a close examination of the texts as given by Tourneur.

LECONTE DE LISLE & ROBERT BURNS

BY

A. LYTTON SELLS

*Professor of French Language and Literature
in the University of Durham*

LECONTE de Lisle felt no very deep admiration for the literatures of modern Europe. He thought that the ancient Greeks
were more truly inspired and produced nobler works than the
modern peoples; and, for his own part, he sought inspiration above
all in the 'légendes glorieuses' of glorious Hellas, of mysterious
Hindustan, of stern Norway, and Finland, and of the Celtic
peoples. But there was one modern literature which he admitted,
in a large measure privately, into his affections: that of our own
country and particularly of the northern kingdom. Lord Byron,
we know, influenced him profoundly. For Sir Walter Scott,
as we have shown elsewhere,[1] he conceived in boyhood an immense
admiration; and he maintained throughout his life a cult for one
who, whatever his defects, remains the writer of deepest humanity
and widest human sympathies that we have had since Shakespeare.

Scott would not appear to have exercised much direct influence
on his writings. But he interested him in Scottish life and scenery,
perhaps in Scottish poetry; he almost certainly, through the inter-
mediary of *The Pirate*, drew his attention to Norway and Norwegian
folklore, and thus perhaps opened the way for the whole series of
Scandinavian poems; and it is more than probable that he predisposed him to study the works of Scotland's national poet. Thus
his indirect influence on Leconte de Lisle was considerable. That
the influence of Robert Burns was to go far more deeply—and also
far more widely—than any critic has recognized, is certain. We
have already touched on this question,[2] and now propose to
explore it in more detail.

I

It is not known how, or when, Leconte de Lisle first became
acquainted with Burns's poetry. He may have found a translation

one day, by chance; he may have read about it in some contemporary book of travel, when reading about Scott. It may even have been mentioned to him by that 'venerable' librarian at Saint-Denis in the Île Bourbon who, probably about 1831, was lending him the Waverley Novels.[3] A book which perhaps fell into his hands at this time was Charles Nodier's *Promenade de Dieppe aux Montagnes d'Écosse*.[4] It is a sketch ('l'esquisse à peine ébauchée d'une promenade rapide') of 336 small pages; the three vignettes by Thompson and the coloured lithographs of a Highland chieftain and of some rare mountain plants add to its character. Now Nodier had been one of the first, in 1817, to realize the importance of Scott, and the main object of the tour he made in the summer of 1821 was apparently to meet Scott in Edinburgh. For some reason he missed him. Nor, strangely, does he say very much about Scott, or anything about Burns. In Edinburgh he fails to find the prison in which Jeanie Deans was confined. By Loch Lomond he naturally thinks of Rob Roy. Reaching Loch Katrine he speaks of 'un poëme délicieux de Sir Walter Scott, *la Dame du Lac*'; but in his own description of this, the most poetical of the lakes, he is more occupied with Ossian than with the adventures of Fitz-James and Rhoderick Dhu. He had come from France, he tells us, convinced that Macpherson's book was 'tout simplement la plus heureuse et la plus magnifique des supercheries littéraires'; he was to leave Scotland no less convinced 'que Macpherson a réellement recueilli des poëmes de tradition fort répandus' and that he changed their character very little. Further on we learn that his companions, who had left him for a time, had visited the island on Loch Leven where Queen Mary was once held in durance (*The Abbot*), had looked for MacGregor's birthplace at 'Balquidar' and the path followed by the Knight of Snowdon through the Trossachs. But in Nodier's personal experiences there is nearly as much question of 'wiskey' as of Sir Walter and—whether this be to his credit or not—more of Ossian than of either. Of Burns, nothing. Yet the chapter on Ayr contains a description of Burns's people, the Ayrshire peasants, which is not quickly forgotten. At Kilmarnock Nodier was greatly impressed by the 'quantité incroyable de jolies femmes' and by the care they gave to 'leur costume élégant'.

L'Ayrshire est d'ailleurs [he continues] le pays de l'Écosse où le peuple nous a paru le plus fidèle au vêtement national et le mieux inspiré dans la manière de le porter. Les hommes, les femmes, les enfants, s'y drapent à l'envi de leurs larges *plaids*, sans aucune règle bien fixe à ce qu'il paraît, mais de manière à charmer l'œil des artistes et à tenter l'émulation des Parisiennes elles-mêmes. . . . J'ai vu un tel groupe qui, pris comme il était, n'aurait pas déparé un tableau de Poussin. Les Écossaises surtout tirent un parti extraordinaire de ce genre de séduction, et la plupart pourraient s'en passer: elles sont charmantes.[5]

Perhaps Leconte de Lisle remembered this page when he was composing *Kléarista*. It is evident that Ayrshire was a land redolent of poetry, something like Sicily in the age of Theocritus, or Tuscany in more recent times. The day Nodier was describing was overcast; great sea-birds were flying with raucous cries over the woodland:

Toutes les ombres des ayeux traînaient en courant de montagne à montagne leurs vêtements à longs plis, et s'entassaient contusément sur un point du ciel; troupe immense et pressée, au-dessus de laquelle on distinguait à peine le front sourcilleux de quelques vieillards à la barbe chenue, et les casques aux ailes d'aigle de quelques guerriers. Ce magnifique aréopage des bardes et des héros ne tarda pas à se dissoudre sur nous en pluie froide et pénétrante mêlée de grêle et accompagnée de toutes les rumeurs de l'orage répétées par tous les échos.[6]

Thus did Ossian console them for the rigours of our island climate. In brief, there is in this book little about Scottish literature (apart from Ossian), but there are charm and a contagious enthusiasm. Most of its readers, including perhaps Leconte de Lisle himself, would be ready to repeat its author's cry: '*Caledoniam! Caledoniam!*'

Nodier was, in this matter, a representative man; for Ossian was still a household name in France at a time when the works and even the name of the national poet of Scotland were familiar only to a few. But Amédée Pichot, who knew more about English and Scottish literature and understood them better, we fancy, than any of his compatriots at that time, not only visited Sir Walter Scott in Edinburgh and at Abbotsford, but gained an immediate understanding of Robert Burns and of that tradition of song and ballad of which he had been the supreme interpreter.[7] Whether, in the course of the ambitious tour he made in 1822, Pichot visited Ayrshire is not quite certain. He went through the Trossachs and saw Loch Lomond; he may have crossed to the Hebrides: but between the foot of Ben Lomond, where he takes leave of the reader at the end of volume III of his *Voyage*, and the English Lakes, where we know he called on Southey at Keswick, it would be very strange if he did not travel through Burns's country. In any event, he well understood the spirit and raciness of Burns's poetry, of the nature-poems and the love-poems; as he understood why our Lake Poets, who had been quick to appreciate Burns's fresh spontaneity, could themselves only attain a similar freshness by conscious effort. Now Pichot's *Voyage historique et littéraire en Angleterre et en Écosse*[8] had perhaps done more than any other work seriously to initiate French readers into the contemporary literature of Great Britain; as its active and sympathetic author, by his translations and his writings on Scott, had been more instrumental than any-one, even than Defauconpret, in spreading in France the fame of the author of *Waverley*. Nor was this all. At the time of which we are writing, Pichot had not yet published *L'Écolier de Walter Scott* nor *Les Chiens de Walter Scott*. But he had contributed the letter-press to the *Vues pittoresques de l'Écosse*,[9] in which he speaks of places immortalized in *The Pirate*, *The Legend of Montrose*, *The Abbot*, *Old Mortality* and *Rob Roy*; and an album of this kind, with its fine lithographs by Pernot and vignettes by Lami, Bonington and Delaroche,[10] would appeal as powerfully to a young initiate as the novels themselves.

Were there copies of the *Voyage historique et littéraire* and of the *Vues pittoresques* in the town-library at Saint-Denis, and did Leconte de Lisle, now or later, come across the books and have the curiosity to open them? If he ever consulted the *Voyage*, his attention may well have been drawn to the figure of Burns, whom Pichot had singled out for special study. He would have seen that Burns's songs, described by Pichot as 'le prisme de la poésie', were in part the outcome of a wonderful tradition. 'La chanson . . . est en Écosse, plus qu'ailleurs, l'écho du peuple.'[11] And if he read a passage like this:

L'Écosse est plus fière de Burns que d'aucun de ses poètes: elle a raison; la poésie de Burns n'est qu'à elle: c'est le fruit de son sol, de son climat, de ses mœurs . . .

or like the following:

Il y a dans ses descriptions une sorte *d'unité de lieu* qui est plus difficile-
ment observée par Walter Scott lui-même, tout sobre qu'il est d'allusions
classiques. Dans les montagnes d'Écosse, il a suffi à Burns, pour embellir
ses paysages, de la grâce de quelques vallées, du contraste de quelques
ruines et du charme particulier de ce jour polaire, qui dédommage les
habitants du Nord de leurs longs hivers. C'est qu'aussi toute la poésie
de Burns naissait de sa sensibilité exquise, qui en trouvait les élémens
dans l'objet le plus insignifiant . . .[12]

—if he read such passages, his curiosity would certainly have been
roused and, not content with reading the poems which Pichot
quoted (*A Vision*, *The Daisy*, *Highland Mary*, and *To Mary in
Heaven*), he would have asked for a translation of Burns himself.
Now a partial translation, entitled *Morceaux choisis de Burns*,
traduits par James Aytoun et J.-B. Mesnard,[13] had appeared in 1826,
the year of the *Vues pittoresques*. The possibility that he read this,
or even had a copy of it, is worth noting, as it may afford a clue.
But in default of clear evidence, it appears more likely that Leconte
de Lisle's familiarity with Burns dates from the appearance of Léon
de Wailly's translation of the *Poésies complètes* in 1843.[14]

This was Vianey's view. Vianey said nothing about the earlier
Morceaux choisis or about Amédée Pichot; but he thought Leconte
de Lisle was 'certainly' one of Léon de Wailly's first readers.[15]
It is very likely. In spite of his legal studies and the business he had
half-heartedly taken up on his return home in 1843, the eighteen
months he spent on the Île Bourbon between 1843 and 1845 were
almost wholly devoted to the reading and writing of poetry; and
it seems to the present writer not improbable that this period of his
imaginative life—perhaps the decisive period in these formative
years—was as deeply marked by the discovery of Burns and the
revelation of Greek poetry (to much of which Burns's work was so
closely akin) as an earlier period had been marked by the discovery
of Scott. The theory is the more attractive in that it would account
for his decision to accept the offer of *La Démocratie pacifique* and
return to France. Had he been less obsessed with literature, he might
have given more thought to the advantages of his native island: a
livelihood assured by his family, the companionship of affectionate
parents, idyllic surroundings and an almost perfect climate. All these

things he exchanged for the long, dolorous winters of north-western Europe and for years of penury and semi-starvation, not to speak of the embarrassment in which his share in the Revolution of 1848 was to involve him. Nature alone had not been enough to retain him, as he saw when he wrote *Ultra Cœlos*[16] (*Revue contemporaine*, 1863); but the poet of *Requies* bitterly regretted what he had lost:

> Comme un morne exilé, loin de ceux que j'aimais,
> Je m'éloigne à pas lents des beaux jours de ma vie,
> Du pays enchanté qu'on ne revoit jamais.
> Sur la haute colline où la route dévie
> Je m'arrête, et vois fuir à l'horizon dormant
> Ma dernière espérance, et pleure amèrement.

Nevertheless, the poetry, which had dazzled him perhaps too much, offered the exile real and lasting sources of consolation. The exploration of Greek myth and legend was a perpetual enchantment, from which he only turned for a time to the *Bhagavata Purana* and the *Rig-Veda* to seek inspiration for some of the best of his *Poèmes antiques*—and also to find a personal philosophy of life. But in the years which preceded the *recueil* of 1852, it is clear that Burns's poems filled an honoured place in his mind.

II

It may be noted that the six *Chansons écossaises* which figure near the end of the definitive edition of *Poèmes antiques* had not all been composed at the same time. *Jane, Nanny, Nell, La Fille aux cheveux de lin*, and *Annie* had appeared in the first edition, in 1852; *La Chanson du Rouet*, 'imité de Burns', in the *Poèmes et Poésies* of 1855. The rather rapid survey of the *Chansons écossaises* in Joseph Vianey's book is far from exhausting the question of Burns's influence, or even the interest of this curious group of poems itself. We do not propose to examine them *ab initio*, but only to add our observations to those of M. Vianey,[17] whose book is the constant companion of students of Leconte de Lisle. We shall also connect these poems with the songs on which they are based, as M. Vianey refers only to Léon de Wailly and Auguste Angellier, so that Anglo-Saxon and Scottish readers, who do not always have access to these writers, are at a loss to see at once where Leconte de Lisle found his material. Vianey observes that the poet did not pretend to offer translations of Burns, still less to condense all the elements of interest in this most varied of the poets of love. *Jane* and *Annie* are the nearest, he considers, to their models, and not the best inspired.

Now *Jane* is a paraphrase of *The Blue-eyed Lass*;[18] but the refrain:

Je pâlis et tombe en langueur:
Deux beaux yeux m'ont blessé le cœur—

is not in Burns; and it is worth remarking that Leconte de Lisle must have been greatly taken with the refrains he did find in Burns, because he invented one for *La Fille aux cheveux de lin*, different from that in the original; for *Annie* he altered the refrain, making it more regular; while for *La Chanson du Rouet*, the original of which has no refrain, he composed one of his own. *Annie* is based on *The Rigs o' Barley*.[19] It is more regular, more classical, perhaps more artistic, than the original. We should hesitate to say that Leconte de Lisle was not as well inspired here as in any other of the *Chansons*. *The Rigs o' Barley* is not one of Burns's major successes; Leconte de Lisle's *Annie*, on the other hand, is a little masterpiece.

Nell (*Chansons écossaises*) contains more of nature and description than the other songs, though here, as often in Burns, nature furnishes the background and imagery for a theme of love. Beyond tracing it to one poem without title in Léon de Wailly's translation, M. Vianey neither appraises nor discusses it. For our own part, we should say tentatively that it seems to combine elements taken from *Phillis the fair*[20] and *Ca' the Yowes*;[21] and for the rest to be a poem as original as *La Fille aux cheveux de lin*. Vianey considered the latter to be the best of the six *Chansons*, and traced the inspiration of it to the *Lassie wi' the lint-white locks*;[22] but neither the 'luzerne en fleur', nor the 'alouette' of the refrain, nor the 'daims', 'lièvres', and 'perdrix' of the last quatrain, occur in this song of Burns. The lark and hare, however, figure prominently in others. We think that for *La Fille aux cheveux de lin* Leconte de Lisle also took a glance at *She says she lo'es me best of a'*, which opens with the line:

Sae flaxen were her ringlets,[23]

as he was, later on, to use the portrait it contains in one of his supposedly original poems: *Kléarista*. One would, then, hesitate to call either *Nell* or *La Fille aux cheveux de lin* adaptations. 'Composed after a reading of Burns' would be the best sub-title for them.

If the second of these is the best of the whole series, the most striking and interesting in our eyes is the one which the French poet entitled *Nanny*. Vianey did not consider it as moving as the song which he believed to be its original—*My Nannie's awa'* [24]— and for which he refers the reader to Angellier's subsequent translation. The reader might well, after perusing it, rub his eyes, for all that Leconte de Lisle seems to have derived from this poem of Burns is the heroine's name and the poet's lament for her absence; and these only come out in the last two lines. The greater part of the poem is an elegy in which woods and hills, lake and water-birds, are called on to lament the author's loss; and these stanzas, so different from anything in *My Nannie's awa'*, evidently struck Vianey, because he adds:

> Leconte de Lisle a essayé de nous donner *ce que Burns ne nous a pas donné une seule fois*, si grand peintre de la nature qu'il ait été, c'est-à-dire un paysage de la Haute Écosse; car, dans son pays, le poète écossais n'a connu et *il n'a peint que les régions qui ressemblent à toutes les plaines cultivées et bien arrosées*. Et je ne dis pas que la description des fameux lacs soit dans la pièce de Leconte de Lisle tout à fait digne de leur réputation. N'est-il pas cependant piquant que la physionomie pittoresque de l'Écosse ait intéressé davantage un poète étranger que le poète national? [25]

But is not there a grand picture of 'la Haute Écosse', generalized, it is true, but vivid and spirited as one could wish, in *My heart's in the Highlands?* [26] and can one say that Burns 'only depicted regions which are like any cultivated and well-watered plains'? It is true that the usual background of his songs and poems is the soft, pastoral landscape of western Ayrshire, or Nithsdale; but often enough he describes the steep braes and foaming streams of the glens (*The Birks of Aberfeldy*) or the rolling moors that cover the higher ground (*Hunting Song*, and *The death and dying words of poor Mailie*). There is lake-scenery, too, in southern Scotland— Leconte de Lisle, who must have read *The Abbot*, would not need to

go to Burns to discover the fact—and fine mountain-scenery, too.
To restrict the 'physionomie pittoresque de l'Écosse' to the Highlands is an error which Amédée Pichot would not have made,
nor Taine. What of the following song, which the French poet
may have read in translation:

> Yon wild mossy mountains sae lofty and wide,
> That nurse in their bosom the youth o' the Clyde,
> Where the grouse lead their coveys thro' the heather to feed,
> And the shepherd tents his flock as he pipes on his reed . . .
>
> Not Gowrie's rich valleys, nor Forth's sunny shores,
> To me hae the charms o' yon wild, mossy moors . . .?[27]

Moreover, to return to the poem we have been considering, *Nanny*,
it is not clear that Leconte de Lisle intended to paint the Highlands
or the scenery of Loch Lomond, Loch Katrine or Loch Achray,
which Vianey presumably had in mind. The greater part of this song
—four out of the five stanzas it contains—was not, as Vianey
seems to have supposed, invented by Leconte de Lisle to give a
Highland background to the story of *My Nannie's awa'*, but taken
from a longer poem which probably escaped Vianey's notice—an
elegy not on a lost love but on a lost friend—the *Elegy on Captain
Matthew Henderson*. However, to enable the reader to judge of all
this, we will quote Leconte de Lisle's poem *in extenso*. Like all the
Chansons écossaises it is good, and some readers may prefer it to the
other songs.

NANNY

> Bois chers aux ramiers, pleurez, doux feuillages,
> Et toi, source vive, et vous, frais sentiers;
> Pleurez, ô bruyères sauvages,
> Buissons de houx et d'églantiers!
>
> Du courlis siffleur l'aube saluée
> Suspend au brin d'herbe une perle en feu;
> Sur le mont rose est la nuée;
> La poule d'eau nage au lac bleu.
>
> Pleurez, ô courlis; pleure, blanche aurore;
> Gémissez, lac bleu, poules, coqs pourprés;
> Vous que la nue argente et dore,
> Ô claires collines, pleurez!

> Printemps, roi fleuri de la verte année,
> Ô jeune Dieu, pleure! Été mûrissant,
> Coupe ta tresse couronnée;
> Et pleure, Automne rougissant!
>
> L'angoisse d'aimer brise un cœur fidèle.
> Terre et ciel, pleurez! Oh! que je l'aimais!
> Cher pays, ne parle plus d'elle.
> Nanny ne reviendra jamais.[28]

My Nannie's awa' is a short song; it gives a picture of Spring with
all its beauty, all its sources of joy, which bring only pain to the
poet. Autumn and winter are more dear.

> Come autumn sae pensive, in yellow and grey,
> And soothe me wi' tidings o' Nature's decay:
> The dark dreary winter, and wild driving snaw,
> Alane can delight me—now Nannie's awa'![29]

Of this feeling nothing is retained by Leconte de Lisle; nothing
in fact of the whole song except the heroine's name and the poet's
grief for her absence. But turn now to the *Elegy on Captain Matthew
Henderson*, which is the real source of *Nanny*. It is a long poem in
sixteen six-line stanzas. A good deal of the flora and fauna of
southern Scotland figures in it. We quote only the stanzas which
were used by Leconte de Lisle.

> Ye hills! near neebors o' the starns,
> That proudly cock your cresting cairns! . . .
> Come join, ye Nature's sturdiest bairns,
> My wailing numbers!
>
> Mourn, *ilka grove the cushat kens!*
> Ye haz'ly shaws and briery dens!
> Ye burnies, wimplin down your glens,
> Wi' toddlin din,
> Or foaming strang, wi' hasty stens,
> Frae lin to lin! . . .
>
> Ye roses on your thorny tree,
> The first o' flow'rs.
>
> *At dawn, when ev'ry grassy blade*
> *Droops with a diamond at his head* . . .

Mourn, ye wee songsters o' the wood;
Ye *grouse* that crap the *heather* bud;
Ye *curlews* calling thro' a clud;
    Ye *whistling* plover;
An' mourn, ye whirring paitrick brood:
    He's gane for ever!

Mourn, *sooty coots*, and speckled teals;
Ye fisher herons, watching eels;
Ye duck and drake, wi' airy wheels
    Circling the lake;
Ye bitterns, till the quagmire reels,
    Rair for his sake! . . .

Mourn, Spring, thou darling of the year!
Ilk cowslip cup shall kep a tear:
Thou, *Simmer*, while each corny spear
    Shoots up its head,
Thy gay, green, flow'ry tresses shear
    For him that's dead!

Thou, Autumn, wi' thy yellow hair,
In grief thy sallow mantle tear! . . .

Mourn him, thou Sun, great source of light!
Mourn, Empress of the silent night! . . .
For through your orbs he's ta'en his flight,
    Ne'er to return . . .[30]

Here, in a form less concentrated, are nearly all the elements used by Leconte de Lisle: the 'collines', the 'lac', the 'bois chers aux ramiers', the 'églantiers', the 'aube' which 'suspend au brin d'herbe une perle en feu'; the 'bruyères' and the 'coqs pourprés' (grouse), the 'poule d'eau' (sooty coots), the 'courlis siffleurs' (curlews, the word 'whistling' being transferred from the plovers); and the spring, summer and autumn, with one line ('Coupe ta tresse couronnée') translated almost literally.

French readers of *Nanny* might be reminded, first of all, of *La jeune Tarentine*. No doubt Leconte de Lisle thought of it, too, when he read the *Elegy on Captain Henderson*. Similarity of feeling, and even of form, is natural among bucolic and elegiac poets; and although Burns, a cultured man, may not have been very familiar with Bion and Moschus, he was well aware of being in the lineage of Theocritus, their predecessor:

> But thee, Theocritus, wha matches? ...
> In this braw age o' wit and lear
> Will nane the shepherd's whistle nair
> Blow sweetly in its native air
> And rural grace;
> And wi' the far-fam'd Grecian share
> A rival place?

But, as we have seen, the rhythm of

> Pleurez, ô courlis; pleure, blanche aurore; ...
> O claires collines, pleurez!

is not a reference to Chénier, but an adaptation from Burns.

Such, then, are the *Chansons écossaises* as they appeared in 1852, accompanying in the *Poèmes antiques* the small but important group of Hindu poems and the larger group of Greek poems, which set the tone for the *recueil*, as indeed they rightly do for the author's work as a whole. One song remained to be added: the *Chanson du Rouet*. In the *Songs and Ballads*, *Bessy and her Spinnin-Wheel* is a poem of four eight-line stanzas: it is of a serene, even gaiety, the notes rippling steadily out like the song of that 'laverock' which Burns so loves to evoke. The concluding stanza expresses the peasant girl's contentment with her lot (she had the good fortune to live before the industrial era):

> Wi' sma' to sell, and less to buy,
> Aboon distress, below envy,
> O wha wad leave this humble state,
> For a' the pride of a' the great?
> Amid their flaring, idle toys,
> Amid their cumbrous, dinsome joys,
> Can they the peace and pleasure feel
> Of Bessie at her spinnin-wheel? [31]

Leconte de Lisle's poem contains three six-line stanzas only. The first two are a development of the first in Burns; but the picture of Spring and the song of northern birds which occupy the second and third stanzas of Burns's poem—all that gladsome nature which

surrounds the girl at her work—are omitted; while in place of the
concluding stanza, quoted above, we have the following:

> O mon cher rouet, ma blanche bobine,
> Vous me filerez mon suaire étroit,
> Quand, près de mourir et courbant l'échine,
> Je ferai mon lit éternel et froid.
> Vous me filerez mon suaire étroit,
> O mon cher rouet, ma blanche bobine!

'Imité de Burns' is almost an exaggeration. There is nothing in
Burns resembling the desolation of this stanza. We have recalled
the fact that the *Chanson du Rouet* appeared in the *Poèmes et Poésies*
of 1855: one might have guessed as much from the difference of
tone. The first five songs, despite the fact that in them Leconte de
Lisle borrows much more widely than Vianey saw, are on the
whole very near the gay, transparent spirit of the original. The
Chanson du Rouet, on the other hand, belongs to the period of the
most sombre verses of *Poèmes barbares*;[32] to the same year as *Les
Hurleurs*, *Le Vent froid de la nuit*, *Le Nazaréen*, *L'Anathème* and
Requies; and it reveals the mark of this proximity. 'Le soleil, ni la
mort ne peuvent se regarder fixement', a great writer had truly said.
Yet the idea of death may become very much of a prepossession;
and the thoughtful soul, when a prey to great misfortune, may
become possessed with the idea that man, that 'marvellous animal',
is a failure. The observation is constantly recurring in Leconte de
Lisle's poems at this time: not merely in the personal poems like
Requies, as piercing in its desolation as anything in Leopardi, but
even in objective, archaeological poems like *Le Runoïa*, where the
ancient prophet unexpectedly becomes the mouthpiece of the
modern pessimist:

> J'ai vu que mieux valaient le vide et le silence.

One thing only during these terrible years attached Leconte de
Lisle to continued existence: his love of beauty, his love of art.
For in this modern world, which is the creation of industrialism,
applied science and the 'Enlightenment' (to give it a name which was
not originally intended to be derisive), for the reflective soul which
no longer believes in God, there is no anchor save in the love of beauty.

And beauty may be found in all sorts of places, the noblest and the humblest; in the life of an emperor and in the life of a poor working-girl. Bess's song made Auguste Angellier think of a Dutch interior. 'N'est-ce pas surtout', he observes, 'avec cette riche demi-teinte de pourpre, un intérieur de Peter de Hooch villageois?' What the Scottish poet describes, however, apart from the girl's reflections, are the stretch of country below the cottage, where the two burns meet, the birches in leaf, the hawthorn blossom, and the birds singing near the little shelter. The notations of wild-life and scenery fit well into the poem as they do into so many epigrams in the *Greek Anthology*, more particularly those of the age of Mnasalkas and Leonidas of Tarentum. [33] And if *Bessy and her Spinnin-Wheel* reminds one of anything in literature, it is surely of the homely epigram which Leonidas wrote for old Platthis who

often repelled from her her evening and morning sleep, keeping poverty away, and near the door of gray old age used to sing a tune to her spindle and familiar distaff. Still by the loom until the dawn she revolved in company with the Graces that long task of Pallas, or, a lovable figure, smoothed with her wrinkled hand on her wrinkled knee the thread sufficient for the loom. Aged eighty years comely Platthis who wove so well set eyes on the lake of Acheron. [34]

It is probable that Burns, and possible that Leconte de Lisle, were not familiar with this epigram; but Burns had only to compose a song about country things, birds, beasts or trees, or simple country-folk, to write in the Greek manner; while Leconte de Lisle in following him [35] was probably conscious of remaining in that great current of Hellenic poetry to which he himself contributed so much.

III

It is acceptable, if not usual, to place Burns in the spiritual lineage of Theocritus and the bucolic poets. [36] Theocritus was, after all, city-bred; whereas Burns was a man of the soil. [37] He had a con-genital knowledge of what he wrote about. Angellier, comparing him with the Greeks, thought his peasants were nearest of all to those who form the chorus in the *Peace* of Aristophanes. [38] He has affinities, too—or so it seems to us—with a few of the so-called minor poets who figure in the *Anthology*. He makes one think of

Theognis or Anyte, but especially of Mnasalkas and Leonidas of
Tarentum. Leonidas was indeed for Magna Graecia very much
what Burns was to become for Scotland. A man of the people, he
wrote for all classes and all ages, for children and old people, for
sailors and country-folk, for rich men and nobles, too, if one may
judge from his epigram on the generous Aristokrates,

> Whose heart no kindness e'er denied—
> Alas, another should have died—

one of the most beautiful and moving poems in the whole of the
Anthology. Even more universal in his appeal than Burns, if he
was less occupied with the 'lassies'—and hardly at all in an
amorous way—he loved the country and the wild creatures, like
Burns, and because he lived longer he knew more about life and its
'bitter taste of tears'—he was more profound. Yet most of his poems
which have survived are poems of circumstance and the similarity
of feeling between him and Burns is, on occasion, striking.

Nevertheless, the parallel between Burns and Theocritus must
always have a major significance. It was clearly present in Burns's
mind,[39] and Scottish Hellenists have often amused themselves by
translating one or other of his poems into Theocritan Greek[40]—
and they go very well; just as, when a British scholar undertakes
to translate the Sicilian bucolic poets, he adopts the dialect of Burns
for the purpose. One has indeed only to study Burns and become
penetrated with his spirit, to perceive that his work as a whole—the
peasant-poems, the elegies, the poems which treat of love and nature
and, as we shall presently show, the animal-poems—constitutes the
most spontaneous and perhaps the most authentic resurgence of the
Greek spirit which the modern world has known. Even the pastoral
life he describes had, despite a terrible difference in climate, close
resemblances with that of ancient Sicily. Much has unfortunately
changed since Burns's time; but it is significant that the pastoral life
with its native industries, and even the clan-system, survived longer
in Scotland than elsewhere in western Europe; Scotland maintaining,
down to the twentieth century, certain affinities of culture with
contemporary Sicily and Greece.

Of the similarity of spirit in Burns and Theocritus, Leconte de
Lisle must very soon have become aware. It is significant that it

was only after publishing the five *Chansons écossaises* in the *Poèmes antiques* of 1852 that he composed a number of Greek and Sicilian poems more or less inspired by Theocritus, and also undertook a translation of the *Idylls* which appeared, with a version of Hesiod's poems and of the Orphic Hymns, in 1861. Now of the poems based on Theocritus of which Vianey traces the sources (without, however, discussing the dates), *Le Vase* had appeared, with *La Chanson du Rouet*, in the *Poèmes et Poésies* of 1855; *Les Plaintes du Cyclope*, *L'Enfance d'Héraklès*, *La Mort de Penthée* and *Héraklès au taureau* in the *Poésies complètes* of 1858; *Symphonie* and *Le Retour d'Adônis* in the 1874 edition of *Poèmes antiques*. In *Hylas* (1846) and *Les Bucoliastes*, while Theocritus affords a starting-point, the share of invention is greater. But *Les Bucoliastes*—an interesting poem for our purpose—appeared in the new edition of the *Poésies complètes*, in 1862. It is therefore clear that the poems inspired by Burns preceded, in date of publication, those inspired by Theocritus, with the single exception of *Hylas*; and to suggest that it was the reading of Burns which led Leconte de Lisle to the study of Theocritus is not going as far as it sounds: the possibility is in fact a likelihood. The longer Greek poems, *Hélène*, *Niobé* and *Khirôn*, all, at least in their original versions, precede these verses of the Burns–Theocritus period (1852–62); so do *La Robe du Centaure*, *Hypatie* and the *Chant alterné*, to name some of the best of the Hellenic poems. On the other hand, between 1862 and 1874 the influence of Theocritus on Leconte de Lisle is less marked. During this period Leconte de Lisle published a number of Greek poems in which the landscape or background appears to us to be drawn with more originality and with more precision. There remain, however, several short poems, more or less idyllic in character, which we have not yet discussed. Vianey groups them with the Theocritan pieces, while adding that, properly speaking, they have no sources. The imitation of Theocritus, he says, is indirect, 'et cependant je ne sais si ce n'est pas dans ceux-ci que le bucoliaste syracusain eût le mieux reconnu la Sicile et les Siciliennes'. They are *Thyoné*, *Glaucé*, *Klytie* and *La Source*.[41] 'C'est surtout', he concludes, '*Thestylis*, *Kléarista* et *Paysage*, trois étonnantes visions de Sicile.'[42]

This is significant for our purpose, and nothing could better illustrate the way in which the inspiration of Burns and the inspiration of Theocritus had become fused in Leconte de Lisle's mind. *Thestylis* had first appeared in the *Revue Contemporaine* of 15 August 1862; *Kléarista* with four other poems, all *really* Hellenic, in the same review on 15 October 1862. Now *Thestylis* may be, as Vianey thought, a more or less original poem. There arises from the landscape an authentic impression of the shores of the Mediterranean, and the tone of this idyll seems to us genuinely Greek. But *Kléarista* contains at least two features which raise a doubt: the portrait of the maiden, with its precise, individual traits, in the first stanza; and the birds and animals in the second. Most of Leconte de Lisle's Greek heroines are ideal figures, 'vierges . . . au corps de neige, aux bras d'albâtre, aux épaules de marbre, au col d'ivoire, aux pieds d'argent', etc., to quote Fernand Desonay's mischievous summary of their charms. Kléarista, on the other hand, might be the portrait of someone whom the poet had seen.

> Kléarista s'en vient par les blés onduleux
> Avec ses noirs sourcils arqués sur ses yeux bleus . . .

She is probably the sister of the cold and cruel maiden in the *Bucoliastes*—'la fille au noir sourcil'—but with this exception, there is no one like her in the other Greek poems of Leconte de Lisle. Again, in an evocation of ancient Sicily, if animals were to be introduced, we should expect to find those that figure most frequently in ancient poetry: a goat, or some white oxen, of the family of those sacred oxen of the Sun which Odysseus's companions so unwisely set upon; or the swallow or nightingale, long dear to Greek poets; or the grasshopper and the cicada which country-children used to keep as pets. Instead, Leconte de Lisle shows us the lark, the blackbird and some hares 'dans le creux des verts sillons tapis'. True, all these creatures are found in Sicily. But the lark and blackbird only occasionally figure in Greek poetry, and rarely receive much notice: the mention we find of the crested lark, in particular, shows that the Greeks, unlike ourselves, felt no special admiration for its song. In short, if it were not for the name of the heroine and the mention of 'les roses de Milet' and 'le berger de l'Hybla'—both rather conventional traits—we might just as well suppose ourselves to be in Scotland—in fact, better. The truth is, as we have shown in an article in the *Revue de Littérature comparée*,[43] that the whole of *Kléarista*, apart from these conventional names, is composed of scenes, features and other traits taken from Burns's *Songs and Ballads*.

We do not disagree with Vianey that this poem is 'une étonnante vision de Sicile'; *Kléarista* can be counted as an Hellenic poem in the sense in which Burns's work and even something of what it inspires belong to the Hellenic tradition. If this were not so, *Kléarista* could not for so long have deceived so many. We do not doubt either, that Leconte de Lisle hoped, or intended, to deceive his readers, or that he enjoyed what was perhaps a pleasantry; for he knew what he was doing. He had only just published a translation of Theocritus, and he could easily have written an idyll with the genuine Sicilian flavour. Now this flavour *Kléarista* does not possess. It is obvious that if the heroine had been a Jeanie or a Margaret, the hero an Ayrshire shepherd, and if the poem had been described as 'a Scottish idyll', the picture and feeling would have been authentic; whereas, in their Sicilian disguise, they are not, or at least not quite.

Les Bucoliastes, which Leconte de Lisle also published in 1862, offers a curious example of what he could write when he wished. It is an eclogue which appears to be inspired partly by the eighth Idyll of Theocritus, partly by Chénier's *Le Jeune Malade*. But the heroine who has worked such ravage in the young goatherd's heart is 'la fille au noir sourcil' whose portrait Leconte de Lisle took from *She says she lo'es me best of a'*:

> Sae flaxen were her ringlets,
> Her eyebrows of a darker hue,
> Bewitchingly o'erarching
> Twa laughing een o' bonnie blue;

and when we read:

> Quand, aux feux du matin, s'envole l'alouette
> Du milieu des sillons de rosée emperlés,
> Je ne l'écoute plus; mes esprits sont troublés;
> Mais pour te ranimer, ô nature muette,
> Il suffit d'une voix qui chante dans les blés—

we at once recognize the lark of *My Nannie's awa'*:

> Thou lav'rock that springs frae the dews of the lawn,
> The shepherd to warn of the grey-breaking dawn,

and also the scenery of the *Rigs o' Barley* and *Comin' thro' the Rye*. Yet the poem as a whole is Hellenic; and if these lines fit harmoniously into the dialogue, it is because, as we have seen, the Scottish and Sicilian pastoral are very closely akin.[44]

Unique among the works of Leconte de Lisle are the various Animal-Poems. They deserve a *recueil*, or part of a *recueil*, to themselves, instead of being scattered through various volumes. There is nothing like them in French literature. Du Bellay's *Épitaphe d'un Chat* affords some idea of what that whimsical poet might have written, had animals enjoyed sufficient prestige to be subjects for serious poetry; but La Fontaine's birds and beasts belong to a literary tradition, they are not 'peints d'après nature'. In modern times, the best stories of wild animals, both in French and English, are in prose. In no modern literature, to our knowledge, is there any body of animal-poetry approaching that of Leconte de Lisle, either in bulk or in interest.

There are, however, in the work of Cowper and Scott, and especially of Burns, hints of the poetic inspiration which might be drawn from the lives of animals, wild or domestic. Such are the episode of the stag, and the death of Fitz-James's horse, in the opening part of *The Lady of the Lake*. Sir Walter had all the country gentleman's love of animals, and Landseer was well inspired in painting him with his deerhounds at his feet. But Burns had written a few poems entirely devoted to animals, and a number of anecdotes show that he was passionately fond of them. *The Death and Dying Words of poor Mailie* and *The Auld Farmer's last words to his auld Mare* could only have been written by a genuine animal-lover. The field-mouse, whose nest Burns one day unwittingly destroyed, inspired the most whimsical of the dialect-poems. On another occasion a hare, wounded by a clumsy and heedless sportsman, came limping past him. Burns, overcome with indignation, could hardly prevent himself from assaulting the man; and the elegy which he wrote on the hare is one of the most moving of his shorter pieces. But, in truth, the wild creatures and especially such birds as the lark, the thrush, the blackbird, the partridge and grouse, recur frequently in the *Songs and Ballads* and often give joy and animation to poems which are love-poems rather than poems of nature.

It is not unlikely that Leconte de Lisle found in Burns's work suggestions for a kind of animal-poem which, in his hands, was to become more objective and more artistic. 'Le seigneur rayé', 'Le roi du Senaar', 'La reine de Java', 'Le roi du Harz', even the shark, that 'sinistre rôdeur des steppes de la mer', are real animal-heroes whose lives are independent of man and who, though some of them come in touch with him, have a place in literature for their own sake and not because they may affect man's life in one way or another. On one occasion, perhaps under the influence of *The Origin of Species*, Leconte de Lisle imagines a kinship with them and expresses this fancy in *Les Hurleurs*. He even feels pity for the shark, whose cruel rapacity he places on a level with man's own:

> Console-toi: demain, tu mangeras des hommes,
> Demain, par l'homme aussi, tu seras dévoré.

Life is maintained by a system of murder, legitimate and infinitely depressing: it is one of the observations which confirm Leconte de Lisle in his pessimism. There is thus, in his animal-poems, more thought as well as more art than in Burns's.

They are almost a new kind of poetry, and although Leconte de Lisle may have found hints for it, not only in Burns, but in the Greek Anthology among the descriptive and sepulchral epigrams, many of which are devoted to the wild creatures, yet he must be reckoned the true creator and the only great practitioner of animal-poetry in the modern world. His influence in this respect has been very important: we believe that he inspired the late Charles G. D. Roberts as regards the spirit, and to some extent the manner, of his animal-stories, which are the best that have ever been written.[45]

All Leconte de Lisle's work bears the stamp of a great personality. He not only assimilated his models, but made the poems they suggested to him an expression of himself. He frequently surpassed the writers who inspired him: this is true of his Scandinavian poems and also, as a rule, of his 'rifacimenti' of Burns. The originals of *Nannie* and *La Chanson du Rouet* are remarkable lyrics; but Leconte de Lisle's rehandlings of them (and this applies to *Kléarista* as well as to all the *Chansons écossaises*) are finished works of art. There has always been a tendency to exaggerate Burns's merits, which are sufficiently remarkable in themselves.

He was a great natural genius, with a spontaneous and abundant flow of inspiration; but the content of his poems is often slight and the form is not perfect. He misses a place in the first rank. With Leconte de Lisle this is not so. Firmness of thought, depth of sensibility, consummate craftsmanship, all unite in his work as in that of the greatest poets; and that is why, in the nineteenth century, he ranks with men like Wordsworth, Arnold and Carducci. His rehandling of Burns shows, in a way which appears decisive, wherein lies the difference between good poetry and great poetry, and it illustrates his own well-founded opinion that in poetry the form should be impeccable.

NOTES

(1) *Leconte de Lisle and Sir Walter Scott*, in 'French Studies', vol. I, no. 4, 1947, pp. 334–42.

(2) 'Kléarista: idylle écossaise', in the *Revue de Littérature comparée*, Paris, janvier–mars, 1947, pp. 39–53.

(3) Le Colonel Staaf, *La Littérature française*, 1884, vol. IV, p. 815.

(4) We owe this suggestion, and the opportunity of consulting this charming little book in its first edition (Paris, J.-H. Barba, 1821), to Professor R. L. Graeme Ritchie.

(5) Op. cit. pp. 291–2.

(6) Ibid. pp. 293–4.

(7) See L. A. Bisson, *Amédée Pichot: a Romantic Prometheus*. Oxford, n.d. (1942), pp. 299–300, 306–7, 313–14.

(8) Paris, 1825, 3 vols. octavo.

(9) Paris, Gosselin, 1826.

(10) See L. A. Bisson, op. cit. p. 329.

(11) *Voyage*, vol. III, p. 242. Cited by Bisson, p. 299. We have drawn freely, in this part of the study, on Professor Bisson's excellent monograph.

(12) *Voyage*, vol. III, pp. 448–9. Cited by Bisson, pp. 313–14.

(13) Paris, Ferra jeune.

(14) Paris, Charpentier, 1843; Delahays, 1857. See A. Angellier, *Robert Burns: La Vie et les Œuvres*. Paris, 1893, t. II, p. 415.

(15) *Les Sources de Leconte de Lisle*. Montpellier, 1907, p. 217.

(16)
Ta coupe toujours pleine est trop près de nos lèvres;
C'est le calice amer du désir qu'il nous faut!
C'est le clairon fatal qui sonne dans nos fièvres:
Debout! Marchez, courez, volez, plus loin, plus haut!
Non! Ce n'était point toi, solitude infinie,
Dont j'écoutais jadis l'ineffable concert;
C'était lui qui fouettait de son âpre harmonie
L'enfant songeur couché sur le sable désert.

(17) *Les Sources de Leconte de Lisle*, pp. 217–24.
(18) *The Poetical Works of Robert Burns*. Oxford, 1911, p. 450.
(19) Ibid. pp. 378–9.   (20) Ibid. p. 517.
(21) Ibid. p. 547.   (22) Ibid. p. 553.
(23) Ibid. p. 548.   (24) Ibid. pp. 566–7.
(25) Our italics. Vianey, op. cit. p. 220.
(26) Burns, ed. cit. p. 444.
(27) *Yon wild mossy mountains.* Ed. cit. p. 459.
(28) *Poèmes antiques*, pp. 297–8.
(29) Burns, ed. cit. pp. 566–7.
(30) Burns, ed. cit. pp. 122–4. Cf. 'Nanny ne reviendra jamais'.
(31) Ed. cit. pp. 469–70.
(32) The reader will recall that most of the pieces in *Poèmes et Poésies* were subsequently redistributed between the definitive editions of *Poèmes antiques* and *Poèmes barbares*.
(33) E.g. *Anthologia Palatina*, Book VII, no. 657.
(34) Trans. W. R. Paton. *Anthologia Palatina*, Book VII, no. 726 (see Loeb edition, vol. II, pp. 384–7).
(35) Whether or not Leconte de Lisle knew this epigram, his disciple Heredia was certainly struck with it, as he used it as the starting-point of *La Fileuse*, one of the posthumous sonnets of 1905. See M. Ibrovac, *Les Sources des Trophées*. Paris, 1923, p. 51.
(36) 'Pour trouver son analogue', says Angellier at the end of his great study, 'il faut remonter, par delà les Latins, jusqu'aux Grecs . . . Les Grecs seuls ont aimé la Nature avec la simplicité, la naïveté que nous trouvons dans Burns . . .' And he concludes: 'On voit assez qu'il a ressuscité un état poétique disparu et qui est bien lointain de nos âges' (vol. II, pp. 391–2).
(37) Angellier (vol. II, p. 392) remarks that of the Greek writers who might be compared with Burns, one would not choose either Hesiod or Theocritus. The latter 'est un artiste achevé mais qui représente plus qu'il ne ressent'.
(38) Op. cit. II, p. 392.
(39) 'But thee, Theocritus, wha matches?'
(40) So my former colleague, Professor Murray, of the University of New Zealand, tells me.
(41) These are all early poems.
(42) *Les Sources de Leconte de Lisle*, p. 329.
(43) 21e Année, no. 1 (janvier–mars, 1947), pp. 39–53.
(44) Cf. art. cit. p. 49, note 1.
(45) Roberts was brought up in the backwoods of New Brunswick, where he obtained that knowledge of 'the kindred of the wild' which underlies most of his stories. Later, he wrote one or two historical romances relating to the French period in the history of the maritime provinces. He was a poet, and, in a sense, the creator of Canadian literature. But he was also professor of English and French at Toronto University, and he had thus become familiar with French literature at an early stage in his career.

PONTIGNY

BY

the late H. F. STEWART

Reader in French in the University of Cambridge

HALF-WAY to Dijon on the P.L.M. between Laroche and Saint Florentin lies the forest of Pontigny, ten miles down the slope. Emerging from it, you come out upon a wide, well-watered plain, with the great Abbey church of Pontigny standing, or in more appropriate terms, sitting in the midst, the village clustering at its gate. To the north rise vineyards and cornland in pleasant but rather unusual combination, and two extremely ancient farmsteads flank the valley this side and that, one with title-deeds older than the abbey, the other in the forest, recalling by its name, La Porcaire, the times when pigs were the main source of wealth and the term swineherd one of honour. The whole picture is a real bit of old France, and the hamlets are as full of history as their names, Heirie, Seignelay, Ligny-le-Chatel, are of music. The abbey church is a noble example of Cistercian architecture. Built in the early twelfth century, the second of St Bernard's reformation, it is a perfect realization of his ideals. He forbade, as we know, all ornamentation; 'works of art only turned men's minds from God'; was he thinking of the carved capitals of Vézelay?—'fantastic monsters, hateful abominations and unclean apes'. Pontigny is free of all such. French genius has come to aid ascetic piety and produced a masterpiece of simple dignity and elegance. Only in the quire is there any lessening of austerity; here the taste of the seventeenth century finds expression in the woodwork of the stalls, and of the eighteenth in the sumptuous high altar behind which is perched the shrine of S. Edme, our Edmund Rich, archbishop of Canterbury, who sought asylum in 1240 with the monks of Pontigny from the bullying of king and pope.

Rich was not the only English prelate in trouble to find harbour here. Stephen Langton and before him Becket were guests and have their names recorded beside the royal visitors Louis IX, Philip

218

Augustus, Louis XI, Henri IV in what the Revolution spared of the monastic buildings adjacent to the church. This consists of *cellier, grenier* and cock-loft, pillared and with walls so thick as to defy destruction. Thither in the course of the last century there crept back a handful of religious mission priests, 'les pères de Saint-Edme de Pontigny', who added dwelling-rooms and continued their modest and beneficent work till the separation of Church and State and the suppression of the Orders in 1905. Then the whole property (the church excluded), 'abbaye', garden and orchard, passed into the hands of one well worthy of it, professor Paul Desjardins, one of the most cultured men of his generation, who proceeded to make of Pontigny a home of light and learning. His purpose had best be told in his own words:

Occupé qu'il était de *l'Union pour la vérité* [of this in a moment] qu'il avait contribué à former, il eut, dès le premier moment, l'arrière-pensée d'essayer, dans ce cadre préparé au xiie siècle par et pour les cénobites cisterciens, un libre et tranquille groupement d'amis, un moderne *Cœnobium*. La persuasion insensible du lieu agit dans ce sens ... La grandeur et l'agencement de l'édifice invitaient à une vie collective, l'imposaient presque ... La simplicité de l'architecture romane et le silence indiquaient que, de plus, cette vie collective devait être repliée, intérieure. Ainsi s'est determinée l'idée des *Entretiens d'été*. Des *retraites* d'autrefois, les *Entretiens d'été* voudraient reproduire le bienfaisant effet de rupture périodique avec ce qui disperse, contrarie et use, de rappel de la pensée à elle-même. Mais la préoccupation du salut au sens théologique n'est pas celle qui inspire les *Entretiens*. Ceux-ci sont laïques en fait et d'inspiration. Ils veulent appliquer discrètement, librement la méthode cénobitique éprouvée efficace, à l'entretien, au raffermissement d'un esprit de pure raison. Si cet esprit, étant libre et ouvert, est irréductible au dogmatisme ancien, dont la prétention était de formuler définitivement l'absolu, d'imposer ses formules et d'en interdire la critique, il s'oppose plus fortement encore, étant un esprit, à cette radicale absence d'esprit que dénoncent, dans la société présente, des mœurs publiques et des mœurs privées sans règles, une concurrence âpre et une servitude dure dans l'ordre économique, enfin un général refus de servir.[1]

This quotation will show, I think, what Paul Desjardins might have been as a writer had he so chosen. But his genius led him another way.

The *Union pour la vérité* of which he speaks in the programme grew out of an *Union pour l'action morale* and was a society for the pursuit and propagation of liberty of thought and action. It held regular meetings in a fine seventeenth-century house in the rue Visconti (*rive gauche*), ran a journal under the title *Correspondance*, discussed topical questions, e.g. l'Affaire Dreyfus, and where possible passed from table to act. Desjardins, who was in fact its chief founder, watched its progress with a parent's care, and it left him little time for other activity; besides, how can a man write who reads as much as he did?

The result was that his literary output was small 'tho' all was gold'. I count it one of my personal achievements that I persuaded him to collaborate in a work, *French patriotism in the nineteenth century*, but that is another story.

My first contact with Paul Desjardins was in 1913 through the good offices of a son, Jacques, of Georges Raverat, one of the organizing committee, for Desjardins needed help in launching such an undertaking. There were ten of them and when I say they included Joseph Bédier, André Gide, Émile Verhaeren and Alfred Loisy, the character and intellectual quality of the *Entretiens* may be gathered. This committee made itself responsible for the subject of discussion and the speakers to introduce it, but Desjardins called the tune. The topic of our particular *décade* (there were three sessions of ten days in sequence each autumn—political, artistic, religious or philosophical) was *le Messianisme* or *la Grande Espérance* and it involved the notion of justice down the ages. Justice in Israel, and students of the Old Testament know how large a place it occupies in the psalms and prophets, was entrusted to the hands of Loisy, and I can see and hear him still as he sat in his fauteuil and held forth for two solid hours, with never a note, on the injustice of man and the justice of Jahweh, which sometimes manifested itself in so strange a form. 'Dès la plus haute antiquité Jahvé est juste, mais il a parfois une façon d'être juste bien inquiétante', and he quoted the 'breach upon Uzzah', struck dead for having handled too familiarly the sacred emblem he was driving! The modern world was called in to redress the balance or want of balance of the old, and a Polish professor with a name full of z's, and an Italian, Signor Bégey, disciples of Towianski, mystic and prophet of the early nineteenth century, described their hero's prowess, while Dr Ostrogorsky elaborated what one can only describe as a Russian theme with variations. It will be clear that the international atmosphere which will always be associated with the name of Pontigny already distinguished these early *Entretiens*, and indeed we stepped into it when the little regional railway discharged us, i.e. my wife, her sister and myself, at the station. There to welcome us was Desjardins with a mixed crowd, Italian, Russian, French, American, English, or a selection of them. I have already named some; but courtesy and the memory of friendships there and then begun and long continued call on me to mention Miss Maude Petre and Mr Lilley, later Archdeacon of Ludlow, Maurice Emmanuel of the Conservatoire, then busy writing accompaniments to his delicious Burgundy songs, and Louis Canet his friend and Loisy's lieutenant, of whom large mention is made in the latter's *Mémoires*, as of Desjardins himself.

The pre-1914 *Entretiens* were at once more and less ascetic, cœnobitic than those that followed the first world war. There was no smoking within doors; the *tisane* was served at 10 p.m. and then quiet descended on the company. No charades, no acting, no parlour games, nothing more frivolous after dinner than a reading aloud by our host (and how well he read!) of a poem, a fable of the *bonhomme*, a passage, familiar or unfamiliar, out of his wide repertoire, illustrative of some point that the afternoon's debate had brought out; Desjardins was modesty incarnate, but he could not help dominating. He had been in touch with all that was of interest in his country during a period of unexampled interest. The salon of his stepfather-in-law, Gaston Paris, was a house of call for the spiritual leaders of the day and Paul had greatly profited thereby. He was a fine classical scholar. Greek and Latin masterpieces lay on the tables of the Abbaye as naturally as novels and magazines do on those of a fashionable boudoir. He had taught in several of the most noted boys' schools in the capital. Marcel Proust was one of his pupils; the young ladies of the Collège de Sèvres were at his feet and a good number of them always attended the *Entretiens* and provided excellent and accurate reports as well as the devotion and admiration of grateful disciples.

We who had every cause to be pleased with this our first experience looked forward with eagerness to the great *Entretien* of 1914, which was to include a tour of visitation to all the other sister foundations of Cîteaux under the guidance of Desjardins; and no one who ever stood with him before the west front of Auxerre cathedral with its mutilated but lovely figurines, or on the terrace at Vézelay where St Bernard preached the second crusade to the warriors grouped around, or accompanied him to the little towns of the neighbourhood or to the nooks and corners of old Paris, but will understand and sympathize with our lively anticipation. But Mars shattered the plan and the Abbaye was turned into a military hospital, with Madame in a nurse's uniform.

When the sick and wounded departed from the great hall and peace returned, things were not quite the same. Events had left their mark on Paul, and Madame had learnt the value of tobacco as a prophylactic and disinfectant; henceforth the cigarette-holder was seldom out of her lips. There was a pause, necessary and natural after the great dislocation, and then the *Entretiens* began again; but they were not quite the same. When after convalescence from serious illness I was able to return to Pontigny, I found a change—a desire *desipere in loco* after the intellectual effort of the day which had been directed by a new chairman, Charles Du Bos, who with suavity and sweet reason managed to curb the discursive tendency of the participants, and so doing could not avoid a slightly magisterial tone. Paul Desjardins with admirable patience played the rôle—not of second fiddle, but of leader of the orchestra under a foreign conductor—but his heart was set on a long-term policy of international amity, especially with Nordic races, and his present policy for Pontigny more and more was to make it a haven of rest rather than an arena of debate. At least, that is how it struck me. When I last saw the Desjardins, on the way back from Grenoble in May 1939, Paul was evidently weary and nearing the end, 'un vieux bonhomme', as he described himself, and Madame at her wits' end to find accommodation for the rising flood of visitors in September. For one of the *décades* was to be a grand tournament between two teams of English and French, on the cultural and political relations between the two countries; the French selected by the Desjardins and the English by M. Denis Saurat of London

University. Once more, however, the god of war forbade the peaceful project.

Before closing this most inadequate account of the Abbaye as it appeared to an outsider to whom it meant and means a world, I must add a word on the part played by Mme Desjardins, whose economic and administrative genius (for it was no less) was responsible for the success of the autumn meetings. It was no light task to cater for the material comfort of a company that sometimes numbered half a hundred and more—and that in a region remote from the Halles and the hub of civilization—but Madame triumphed over difficulties of import and managed to entertain her hungry and exacting guests with Burgundian hospitality. Nor was it only in the domestic sphere that she made her influence felt. During a *décade* she would sit quietly in a corner, apparently absorbed in her knitting or needlework, and puffing an endless sequence of cigarettes, but following closely the discussion which she would recall to reality by a pertinent observation from the vague regions into which it was inclined to wander, and proving herself thereby not the mere *paysanne* of her husband's ironical description, but a person of high intelligence as well as practical sagacity, a perfect example of the marriage of mind and matter which is the mark of the woman of France. Paul happily did not live to see the collapse of his country, which would have broken his heart; for he passed into another world in April 1940; and Madame betook her to her Norman property before the Germans laid hands on the Abbaye. And this is the point at which I am glad to tell a little story that reflects a pleasing light upon the invader. A German officer, in uniform and clicking his heels, presented himself before Mme Heurgon, the Desjardins' daughter left in charge of the house, and demanded to see the master. On learning that he was no more, he expressed regret, for he understood him to be a friend of peace who had shown kindness to Germans. His own wife (or sister-in-law) had benefited by an *Entretien* in the past and he would have been glad to thank him. 'Now, Madame, is there any way in which I can serve you?' 'Yes, you can lend a car to help my mother make contact with my brother lying wounded in hospital.' This was done and the contact was duly made. But it was too late; Blaise Desjardins did not recover, and Anne Heurgon with her three children is now the sole *rejeton* of a family which did indeed labour for peace between the nations and to which Pontigny the ancient home of peace, whatever be its future,[2] owes a place in the annals of those who are called the children of God.

NOTES

(1) From the programme of the *Entretiens d'été de l'abbaye de Pontigny*, first year, 1910, August–September.

(2) I understand that house and church suffered hurt from the explosion of an ammunition train standing in the railway station—how great I do not know—and that the Pères de Saint-Edme have recovered possession of the property which passed from them forty years ago.

TWO FRENCH ATTEMPTS
TO INVADE ENGLAND DURING THE
HUNDRED YEARS' WAR

BY

G. TEMPLEMAN
Lecturer in History in the University of Birmingham

FROM November 1384 for two years, Charles VI of France, his uncles and his allies strove to launch an invasion of England. Their efforts, together with preparations made here to meet the expected attack, form one of the more curious episodes of the Hundred Years' War. As such the whole matter, particularly from the English standpoint, is worth rather more careful scrutiny than it has hitherto received.

After 1380 both sides drifted into the unenviable position of being unable to wage effective war or to make an enduring peace. Edward III's dotage, his grandson's minority, Gaunt's Castilian schemes and the social crisis of 1381 all helped to make the English more feeble and more intransigent. For the French, the death of Charles the Wise was a disaster. The youthful Charles VI was ill-fitted to carry forward his father's work of repairing the realm and chastizing the English. Like Richard II he also had to reckon with powerful and ambitious uncles. Both kingdoms were now caught in the toils of the Great Schism, and their differences were further acerbated by the remorseless feud between Rome and Avignon.[1]

The situation which provoked the invasion attempts of 1385 and 1386 began to take shape in the summer of 1383. Then the bishop of Norwich was mismanaging his so-called crusade in Flanders, and destroying the already slender military prospect of organizing a great league of Urbanists against France. While this was happening the Clementist cardinal, Walter Wardlaw, bishop of Glasgow, was busy at Orleans negotiating a new Franco-Scottish treaty. Agreement was reached in August 1383, when the Scots undertook to invade England on condition that Charles VI provided them with 1,000 French men-at-arms, equipment for a like number of Scottish knights and 40,000 gold florins.² The English government was thus confronted with an ugly situation, for its truce with the Scots expired in February 1384. The chancellor, De la Pole, spared no effort to convince his hearers of the peril when he addressed the parliament which met in November 1383, advocating a vigorous campaign across the Border.³ Meanwhile John of Gaunt set himself to undo the Franco-Scottish agreement and succeeded at least for the moment, because the Scots were excluded from the truce he made with the French at Lelinghen in January 1384.⁴ The pleni-potentiaries agreed to meet again in June for further talks, and in the meantime the English were free to move unhindered against their northern foes. In April Gaunt himself captained a leisurely and surprisingly well disciplined raid through Teviotdale and Lothian to Edinburgh. It failed to bring the Scots to battle, but persuaded them to adhere to the Truce of Lelinghen in July.⁵ Discussions between the English and French were somewhat tardily resumed at Boulogne in August, with the ostensible purpose of enlarging the truce into a more permanent settlement. These conversations dragged on through the autumn and hope of agree-ment steadily diminished. As claimant to Castile, Gaunt was resolute against a general peace which included that kingdom, and the French demand for Calais was a further stumbling-block. The dukes of Berry and Burgundy, who represented Charles VI, were importuned by Scottish envoys demanding to know why the French had not honoured their obligations, and when they proposed to do so. The sole achievement of this tortuous diplomacy was a further truce, made on 14 September and designed to last until 1 May 1385, although the knowledgeable both in France and Italy thought it was only the calm before the storm, and expected a renewal of the general war in the next summer.⁶

This view was shared in England, for on 20 October the king wrote to the English bishops bidding them use their influence to make known the peril which threatened the kingdom, and to stimulate the will to resist invasion among the people. Richard alleged that the French envoys, to whom he referred in most in-temperate language, had deliberately wrecked the negotiations at Boulogne. They had done this in order to frustrate the well-meant English plan for a general settlement, 'boasting that they would invade not only the king's territory overseas, but also his realm of England, do away [with] his place and people, destroy all the English tongue without regard to state, age, sex or person, and imbue the realm with a new tongue'.[7] This highly coloured account of the situation shows that the English government was now reckoning seriously with the prospect of a concerted attack by the French and Scots in the following summer. Active preparation for the assault began in November 1384.[8] The French plan provided for the Admiral, Jean de Vienne, to take an expeditionary corps to Scotland, and organize an invasion across the Border, while the Constable, Olivier de Clisson, landed another force in Kent.[9] It is uncertain whether Charles VI and his advisers hoped to conquer the country, or just to scare the English into accepting a general peace on French terms. Jean de Vienne was said to have vowed that he would harry the kingdom from Berwick to Dover,[10] but there was no one to boast, as Eustache Deschamps did in the following year, that this was to be the Norman Conquest all over again.[11] Richard II's horrific account of what the French proposed to do cannot be taken as a sober estimate of the enemy's purpose. It was a propagandist formula, later repeated, and apparently found useful in securing the financial co-operation of the clergy.[12]

The government here first began to bestir itself in January 1385. Then, apart from the Scottish venture, nothing more was anticipated than a French attack upon the Kentish coast, with the particular purpose of seizing Rye. Accordingly the veteran, Simon de Burley, once the king's tutor, and now constable of Dover and warden of the Cinque Ports, was instructed to acquaint the men of Rye with their peril, and, if necessary, compel them to put their town in proper order for defence.[13] With singular foresight large quantities of timber were fetched from woods at Brede in Sussex, belonging to the abbey of Fécamp, and a levy of threepence on every noble's worth of fish landed between Seaford and Reculver was authorized to forward the work of defence in Rye and the neighbouring coast towns.[14] Then on 24 January a peculiarly stringent commission of array was issued for Kent, designed to put the whole county on a war-footing.[15] All the able-bodied were to be armed, the unfit must contribute, those assigned to defend their own homes were to serve without wages, while others not so required were to be kept ready to move with all speed to the coast. Finally the recalcitrant were to be imprisoned, and beacons built in the accustomed places to give early warning of the enemy's advent.

These Kentish preparations are typical of the arrangements made in many other counties as the summer drew nearer. The chief burden of defence was to be shouldered locally. Townsmen must mend and man their walls at their own cost. Country folk, who could afford it, were expected to arm themselves and to contribute towards the equipment of their poorer neighbours, while, on the instructions of the king's officers, all the able-bodied of every degree must hurry to the defence of their district. Orders, exhortations, threats and cajoleries from London initiated and maintained these efforts at local self-help. As the peril loomed nearer, drastic powers to distrain, compel and imprison everyone, even aliens and ecclesiastics, were given to local officials. Yet the government provided very little direct assistance in men or money even for the regions most gravely threatened.[16] What help was forthcoming often took peculiar forms. The monastery at Abbotsbury on the Dorset coast was permitted to appropriate the church of Tolpuddle as a contribution towards its military expenses.[17] Canterbury received the dubious privilege of raising some of the money required for its defence by a tax on the enterprise of its citizens. Fines were to be levied on Canterbury folk who used the cheaper and better method of fulling their cloth at mills outside the walls in preference to employing fullers working by hand in the town. Not surprisingly the grant was revoked after a few months because 'of the great loss [it] would cause to many of the commonalty of the city and the parts adjacent'.[18]

In February 1385, fears that the enemy attack would fall on other districts besides Kent first show themselves. Remote Cornwall was put on the alert,[19] and by the end of April there was furious activity all along the coast from Great Yarmouth to Helston. Dilapidated castles were being hurriedly repaired, crumbling walls and choked ditches round the towns set in order, and special arrangements made for vulnerable districts.[20] Although Corfe Castle had been strengthened, the people of Studland and Swanage in the Isle of Purbeck were licensed to buy off the enemy, if no other alternative presented itself.[21] In Kent the inhabitants of Oxney and Thanet, together with those living within six miles of Dover, Rye and Sandwich, were to assemble in these towns by 3 May at the latest. Only the clergy were exempted.[22] Finally between 26 and 29 April, when last-minute negotiations at Calais to prolong the truce had failed, commissions of array went out for all counties save Derby, Nottingham, Cheshire, Lancashire, Westmorland, Cumberland, Northumberland and Durham.[23] A few days later the constables of ten great Welsh castles received strict orders to take up their duties in person within a fortnight.[24]

In May some of the ships collected in the ports of Brittany, Normandy and Picardy moved to Sluys and took Jean de Vienne's expedition on board. They then sailed for Scotland, arriving off Leith on 1 June.[25] On its way north the French fleet sailed close inshore near Orford in Suffolk. Alarm reverberated through the eastern counties, where an enemy descent upon the coast of East Anglia was generally expected.[26] At Lynn, Yarmouth and Norwich all men between sixteen and sixty stood to arms, in Suffolk the abbot of Bury with a great company was at his manor of Elmswell, a convenient point for speedy mobilization about 10 miles from the coast, and the earl of Pembroke and his fellows were threatened with the direst consequences should they slacken their efforts to make the array.[27] In Norfolk the constable of Castle Rising was shepherding folk from the neighbourhood into the fortress, and it seems that the sheriff of Lincolnshire, moved by excessive zeal, was preparing to lead his levies into Norfolk.[28]

Despite these alarms the government kept a wary eye on the south coast, where the Constable of France with his host was daily expected to appear. Chichester provides an example of the stringent last-minute measures thought necessary. To facilitate defence there, buildings within 100 feet of the walls were to be razed as were parts of the suburbs, should that be considered desirable.[29] On 20 June, when the danger still seemed great, all pleas in both Benches and in the Exchequer were adjourned until Michaelmas, and the sheriffs, with more urgent things to do, were instructed to take no action on any original or judicial writ for the next three months.[30]

So far as the English were concerned, the tension reached its height about midsummer, and then quickly relaxed. For this there were good reasons. It is true that Jean de Vienne and his Scottish accomplices were raiding and harrying in Northumberland as far south as Morpeth, but early in July events in Flanders removed the immediate danger of a French descent on the south coast. With a little English support, the men of Ghent under their Captain, Frans Akermann, made what proved to be their last gesture of defiance towards Philip the Bold, now master of Flanders in the right of his wife. They captured Damme, the port of Bruges, where, if the story in the *Chronicon Angliae* may be credited, they also took over a thousand casks of wine.³¹ This sea of liquor, it is said, was the cause of their undoing, but not before their occupation of the town had provoked Charles VI and his uncle of Burgundy to lead most of the forces collected at Sluys and elsewhere for the English invasion against them. Damme was re-taken within a day or two of Richard's crossing into Scotland, but the operations dragged on until December 1385, when Ghent made its final submission at the peace of Tournai.³² By this time the English had settled with the Scots, Jean de Vienne was back home discomfited and the invasion season was over.

Richard II had crossed the Tweed on 6 August, nearly a month after the muster had been ordered at Newcastle. He commanded about 16,000 men, the best equipped force which had yet invaded Scotland.³³ The size of the host—about a third of them Gaunt's men—and the lateness of the campaign both indicate that the government had waited until it was satisfied that the risk of invasion in the south had sensibly diminished.³⁴ Only routine precautions were taken like the appointment, made at Durham on 28 July, of seventeen principal captains, including six prominent ecclesiastics, with full power to enforce all necessary measures to protect the south while Richard was absent in Scotland.³⁵ It seems odd, had the king expected trouble, that he delayed issuing this commission until the eve of his departure into Scotland. If real apprehension had been entertained, the obvious time to make such arrangements was before Richard left London, nearly a month earlier. What is not less significant, after the beginning of July there were no more of those hurried orders to improvise defence measures here, and mobilize the people there.

The details of the Scottish campaign are well known and need no more than a passing mention here. As usual the Scots avoided battle, contenting themselves with a sharp diversionary raid into Cumberland, in the hope of deflecting the English army from its northward march. This manœuvre failed in its purpose, and the English moved forward, burning and slaying everywhere. Melrose Abbey went up in flames, and was quickly followed by Edinburgh, deserted by its defenders. Then Richard, despite Gaunt's advice, ordered a retreat on Berwick. This safely accomplished, the expedition was successfully concluded. The country between the Forth and the Border had been thoroughly ravaged, and Jean de Vienne was packing up at Dunbar in disgust to go home. The Admiral cherished the belief that he had come north to fight the English, but he soon discovered that this practice was not much in favour with his allies. He quickly acquired a lively distaste for them and their country, which he thought a second Prussia, and his cup was filled to overflowing when the English straggled to the Forth and back without hindrance. In September he sailed for France, and, with his going, any real prospect of Franco-Scottish military co-operation faded away.[36]

The Scottish campaign had scarcely ended, when news reached England of the Portuguese victory over the Castilians at Aljubarrota on 15 August. English archers, recruited by Portuguese agents earlier in the year, had taken a prominent part in the battle, and it now seemed that Gaunt might be able to launch his long-meditated campaign in Castile. The Parliament, which met at Westminster in October, contributed 20,000 marks towards the cost of what Mr Steele rightly calls the Duke's private expedition to Spain, and vigorous preparations were immediately begun.[37] Meanwhile, during the winter of 1385, the English government laid aside its fears of invasion, halted its defence measures and resumed the more congenial business of negotiation. In December that peripatetic diplomat, the King of Armenia, now self-appointed mediator between the French and English, arrived in London. Despite a rather chilly reception, he was able to arrange a meeting in February 1386 between representatives of both kingdoms in the now familiar surroundings of Lelinghen. Those who spoke for Charles VI came prepared to negotiate a general truce for five years, in which the Scots and the Castilians were to be included.[38] This suggestion caused Suffolk and the other English envoys con-

siderable embarrassment since they were deeply committed to
Gaunt's Castilian enterprise. Moreover on 23 March Charles VI
himself made it crystal clear that if this undertaking was persisted
in there would be no truce.[39] A little before this pronouncement
Richard II and his advisers seem to have recognized that they could
hope for nothing from the parleys. On 15 March commissions of
array were prepared for most of the English counties 'as he [sc. the
King] has information that his enemies of France and their allies,
gathering their power on every side, are purposing shortly to
invade the realm'.[40] Less than a fortnight later special measures
were taken to safeguard the Border.[41] From then until the end of
August a succession of precautions, closely modelled on those
enforced in the first half of 1385, were gradually brought into
operation.[42] There was good cause for such action, for this time
the French were preparing in earnest to repeat the Norman
Conquest.

Sir Charles Oman dismissed these French efforts as a 'sudden
freak of the young king'. Certainly the enterprise was grossly
mismanaged, particularly in its later stages, but the scale of the
preparations leaves little room for doubt that it was intended to
be a huge menace. This was the opinion of the Londoners when
they realized what was being laid up for them. They were, so
a contemporary says, 'timidi sicut lepores'.[43] In July, Crotoy,
Cayeux, Harfleur and Leure were piled high with stores and bulged
with ships ready to be concentrated at Sluys, whither troops from
all parts of France were beginning to make their way.[44] Then there
was that celebrated portable wooden enclosure. Made in sections
at a dockyard near Rouen it had palings 20 feet high, strengthened
at intervals of 60 feet by towers and turrets.[45] It was designed to be
erected on the English coast to serve as the invaders' base; a fact
which seems to confirm the English suspicion that the attack was
to be delivered somewhere in the low-lying region between the
Wash and the Thames estuary.[46] Seventy-two ships were required
to move the fortification from Rouen to Sluys. On the voyage a
few of them, together with the contractor, a renegade Englishman,
were captured off Calais by the Constable, William de Beauchamp.[47]
Evidence of this kind argues a considered plan and a serious purpose
on the part of the French. It seems likely that Charles VI and his

ministers aimed to seize the opportunity of Gaunt's departure for Spain. They had known for months that the expedition was projected, and they could hardly have remained ignorant of its departure on 8 July. Gaunt himself saw to that, for on its way out the fleet made a provocative demonstration off Brest.[48] From the last Scottish campaign they knew how formidable the Duke's military power was, and they probably calculated that, bereft of it, Richard's kingdom would be an easy prey.

In any case, from the beginning of September, when the concentration at Sluys began, the most serious alarm was felt in England. A large fleet was hastily collected in the Thames to be stationed off Dover, and the movement of all other shipping along the East Coast was stopped.[49] Chains were stretched across the entrance to the port of Great Yarmouth, behind which all vessels from the neighbouring harbours were massed, and round Yarmouth itself instructions were given for extensive demolitions.[50] The abbot of Bury was once more sent packing to his war-station with the threat 'that if he do not, and if any peril happen in those parts, the king will so deal with him that his punishment shall be for an example to others', while the arrayers in Suffolk were urged to their task under pain of forfeiting life and limb.[51] On the south coast there was feverish activity, and the extent of the crisis can be gauged by the fact that private interests were ruthlessly disregarded, and no exemptions from service were permitted.[52] At the same time attempts were made to keep down the price of arms in London and the provinces, for enterprising dealers were making their fortunes.[53]

Then, on 12 September, a step not thought necessary in the emergency of the previous year was taken. The arrayers in each county were instructed to despatch contingents of archers to London by Michaelmas. The Border counties and Cornwall were naturally not included, but neither were those along the coast from the Wash to Southampton Water. It was here that the attack was expected. The largest companies, in each case 1000, were required from the king's own palatinate of Chester and from his uncle Gaunt's duchy of Lancaster.[54] The immediate results of this order showed that Richard's government did not lag behind that of his adversary of France in a capacity for mismanagement. The troops began to arrive by the end of the month, although some did not start their journey until early in October. They were quartered in towns and villages to form a wide circle round the capital. None were supposed to approach within 20 miles of the city.[55] Unfortunately no one had remembered to arrange for the payment of the levies. On 2 October the king wrote to all the sheriffs ordering them to levy wages for the men in their own counties, and protesting that this had always been his intention.[56] The soldiery were apparently difficult to handle, and a week later there was a further change of policy. The Council decided to send home all those coming from counties within fifty miles of London.[57] A day or two later they were compelled to disband most of the others as well. The arrayers in Stafford, Derby and Devon were told that their men had come without wages, and, as the writ put it, 'for their ease and peace and for the peace of the country' the Council had sent them home again. There they were to remain in constant readiness, and if they were summoned afresh the sheriffs were to see that they came provided with three weeks' wages at the rate of 6d. a day.[58] The Leicester chronicler supplies some lurid details of the homeward march of those from North Wales, Cheshire and Lancashire; how they plundered the Warwickshire countryside, taking horses to ride on and pigs, sheep and poultry to eat.[59] At Sapcote, in Leicestershire, one of them stole a horse from a ploughman. The infuriated owner with a crowd of neighbours set upon the thief and beat him soundly. He escaped to return with some of his fellows, who bent their bows threatening to kill and burn unless they were given ten pounds, which was duly provided. While this was happening the so-called Wonderful Parliament was meeting at Westminster, and to add to his other difficulties Richard embroiled himself in an open quarrel with the magnate opposition, led by Gloucester, Warwick and the Arundels.[60]

The crisis came during October, for the invasion was expected about All Saints'-tide, when Charles VI arrived at Sluys after a leisurely journey from Paris, which he had quitted on 6 September. As it happened, the great armada never sailed. The reasons for this fiasco have still not been satisfactorily determined.[61] Those who were at Sluys, and who might have been presumed to know why the enterprise was suddenly abandoned, offer very conflicting testimony. Some thought the Duke of Berry was to blame, and a remarkable selection of the arguments against sailing, which he was supposed to have used, has been preserved for our instruction. Others thought Philip the Bold lost interest, that perhaps he had never intended the invasion at all, merely desiring a display of French might in Flanders to impress his truculent subjects in the County. Still others pointed to the apparently remarkable fact that the sea was cold and rough in winter as a sufficient explanation.[62] The Monk of St Albans had his own more appropriate though less accurate version of the matter. According to him the fleet sailed but was providentially dispersed by a violent storm just off Sluys.[63]

Charles VI began his journey homewards on 16 November and was back in Paris on 5 December, but the English government was still not quite sure that the danger had passed.[64] A commission of array for the defence of Scarborough 'against the threatened invasion of the French' was issued on 28 November.[65] A fortnight later, however, the Council thought it safe to remove all restrictions on the fishermen of Blakeney, Cley and Cromer.[66] Otherwise the business of demobilization seems to have been both spontaneous and unofficial. The last traces of all this excitement occur early in 1387. On 28 January there was a special commission of *oyer* and *terminer* for Wiltshire. Those named in it were instructed to deal with the constables and bailiffs, who had diligently converted to their own use money raised to pay archers from the county in the previous October.[67]

NOTES

(1) E. Perroy, *La Guerre de Cent Ans*, chaps. 4, 5; the same author's earlier work *L'Angleterre et le Grand Schisme d'Occident*, chaps. 1, 2; J. Calmette and E. Déprez, 'La France et l'Angleterre en conflit', vol. VII, part I, of *L'Histoire du Moyen Age*, in *L'Histoire générale'*, ed. G. Glotz, chaps. 1, 3, 4; A. Steel, *Richard II*, pp. 1–120.

(2) Rymer, *Foedera*, VII, 406–7.   (3) Rot. Parl. III, 149–50.

(4) In her paper 'The Lancastrian Faction and the Wonderful Parliament' (*Fourteenth Century Studies*, pp. 44–6) Miss M. V. Clarke argued that this move initiated a new English policy inspired by Gaunt. It involved separating Charles VI from his allies, who were then to be destroyed piecemeal; first the Scots then the Castilians. Afterwards the French would be compelled to negotiate on English terms. The evidence given below points clearly to the existence of some such plan. Gaunt's failure to foresee the French reaction to his departure for Castile in July 1386 seems to indicate that he was either more stupid or less disinterested than Miss Clarke will allow. Above, pp. 232–3.

(5) C. Oman, *The Political History of England*, 1377–1485, p. 92.

(6) Calmette and Déprez, op. cit. pp. 235–6. The Scots must have been painfully surprised by the naïve explanation of their exclusion from the January truce vouchsafed by the Dukes. It amounted to the statement that the English wanted them kept out.

(7) Rymer, *Foedera*, VII, 444–5.

(8) Calmette and Déprez, op. cit. p. 237.

(9) Terrier de Loray, *Jean de Vienne*, chap. IX; L. Mirot, 'Une tentative d'invasion en Angleterre pendant la guerre de Cent Ans' (*Revue des Études historiques*, 1915).

(10) Kirstall Chronicle in *Bulletin of John Rylands Library*, XV, 123.

(11) Eustache Deschamps, *Poésies complètes*, ed. A. le Queux de Saint Hilaire and G. Raynaud (Société des anciens textes), vol. VI, no. 1145.

(12) Cal. Close Rolls (1385–9), 86, 3 September 1385.

(13) Cal. Patent Rolls (1381–5), 519, 14 January 1385.

(14) Ibid. 588, 18 January; 525, 16 February; 532, 6 February.

(15) Ibid. 588.

(16) A grant such as that made to citizens of Canterbury was strikingly unusual. They were given £100 for two years from the issues of Kent towards the cost of fortification. Cal. Patent Rolls (1385–9), 103, 9 December 1385.

(17) Ibid. 47, 15 November 1385.

(18) Cal. Patent Rolls (1385–9), 62, 6 December 1385. The revocation is dated 5 April 1386. Ibid. p. 132.

(19) Ibid. (1381–5), 588, 28 February.

(20) Ibid. 543, 545, 555 (2), 546, 597.

(21) Ibid. 545, 554. The licence was for two years and meant that in so doing, as the writ put it, they would be 'without impeachment of the king'.

(22) Cal. Patent Rolls (1381–5), 553.

(23) Ibid. 589–90, 590–1. For the April negotiations see Calmette and Déprez, op. cit. p. 236.

(24) Cal. Close Rolls (1381–5), 549, 8 May. The castles were Harlech, Criccieth, Carnarvon, Beaumaris, Conway, Rhuddlan, Flint, Carmarthen, Dryslwyn and Dynevor. The two latter were both in Carmarthenshire.

(25) Oman, op. cit. p. 94.

(26) Cal. Close Rolls (1381–5), 551, 1 June.

(27) Cal. Patent Rolls (1381–5), 598; Cal. Close Rolls (1381–5), 542, 555–6. The Abbot's manor of Wirlingworth was nearer the coast, but the roads to and from it were bad.

(28) Cal. Patent Rolls (1381–5), 566, 599.

(29) Ibid. 567, 10 May. All religious houses near the south coast were to garrison their estates, and the bishop of Winchester, when arraying all men from 16 to 60 on the Isle of Wight, was told to make the clergy serve in defence of the district. Cal. Close Rolls (1381–5), 538–9, 551–2.

(30) Ibid. 556.

(31) *Chronicon Angliae*, edited E. M. Thompson (Rolls Series), 365.

(32) H. Pirenne, *Histoire de Belgique*, II, 214. Pirenne holds that Philip the Bold only intended the French preparations against England as a cloak to disguise his real purpose of assembling a large force to deal once and for all with his rebellious subjects in Ghent. If this was so, Richard II's spies must have

served their master with singular inefficiency, and many others besides Jean de Vienne were nicely deceived. Froissart gives 17 July as the date of the capture of Damme and for its recapture 27 August (*Chroniques*, edited Kervyn de Lettenhove, X, 354, 366).

(33) Oman, op. cit. p. 95.

(34) Sir Sidney Armitage-Smith, *John of Gaunt*, pp. 437–46. In view of the evidence given here it is difficult to accept Mr Steele's contention that 'the extreme risk was taken of continuing to ignore French menaces and staking everything on a campaign in force against the Scots' (*Richard II*, p. 105). The risk run was not from the French but from the weather, and from the danger of mobilizing so large a force at harvest-time.

(35) Cal. Patent Rolls (1385–9), 80.

(36) Armitage-Smith, op. cit. pp. 292–9; Oman, op. cit. pp. 95–6. The story of Jean de Vienne's discomfiture is related in lively fashion by Froissart in a much-quoted passage (*Chroniques*, ed. Kervyn de Lettenhove, X, 333–9).

(37) Steele, op. cit. p. 108.

(38) Calmette and Déprez, op. cit. pp. 238–40. When the King of Armenia applied for permission to return to England at the end of 1386 this was politely but firmly refused (E. Perroy, *Diplomatic Correspondence of Richard II*, Camden third series, XLVIII, 42–3).

(39) Calmette and Déprez, op. cit. p. 238.

(40) Cal. Close Rolls (1385–9), 60.

(41) Ibid. 153, 27 March.

(42) Cal. Patent Rolls (1385–9), 123, 134, 140, 177, 181, 190, 254–5, 258; Cal. Close Rolls (1385–9), 161. The order compelling the inhabitants of Thanet and Oxney with those living in the neighbourhood of Dover, Rye and Sandwich was imposed on 30 April, revoked on 14 May and re-imposed on 18 June (Cal. Patent Rolls (1385–9), 175, 180; Cal. Close Rolls (1385–9), 77). On 22 July Thomas Tredyngton, a versatile priest, 'an expert in guns and the management of artillery', was appointed to the New Tower at Southampton (Cal. Patent Rolls (1385–9), 196).

(43) Oman, op. cit. p. 100; *Chronicon Angliae*, 370.

(44) Calmette and Déprez, op. cit. pp. 240–3, contains an admirable account of these preparations.

(45) L. Puiseux, 'Étude sur une grande ville de bois construite en Normandie pour une expédition en Angleterre en 1386', *Mémoires Soc. Antiq. Normandie*, XXV.

(46) *Chronicon Angliae*, 371; Cal. Close Rolls (1385–9), 186–7, 20 September 1386. This writ states that the 'King has particular information [that the French] are preparing to land with a great navy in the port of Orwell, or in Suffolk or in other neighbouring parts'.

(47) *Chronicon Henrici Knighton*, ed. J. R. Lumby (Rolls Series), II, 212; *Chronicon Angliae*, 371; Walsingham, *Historia Anglicana*, ed. H. T. Riley (Rolls Series), II, 147.

(48) *Knighton*, II, pp. 209–10.

(49) Cal. Close Rolls (1385–9), 169, 175.

(50) Ibid. 175, 169; Cal. Patent Rolls (1385–9), 259.

(51) Cal. Close Rolls (1385–9), 174–5, 169.

(52) Cal. Patent Rolls (1385–9), 208, 212, 214, 259, 260.

G. TEMPLEMAN

(53) Cal. Patent Rolls (1385–9), 261.

(54) Ibid. 217. The details were as follows: Chester and the Duchy of Lancaster 1000 each, York and Lincoln 400 each, Oxford, Berkshire, Somerset, Gloucester, Stafford and North Wales 200 each, Wiltshire 160, Warwick, Leicester, Derby, Nottingham 150 each, Surrey, Middlesex, Hertford, Cambridge, Huntingdon, Dorset, Devon, Salop and Hereford 100 each, Bedford and Buckingham 60 each, Rutland 40. Originally only 400 were demanded from the duchy of Lancaster; on 26 September this number was raised to 1000 (ibid. 214). See also Cal. Close Rolls (1385–9), 187.

(55) *Knighton*, II, pp. 212–13.

(56) Cal. Close Rolls (1385–9), 187.

(57) Ibid. 194, 9 October.

(58) Ibid. 193–4, 11 October. Presumably similar writs, not enrolled, were sent to other counties as well.

(59) *Knighton*, II, pp. 213–14.

(60) Steele, op. cit. pp. 120–6.

(61) E. Perroy, *La Guerre de Cent Ans*, p. 162.

(62) Calmette and Déprez, op. cit. pp. 243–4.

(63) *Chronicon Angliae*, 373.

(64) E. Petit, 'Séjours de Charles VI' in *Bulletin du Comité des travaux historiques*, Section d'histoire et de philologie, 1893, pp. 433–4.

(65) Cal. Patent Rolls (1385–9), 263.

(66) Cal. Close Rolls (1385–9), 195.

(67) Cal. Patent Rolls (1385–9), 315, also 322.

ERNEST RENAN & ALFRED LOISY

BY

H. G. WOOD

*Formerly Professor of Theology in the
University of Birmingham*

IN the study of Christian origins, British and American scholars are more familiar with the German contribution than they are with the French. This is no doubt due in part to the strength of Protestantism in Germany and its weakness in France. The British scholar is apt to find French Catholics too conservative and French non-Catholics too radical. This overshadowing of the French contribution is unfortunate, since contact with the French mind is at once a refreshment and a discipline. The clarity which charms us in French writers is a challenge to confused thinking and slovenly expression. Two names, however, stand out as compelling attention. Renan is the only French savant whose work is discussed at any length in Schweitzer's *Quest of the historical Jesus*. His *Vie de Jésus* is there made the subject of a highly critical chapter. To-day the work of Renan is inevitably associated and compared with that of Loisy. One is tempted to say that Loisy picked up Renan's mantle, but if so, he wore it with a difference.

It is interesting to make a comparative study of two men in some ways so closely allied and in others so strikingly diverse. The comparison is facilitated by the published reminiscences of both of them. Renan's *Souvenirs d'Enfance*—the work which Sir Charles Dilke liked best of all Renan's writings—has now become a classic. Loisy's *Choses Passées* may never attract so large or so admiring a circle of readers. Though Loisy disclaims the description, it is a kind of apologia, an account and a justification of his judgments and actions up to and during the modernist controversy. As a source for the history of that controversy it has been superseded by Loisy's own massive collection of *Mémoires* in three volumes. As an apologia, it will not rank with Newman's autobiography, partly because for the modern mind there is no 'mystère de Loisy' comparable with the 'mystery' Henri Bremond found in Newman.

239

Nevertheless, *Choses Passées* is a finely-written book of absorbing interest. It is not unworthy of a place alongside Renan's *Souvenirs*. The two books enable us to appreciate Renan and Loisy as personalities and as writers.

Renan was born and brought up in Tréguier in Brittany. Writing of Brittany in 1846, Dean Church said: 'Brittany is a religious country, if ever the term could be applied to a country.' 'In these times of unbelief . . . it is a solemn and an awful sight to see a whole population visibly, and by habit, religious; believing in God, and instinctively showing their belief all day long, and in all possible circumstances.' To be born in Brittany in 1823 was to find oneself in a world where faith and life were closely interwoven and where the past overshadowed the present. The boy was cradled in legend and romance. The bells of the lost city of Is were ever sounding in his ears. Renan was not himself of peasant stock though he lived in a land dominated by peasant farmers. As Dean Church says, 'the peasantry represent Brittany as the middle classes represent England.' But through his father, Renan inherited the traditions of the Breton sailors and fisher-folk, while his mother belonged to the *petit bourgeois* trading class and conveyed to him some sympathy with a class little appreciated in Brittany. Readiness for adventure and respect for the past were thus blended in his social inheritance.

Les vrais hommes de progrès sont ceux qui ont pour point de départ un respect profond du passé. . . . Pour moi, je ne suis jamais plus ferme en ma foi libérale que quand je songe aux miracles de la foi antique, ni plus ardent au travail de l'avenir que quand je suis resté des heures à écouter sonner les cloches de la ville d'Is.[1]

In retrospect Renan may have idealized the faith and life of Breton peasants, and in consequence he discovered the more readily the Brittany of his youth in the Galilee of the first century of the Christian era. His *Vie de Jésus* owes much to his close acquaintance with Palestine—the fifth gospel as he called it—but perhaps it owes even more to his early environment. Renan's quick eye for traits of peasant life and thought in the story of Jesus was trained in Brittany.

Loisy came of peasant stock. His folk were farmers in a village called Ambrières in the neighbourhood of the Marne where it turns south from Saint-Dizier. He had no share in the poetry and romance of Celtic Brittany. The religious background was not so insistent. His ancestors, he tells us, were 'médiocrement dévots; ils respectaient beaucoup la religion, la pratiquaient peu et la laissaient pratiquer à leurs femmes'.[2] Loisy lived closer to the soil than Renan did. He was better acquainted with the hard realities of the farmer's lot. His imaginative powers were not stimulated as Renan's were, but he had a more shrewd, level-headed, critical judgment. Both were fortunate in being educated in communities where Christianity was taken seriously, as a wise and austere discipline. Both valued the moral training which they received in Catholic schools.

Renan and Loisy were alike in that both were inclined to the clerical profession and to the life of a scholar by delicate health and poor physique, though both proved to have reserves of strength and endurance. Neither of them was any good at games. The world of scholarship became the natural habitat of each of them, though Loisy never ceased to hanker after the farmer's life. When he finally retired, he took to keeping hens much as Diocletian took to growing cabbages.

One of the most attractive features of Renan's *Souvenirs d'Enfance* is the account he gives of his education both in school and seminary. 'M. Renan . . . is very just to his education, and to the men who gave it. He never speaks of them except with respect and gratitude.'[3] The imprint of his youthful training was never effaced. He claims to have retained from his education the virtues of frugality, modesty, politeness and chastity. The priests who first instructed him represented an old world which he loved. The otherworldliness of the principal and staff of the seminary of Saint-Sulpice at Issy was likewise for Renan a treasured memory. He recalls how a student, stirred by a political speech, read the newspaper report to the superior, M. Duclaux. 'Le vieux prêtre, à demi plongé dans le Nirvana, avait à peine écouté. A la fin, se réveillant et serrant la main du jeune homme: "On voit bien, mon ami," lui dit-il, "que ces hommes-là ne font pas oraison."' Writing in 1882, Renan comments, 'Le mot m'est dernièrement revenu à l'esprit, à propos de certains discours. Que de choses expliquées par ce fait que probablement M. Clemenceau ne fait pas oraison!'[4] If Renan thus writes of his educators with justice and kindliness, indeed with affection,

Loisy is more restrained and more critical, though still appreciative. The difference was no doubt partly temperamental, but it was due still more to the fact that Loisy became a priest and Renan did not. Renan's intention to enter the priesthood had the full approval of his mother, and he had some difficulty in explaining to her the reasons of his change of mind. But he was fortunate in that he discovered the incompatibility of the Catholic faith with the findings of historical and literary inquiry before he had taken the step of being ordained. Loisy, on the other hand, determined to become a priest against the wishes of his parents. His mother, he says, was very surprised and by no means pleased, and his father lost at least a night's sleep. Then he only discovered the weakness of scholastic theology and apologetic after he was already committed to the priesthood. Consequently, Loisy felt more acutely than Renan the defects and limitations of his early training.

In October 1845, the Roman Catholic Church lost Renan and gained Newman. It is often supposed that the defection of the one and the adhesion of the other were due to the former's knowledge and the latter's ignorance of German. This explanation is much too simple. Renan certainly abandoned Catholicism because German criticism seemed to him to undermine its foundations. But then he assumed that 'L'Église catholique s'oblige à soutenir que ses dogmes ont toujours existé tels qu'elle les enseigne, que Jésus a institué la confession, l'extrême-onction, le mariage: qu'il a enseigné ce qu'ont décidé plus tard les conciles de Nicée et de Trente. Rien de plus inadmissible.'[5] Newman could embrace Catholicism because his *Essay on the Development of Christian Doctrine* convinced him that he was not thereby committing himself to any such inadmissible contention. If the developments of doctrine at Nicaea and Trent can be shown to be legitimate and necessary, there is no need for the Catholic Church to maintain that they have existed or been taught from the beginning. Had the Essay appeared in time for Renan to read it, it might have shown him an alternative solution to his problem.

Loisy, who found himself in Renan's predicament, was reluctant to accept Renan's solution, and Newman's Essay encouraged him to seek another way out. The problem as he formulated it in 1882 was to find the true harmony of faith and science. Anyone who could do that would be his master. When von Hügel whom he came to know in 1893 introduced him to the writings of Newman, he thought he had found the master he needed. When he was sent to the convent at Neuilly, with ample time for reading, he devoured Newman's books. 'The spirit of Newman pleased me much more than that of the Protestant theologians. I studied, above all, the *Essay on the Development of Christian Doctrine*.'[6] It would be quite unjust to hold Newman responsible for any of Loisy's ultimate positions but the Essay suggested to Loisy the possibility of a new apologetic for Catholicism which would, he hoped, open the door for the recognition of the value of Biblical criticism in Catholic circles. He offered this new apologetic in his critique of Harnack's *Das Wesen des Christentums*, entitled *L'Évangile et L'Église*. He tried to show that what was truly essential in primitive Christianity had been preserved in Catholicism and that its transformations had been anything but a constant falling away from a primitive purity. His attempt was too daring and it subsequently became clear that he had moved too far from essentials for the Church to accept his new apologetic. It is interesting to speculate on the possibility that Renan might have won a hearing for some *eirenicon* between faith and criticism, if only he had visualized the possibility of it. Renan had more tact, more sympathy than Loisy. Some would say he had less conscience. Renan says that it was impossible for him to be harsh towards any one, *a priori*.[7] Loisy's was a more difficult nature—stiff as well as upright. 'Cet homme a l'esprit perpendiculaire', was M. d'Hulst's verdict, and Loisy records it with satisfaction as a compliment.[8] In the upshot, Renan had many critics but no enemies. He is now well on the way to at least a literary canonization. Loisy was convinced that many of his critics were his enemies and that some who were or should have been his friends had let him down. Sweetness and light characterize Renan's career and his reminiscences. Conflict, strain and disappointment find all too large a place in *Choses Passées*. Looking back at his life, Renan could say, 'Tout pesé, si j'avais à recommencer ma vie, avec le droit d'y faire des ratures, je n'y changerais rien.'[9] Loisy could not say that. He felt that his acceptance of orders had been a mistake and that much of his life had been spent in fruitless controversy. He may well have envied Renan the good fortune which enabled him to pursue his studies at the Collège de France—a good fortune which Loisy was to share only late in life and when he had secured his freedom at great cost.

Setting out to criticize Renan, Loisy found in him a master and guide. He was attracted to Renan as scholar and teacher. He attended Renan's courses in Hebrew, though he never conversed with him. But it was Renan's attitude to religion that appealed to him. Loisy writes of Renan:

> A aucun titre je ne prétendais être son successeur; mais il pouvait m'être un modèle utile à suivre en beaucoup de choses. Part faite au scepticisme souriant et à l'ironie bienveillante que Renan affectait peut-être par coquetterie intellectuelle, il estimait la religion, respectait le sentiment religieux, gardait une véritable reconnaissance à l'Église pour le bien moral qu'elle lui avait fait. Cette attitude-là n'était point d'une âme vulgaire, et elle se recommande à quiconque se trouve à l'égard de la religion et de l'Église dans une situation analogue à celle de Renan.[10]

Circumstances made it easier for Renan than for Loisy to maintain this attitude, but here Loisy was certainly Renan's loyal disciple.

Loisy saw clearly that experience of the things of religion is a great assistance for the historical understanding of religions. Renan encouraged him to recognize this by noting in his *Souvenirs* that 'Saint-Sulpice knows from the start what Christianity is: the Polytechnic School does not'. Renan was also justified in saying that 'in reality, few persons have the right not to believe in Christianity'.[11] He valued religion and respected the religious sentiment too sincerely and too intelligently to be duped by facile accounts of its origin and nature. Burckhardt, in his *Reflections on History*, says:

> Renan contests the *primus in orbe deos fecit timor* by pointing out that, if religion had been originally born of the calculation of fear, man would not be religious at his supreme moments: nor were religions invented by the poor in spirit and the weak, as the Italian sophists of the sixteenth century taught, otherwise the noblest natures would not be the most religious. On the contrary, he says, religion is a creation of the normal human being. That is true, yet there are plenty of religions of fear.[12]

The Italian sophists of the sixteenth century have their successors to-day, and Renan and Loisy still witness against them. But while

Renan and Loisy thus protest against superficial psychologies of religion, the view of the nature of religion in which they united, though deserving of respect, is still inadequate. 'Religion is a creation of the normal human being.' This is to treat religion as the outcome of human aspiration. 'As a philosopher, Renan held that what is most enduring in religion is the moral ideal which it sustains and that this ideal, ever perfectable, is immortal.' Loisy thinks this is a truth it would be well to hold fast. Indeed it is, but it still leaves out revelation and the supernatural. It is noteworthy that Loisy was puzzled by Bergson's *two* sources of religion and morality, and argued that they should be reduced to one. Both for Renan and Loisy religion was understood too exclusively in human—all-too-human—terms.

It remains to say a little of their characteristics as writers. Though Loisy was undoubtedly influenced by Renan's style, he did not deliberately imitate it. If Renan's irony is kindly and good-humoured, Loisy's is often biting. In controversy he wields a rapier, and one cannot but appreciate the skill with which he delivers his thrusts. Yet, as I have already suggested, he will not find a place comparable to Renan's in French literature. I have neither the space nor the knowledge that would enable me to trace here the development of Renan's style, but I may bring together a few references which throw light upon it. The ease and charm of Renan's writing were not achieved without effort and discipline. R. H. Hutton, after noting in Renan's *Souvenirs* a ring of calm self-complacency, similar to that of Gibbon's autobiography, continues:

Of course, there is nothing in M. Renan of Gibbon's old-fashioned pomp. Renan is, as he says, a man of his age, and the culture of his age ridicules the pomp of manner which the culture of Gibbon's age admired, though, by the way, there is a little of the same stiltedness in the records remaining from Renan's youth. The letter to his Director in which he avowed his doubts and his inability to return to Saint-Sulpice, has the air of a somewhat pompous young man.[13]

It is not surprising if both the elegance of the classicists and the exuberance of the romantics appealed to him in youth. The writer of the biographical article in the *Encyclopaedia Britannica* says that his marriage brought a naturalness into his style as well as much brightness into his life. But the pruning of any tendency to stiltedness really began much earlier than his marriage. Renan says that his earliest teachers were almost studiously unliterary. The desire to present one's thought in a pleasing light would have seemed to them a frivolity. 'En tout cas, si j'étais resté en Bretagne, je serais toujours demeuré étranger à cette vanité que le monde a aimée, encouragée, je veux dire à une certaine habileté dans l'art d'amener le cliquetis des mots et des idées. En Bretagne, j'aurais écrit comme Rollin.'[14] We may be thankful that he did not stay in Brittany. The contempt of his first instructors for literary style may well have caused a reaction towards something affected and mannered. But Saint-Sulpice had a more wholesome effect. It taught one great essential of true literature. The American schoolboy who began an essay with the sentence, 'It is very difficult to convey in words to other people ideas which you haven't got yourself', would have been greatly helped by residence at Saint-Sulpice. For Renan tells us that 'without intending it, Saint-Sulpice, where they despise literature, is then an excellent school of style: for the fundamental rule of style is to have in mind only the thought you want to inculcate, and in consequence to have a thought'. To think to some purpose is the groundwork of good writing. Renan, however, was not without literary guides and models. Sainte-Beuve had a great influence upon him, and he pays an interesting tribute to M. Augustin Thierry, whom he regards as a true spiritual father: 'Ses conseils me sont tous présents à l'esprit, et c'est à lui que je dois d'avoir évité dans ma manière d'écrire quelques défauts tout à fait choquants, que de moi-même je n'aurais peut-être pas découverts.'[15] The outcome of these and other influences is the style which will continue to win readers for the *Vie de Jésus*, though its critical assumptions are no longer tenable.

It is sometimes suggested that the excellence of Renan's style throws a cloak over the weaknesses of his scholarship. On this Loisy has said all that needs to be said.

Tout ne me plaît pas également dans la production littéraire de Renan, mais ses œuvres historiques sont plus solides que beaucoup de ceux qui font profession d'être ses admirateurs ne veulent bien le dire. Ne le blâmons pas trop d'avoir été merveilleux écrivain en même temps que savant. Il y aura toujours assez d'érudits qui écriront mal.[16]

There will indeed always be a sufficiency of learned men who will write badly. The world must not neglect two scholars who have written so extraordinarily well.

NOTES

(1) *Souvenirs*, p. 20.

(2) *Choses Passées*, p. 3.

(3) Church, *Occasional Papers*, II, 246.

(4) *Souvenirs*, p. 206.

(5) Cf. *Choses Passées*, p. 61.

(6) *Choses Passées*, p. 164.

(7) *Souvenirs*, p. 255.

(8) *Choses Passées*, p. 137.

(9) *Souvenirs*, p. 259.

(10) *Choses Passées*, p. 373.

(11) *Souvenirs*, p. 110.

(12) Op. cit. p. 43.

(13) *Contemporary Thought and Thinkers*, I, 227.

(14) *Souvenirs*, p. 117.

(15) *Souvenirs*, p. 264.

(16) *Choses Passées*, p. 373.

A PROBLEM OF INFLUENCES: TAINE
AND THE GONCOURT BROTHERS

BY

J. S. WOOD

Lecturer in French in the University of Birmingham

DURING the period 1860–70, the Goncourts wrote six novels which have been called 'realist'; if we accept that definition, we are naturally tempted to conclude that there are affinities between the Goncourts and other novelists who have been grouped under the same heading, and to say that the Goncourts followed in the path marked out by their predecessors. But such statements need the support of evidence; can the history of literary realism supply it?

We are immediately struck by the fact that the realist 'school' of French novelists, in the nineteenth century, is marked less by the measure of unanimity among those who were considered to be its adepts than by the hostility which they displayed towards it. The generation that reached maturity about 1825 does not appear, on the whole, to have resented the title of 'romantics'; if there were some discordant voices, notably Musset's, the group of young writers was more conscious of its fertility than of its disunity. The same is not true of the realists; the history of the realist movement indeed shows quite clearly that 'realism' was adopted by the critics, invested by them with an ideological sense possessed of wide implications, and applied to writers who were as intensely individualist as the romantics—if not more so. 'J'exècre ce qu'on est convenu d'appeler le réalisme, bien qu'on m'en fasse un des pontifes', exclaimed Flaubert; the Goncourts shuddered at the word—'le mot bête, le mot drapeau'. An attempt had been made, earlier in the century, to formulate a doctrine of literary realism, but it was a movement of self-defence; 'the word', in fact, created 'the thing'. To his evident embarrassment Champfleury, who, in the name of 'realism', undertook the defence of Courbet when the latter's picture, *Baigneuses* (1853), was attacked by the traditionalist painters, found himself acclaimed—and condemned—as the leader of the realist writers, thanks to an easy formula which *La Revue des Deux Mondes* and other right-thinking journals seized upon with alacrity: 'Champfleury fait du réalisme en littérature à peu près de la même façon que Courbet en fait en peinture.' The school, established despite itself, had to have a doctrine; Champfleury, and more particularly *Le Réalisme*, the review founded by Duranty in 1856, tried to give it one. They succeeded in doing so, if by 'success' one means that they erected into conscious principles their own limitations. They would not have written otherwise than they did, even if they had not deemed it necessary to adopt ideas consonant with the greatness thrust upon them.

But those ideas—namely, that art must embrace all classes of humanity, and not merely the aristocracy; that it must study the period contemporary with it, and not linger in the past; that it must reproduce reality as faithfully as possible, and in consequence select subjects and characters which are not creations of imagination or of fantasy but which have their origin in real life—were not new ones. Nor were they of sufficient vitality to produce a literary school. The remarks of Jean Pommier, in his review of the history of French poetry in the nineteenth century, apply even more closely to prose; even despite the great poets who were appearing around 1845—Leconte de Lisle, Baudelaire, Ménard, Banville—there is no distinct grouping: 'Cette génération s'est . . . elle aussi, manifestée à l'heure dite. Seulement, elle ne s'est pas mise d'accord sur un nom d'école qui la représente, elle ne s'est pas nommée. . . .'[1] Still less do the prose writers form a school. George Sand and Balzac represent an earlier generation; 1845, and the ten or more years that follow, produce, with the magnificent exception of Flaubert, no author of first rank, capable of giving new inspiration to the novel. The work of Eugène Sue, Champfleury, Murger, About, Feuillet, Feydeau is formidable in its volume, but not outstanding in its quality.

Between these writers there are many diversities; none of them, before Champfleury's campaign, wrote in conformity with any general theory of art; even Champfleury said that he was 'comme un chat qui se sauve traînant à sa queue la casserole du réalisme que des polissons y ont attachée'.[2] Nor did they bring a new technique to the novel. That had already been done by Stendhal and by

Balzac; the latter, indeed, was proclaimed by the majority of them as their master. The origins of the realist movement are in fact more sociological than ideological, and more a creation of the critics than of the writers who are grouped within it. 'Realism' entered the vocabulary of literary criticism soon after 1830—that is to say, when romanticism was on the decline; one of the first examples of its use can be found in *La Revue des Deux Mondes*.[3] It received widely varying interpretations and experienced many vicissitudes during the next twenty years; its supporters called it 'sincerity in art', and its detractors diagnosed it as the 'reproduction of the base and ugly', not to speak of the immoral; after about 1860, it was reinforced with a scientific armature.[4] But most of the earlier writers who received the name of realists were young men who had come from the lower-middle or working classes, and whom the greater freedom permitted to literature in the early days of the July Monarchy, the triumphs of romanticism, the ferment of new socialist ideas, the political and social changes that were slowly democratizing society, had encouraged to attempt careers which had previously been the preserve of the more favoured classes. They belonged to 'La Bohême', a social phenomenon peculiar to the post-1830 period; the early 'Bohémiens' were more romantic than the romantics themselves; but by about 1845 a new 'Bohême' had constituted itself, which was a real intellectual proletariat.[5] To that proletariat belonged Murger and Champfleury; it was inevitable that they should choose 'des sujets modernes et populaires', as Champfleury said in the preface to *Les Aventures de Mlle Mariette*, for they knew no other environment; it was not to be wondered at that they were critical of social conventions and of high society, that they proclaimed their scorn for lofty idealism and for sentimentality, and that they placed virtue only among the humble of this world—although they were unable to portray these humble folk without falling into a somewhat mawkish lyricism, and without turning them, on occasions, into eccentric and grotesque figures, in their effort to make them original.

The ideas developed in *Le Réalisme* are not therefore significant from the point of view of their novelty; their only significance to the student of French literature is that they formed the basis of most of the subsequent definitions produced by the critics, and that they were accepted as essential conditions of the novel by later and greater writers, chief among them the Goncourts.

But the Goncourts did not accept these ideas because they had been promulgated by *Le Réalisme*; by 1860 the group that had centred round Champfleury had dispersed; and before that date there is nothing to show that the two brothers had the slightest interest in realism, however it was defined. Few writers have left us a more complete record of their daily lives, and, what is more important, of their associations with their contemporaries, than the Goncourts, yet the *Journal* has little or nothing to say about the early realists; such scant references as it does contain are not enough to suggest that the Goncourts had any particular respect for Champfleury, Duranty, Feydeau and the others, nor even that they considered them worthy of contempt. We certainly cannot conclude that these men influenced the Goncourts in any way, for between them and the two brothers there was a wide gulf, partly social but also intellectual. Their whole outlook inclines the Goncourts away from their century rather than towards it: before 1860 they have two main interests, both of which seek their satisfaction in the past—one is the collection of curios and 'objets d'art', the prettier and more picturesque the better; the other is the study of the eighteenth century, which attracts them by its grace and elegance. They are hyper-sensitive beings, 'splénétiques, névropathes, écorchés, crucifiés physiques', quivering at the contact of brutal reality; their extreme sensibility is aggravated by their morbidly vain pride in their aristocratic origin; they rail against a coarse, stupid, bourgeois society, the product of the French Revolution from which all evils are sprung. Even the fortnightly reunions at Magny's leave them with a sense of isolation and dejection.

How different is the position after 1860! True, their natures have not changed overnight; they remain all their lives the slaves of their nerves and feelings. Yet the *Journal* reveals them on a determined, almost feverish search for material from which they can construct novels illustrating aspects of contemporary reality. *Charles Demailly* is published in 1860, *Sœur Philomène* in 1861, *Renée Mauperin* in 1864. *Germinie Lacerteux*, published in January 1865, is preceded by a defiant preface, which declares that it is the duty of the novelist to study all classes of society, particularly the lower classes. In the same year they declare that history no longer satisfies them, that the sole source of interest for them is henceforth in the study of their own time, and of that which exists and evolves— and suffers—around them: 'Maintenant, il n'y a plus dans notre vie qu'un grand intérêt: *l'émotion de l'étude sur le vrai.* Sans cela, l'ennui et le vide. Certes, nous avons galvanisé l'histoire, et galvanisé avec du vrai. . . . Eh bien, maintenant, le vrai qui est mort ne nous dit plus rien. Nous nous faisons l'effet d'un homme habitué à dessiner d'après la figure de cire, auquel serait tout à coup révélée l'académie vivante—ou plutôt la vie même avec ses entrailles toutes chaudes et sa tripe palpitante.'[6] All the intentions assigned to 'realism' are implicit in the novels that the two brothers published between 1860 and 1870; their *Journal,* particularly between 1860 and 1865, shows their increasing preoccupation with the relation between literature and society; the preface of *Germinie Lacerteux* is merely the open avowal of principles which they had already accepted in fact, and which, largely to avoid being cited by the government for immorality, they felt it necessary to defend.

This change of viewpoint on the part of the Goncourts is the more significant because it is a victory over their own temperament, a victory maintained for ten years by a ruthless discipline that was only finally broken by two events that shattered their little world: the death of Jules and the invasion of France. With all the intensity of their beings they hated the task which they carried through with such uncompromising thoroughness. Wherein is the explanation to be sought? What influences combined to bring it about? The source from which one would hope to obtain this information is disappointing; the *Journal,* which covers a period of over forty years, gives practically no direct evidence; only once do they acknowledge any debt to a contemporary, when they describe how they arrived at the dénouement of *Madame Gervaisais.*[7] But their approach to literature is so different after 1860 from what it was before, and so repugnant to their own natures, that reasons for the change must exist. Can this change be explained by factors exterior to themselves? There are no irrefutable proofs of this, but it is the conclusion to which one is led almost inevitably by certain considerations.

Against what background did they move during this period? They were in close association with Flaubert, Gautier and Maupassant, with whom they shared a bond of weariness and discouragement which would not in itself have predisposed them towards their own time; but it was in the salon of the Princesse Mathilde, and at the Magny dinners, that they met many of the philosophers and scientists whose names were already becoming famous. The Magny dinners in particular—their sole regular contact with contemporary thought—influenced them far more profoundly than their *Journal* admits. They appear to have taken little part in the wordy battles that were fought out at these reunions; they had little to contribute that was original; on the other hand, with their astonishing degree of impressionability,[8] they were incapable of resisting the domination of stronger personalities and the seduction of their theories and arguments. The long accounts of the dinners given in the *Journal* are a tacit admission of it—not indeed an open one, for like many over-sensitive beings they suffered from an inverted sense of superiority that refused to recognize any merit in the ideas of others, and took refuge in irony. But if there is no conscious adoption on their part of the ideas of their contemporaries, it is nevertheless certain, as P. Martino points out, that the literary movement to which the Goncourts have been attached willy-nilly does coincide with tendencies that were common to all forms of intellectual activity in the nineteenth century.[9] Like Martino, we must perforce set aside 'doubtful synchronisms', but the positivist spirit of the age, which sought to apply experimental, objective methods to the study of human and natural phenomena, and which proclaimed the supremacy of science in all the domains of thought, affected to a greater or less degree the majority of contemporary writers. Flaubert did not escape it; neither did Leconte de Lisle. How then could the more receptive and less positive minds of the Goncourts do so?

Again, did they undergo the influence of any particular individual? It is at least extremely probable. There is between the conceptions and methods of the Goncourts and those of many of their contemporaries a parallelism that cannot be readily ignored, and it is a particularly close one in the case of Taine, 'le vrai philosophe et théoricien du réalisme',[10] whose statements at the Magny dinners are reported with special care by the Goncourts, despite the lack of sympathy which they profess for his ideas.

The fundamental principle of Taine's philosophy is that man must be studied according to rigidly applied laws, which leads him naturally to assimilate human phenomena and scientific phenomena: 'Tous les sentiments, toutes les idées, tous les états de l'âme humaine sont des produits, ayant leurs causes et leurs lois, et ... tout l'avenir de l'histoire consiste dans la recherche de ces causes et de ces lois. L'assimilation des recherches historiques et psychologiques aux recherches physiologiques et chimiques, voilà mon objet et mon idée maîtresse. ...' It is the physiologists and the anatomists who can teach us the laws governing human activity; the task of the historian is essentially the same as that of the naturalist—the same theme, expressed in varying ways, returns continually in the writings of Taine.[11]

Certain passages of the *Journal* suggest that the Goncourts would not be offended if they were mistaken for scientists, and especially for doctors and surgeons. They style themselves 'à la fois des physiologistes et des poètes'; they reply to those who criticize their portrait of Sainte-Beuve: 'Nous avons été tout bonnement poussés par ce désir d'analyste de pousser à fond la psychologie d'une individualité très complexe, ainsi qu'un naturaliste, amoureux de la science, disséquerait et redisséquerait un animal...'; Edmond, at a later date, sees himself 'comme un chirurgien qu'on arracherait à d'aimables curiosités, obligé de reprendre la cruelle autopsie, la brutale prose', and he is not displeased at the term 'érotico-médical' that is applied to his books.[12] Such phrases reveal a somewhat naïve deference for science, not a contempt for it; they show that the comment of Lanson, who, speaking of the writers of the period, notes 'l'assimilation que leur imagination, complice de leur amour-propre, établit entre leur travail et le travail scientifique, fascinés qu'ils sont par les miracles et la popularité de la science',[13] is not without foundation. In the same way as Taine associates history and science, the Goncourts associate the novel and science: it is one of the themes of the pretentious preface of *Germinie Lacerteux*; it is the subject of a letter to Jules Claretie in 1865: 'Vous croyez, comme nous, à un grand mouvement du roman, marchant à l'exactitude des sciences humaines et à la vérité de l'histoire'; and they call their novels 'des romans de science humaine'.[14]

These novels, moreover, are so many examples of the application to literature of Taine's celebrated 'faculté maîtresse', for all the principal characters of the Goncourts are presented as types—Charles Demailly is *the* man of letters, Renée Mauperin *the* young bourgeoise of the Second Empire, Coriolis *the* artist rentier, Madame Gervaisais *the* educated middle-class woman of the reign of Louis-Philippe. Unfortunately, they are more than that: they are also illustrations of different pathological cases. The Goncourts are impressed, far too much so, by the ideas of Taine, as well as by the morbidly fascinating stories which they glean from their medical friends; they are attracted not only by psychological determinism, but also by disease and death. Not only the minds but also the bodies of their personages must be subordinated to forces that are inexorably at work upon them, and distortion results. Many of the characters of the Goncourts are admirable psychological studies—until the moment is reached when they must meet their destruction; they succumb rapidly; madness, heart disease, sexual depravity, alcoholism suddenly attack their victims, who cease to be human beings and become subjects for the pathologist. The very accuracy with which the stages leading to their downfall are described is an indication of the importance which the Goncourts attached to this aspect of their work.

Their preoccupation in this direction carries them beyond their intentions, for they insist that the primary task of the novelist is the psychological analysis of characters. Taine stresses the same point: 'L'art et la science sont deux ordres différents'; the artist and the writer must follow the methods and the disciplines of science, but their function is none the less that of the psychologist; what literature must portray is the psychology of the human being: 'avant tout . . . il s'agit de faire des âmes vivantes'; that is the essential aim, the intrigue and the décor are only means to that end.[15] The Goncourts likewise express a clear preference for psychological analysis in the novel, and endeavour to dispose their material so as to keep the attention fixed on the evolution of their characters.[16] They do not succeed, because in their attempt to solve an antinomy that is only apparent they weight the balance too heavily in one direction.

In many other respects the ideas of the Goncourts bear resemblances to those of Taine. The novelist, affirms Taine, must study the present, the 'modern', and not the past; the Goncourts are of the same opinion. Painting and sculpture are for them, as for Taine, essentially plastic arts, destined not to appeal to the mind, but to please the eye by their reproduction of form, light and colour; on both sides there is the same admiration for the same masters. But it is in the field of history that the resemblances are the most striking. For them, as for him, history is the resurrection of the past through the study of human beings. History for Taine is 'un vaste champ d'expériences psychologiques';[17] the historian must seek to establish the psychology of a given period: 'Tout historien perspicace et philosophe travaille à celle d'une époque, d'un peuple ou d'une race . . . il s'agit toujours de décrire l'âme humaine, ou les traits communs à un groupe d'âmes humaines; et, ce que les historiens font sur le passé, les grands romanciers et les dramaturges le font sur le présent.'[18]

The Goncourts had already expressed the same idea on several occasions: 'L'histoire est un roman qui a été; le roman est l'histoire qui aurait pu être.'[19] Like Taine, they demand that history should imbue with life the individuals and the societies of the past, just as the novel should depict contemporary man. It is through the study of individuals that they endeavour to recreate the age of Louis XV, through the study of society that they endeavour to recreate the period of the Revolution. 'L'histoire humaine, voilà l'histoire moderne; l'histoire sociale, voilà la dernière expression de cette histoire.' History must be 'la déposition de l'humanité'.[20] The conception of the 'faculté maîtresse' appears in their historical works, as in their novels; in *La Femme au Dix-huitième Siècle* their aim is to explain the three periods into which they divide the century in terms of a distinctive characteristic, dominant in each; and in this work, as in their histories of the Revolution and of the Directory, there are passages admirably documented, developed with a prodigious wealth of detail, that recall to one's mind the evocative power—if also the fundamental errors—of the *Origines de la France Contemporaine*.

*   *   *   *   *

Our examination of the reasons which led the Goncourts to enter the field of 'realism' divides therefore into two parts: the period before 1860, and the period after 1860. There is no likelihood that they were influenced by any literary doctrines before 1860, partly because they wrote no novels before that date except *En 18...*, which was published as early as 1851, and bears no resemblance to any of their later novels, partly because the early realists were not men of sufficient stature to command their attention, and partly, also, because it was not until they published *Charles Demailly* that we can begin to detect on their part any interest in the age in which they lived. But from about 1860 they came into much closer contact with their contemporaries; the latter—and chief among them Taine—exercised upon the Goncourts an influence that was not the less potent because they resented it, without however denying it. A number of tendencies common to both sides can be distinguished. It would doubtless be more satisfying if one could adopt a strict chronological method, designed to show that each statement of Taine was echoed shortly after by the Goncourts, but conclusive results would not be obtained in that way. It was, however, between the ten years from 1860 to 1870 that the majority of the ideas of the Goncourts quoted above took definite shape, and it was during that period that Taine wrote many of the letters published in his *Correspondance*, a number of his *Essais*, all his art criticism, and finally his greatest philosophical work: *De l'Intelligence*. When the unpublished documents still in the care of the Académie Goncourt are made accessible, they will throw further light upon the evolution of the Goncourts, and upon the problem of influences, of which we have merely touched the fringe.

NOTES

(1) *Conférences*, Droz, 1945, p. 11. He establishes a suggestive chronology: 1800, the date around which the majority of romantic poets were born; 1825, crystallization of romanticism. For the Parnassians, the same pattern: 1840; 1865. For the symbolists, the same: 1860; 1885. But to what does the rhythm 1820; 1845 correspond?
(2) J. Troubat, *Une Amitié à la d'Arthez*, Duc, 1900, pp. 87–8.
(3) 1 November 1834, in the sense of exact reproduction of reality.
(4) See A. Nettement, *Le Roman Contemporain*, Lecoffre, 1864; E. Maynial, *L'Époque Réaliste*, Œuvres Représentatives, 1931, pp. 7–11; R. Dumesnil,

J. S. WOOD

Le Réalisme, de Gigord, 1936, chap. III; and B. Weinberg, *French Realism: The Critical Reaction, 1830–1870*, New York, Modern Language Assoc. of America, 1937, *passim*.

(5) See P. Martino, *Le Roman Réaliste sous le Deuxième Empire*, Hachette, 1913, chap. I.

(6) *Journal*, Charpentier, 9 vols., 1887–95; vol. II, p. 273.

(7) *Journal*, III, 263.

(8) The most vivid and accurate character-study of the Goncourts is one made by themselves; see *Charles Demailly*, Flammarion, 1926, pp. 71 et seq.

(9) Op. cit. pp. 52–3.

(10) Ibid. p. 213.

(11) See *Correspondance*, Hachette, 4 vols., 1904; vol. II, pp. 305, 320. Also *Essais de Critique et d'Histoire*, Hachette, 1904, pp. xxiv et seq.; and *Origines de la France Contemporaine*, vol. I: *L'Ancien Régime*, Hachette, 1927, p. viii.

(12) *Journal*, III, 268, 257; V, 281; IX, 346.

(13) *Hommes et Livres*, Oudin, 1895, pp. 323–4.

(14) J. de Goncourt, *Lettres*, Charpentier, 1885, p. 222; *Journal*, V, 62.

(15) *De l'Idéal dans l'Art*, Baillière, 1867, pp. 76, 142–3. See also *Nouveaux Essais de Critique et d'Histoire*, Hachette, 1905, p. 228; *Derniers Essais de Critique et d'Histoire*, Hachette, 1903, p. 234; and *Correspondance*, II, 44.

(16) *Journal*, II, 112–13, 281; *Lettres*, p. 161.

(17) V. Giraud, *Essai sur Taine*, Hachette, 1901, p. 36.

(18) *De l'Intelligence*, Hachette, 2 vols., 1870; vol. I, pp. 8–9.

(19) *Journal*, I, 393; II, 229, etc.

(20) *Préfaces et Manifestes Littéraires*, Charpentier, 1888, pp. 202–6; *La Femme au Dix-huitième Siècle*, Charpentier, 1878, pp. x–xi.

LIST OF CONTRIBUTORS

The editors acknowledge the gift of a part of the sum of money subscribed by old students for a presentation to Professor Ritchie. The list of contributors follows:

E. Marjorie Alcock	1922	Florence Winifred Evans	
J. B. Anderson	1936	(*née* Sidaway)	1929
Joan F. Ashworth		H. B. Evans	1936
(*née* Warrington)	1938	Margaret G. J. Evans	1940
Dorothy M. Aspinall	1936	R. L. Evans	1931
F. Astley	1926	Renée Evans (*née* Mitchell)	1939
D. M. Auld	1928	S. C. Evans	1940
H. C. Ault	1927	W. T. Faulks	1929
Doreen M. Bailey	1945	Iris E. Favell	1942
Olive H. Baker	1937	Constance M. Foley	1925
Dorothy E. Barker	1938	Hilda L. Forster	1929
N. Rosalind Barker	1936	Yvonne M. Forster	1944
Vera S. Barker (*née* Farrington)	1942	Margaret Foulkes	1939
Kaye M. Barnes (*née* Scoltock)	1936	A. R. Foxall	1928
Constance M. Bedson	1941	Barbara M. Foxall (*née* Morgan)	1929
N. Freda Blakeston	1938	Elsa F. Freeman	1932
C. P. Boardman	1928	E. Gamble	1939
Agnes M. Boore	1922	Margaret E. Gayner	1942
Cicely M. Boote (*née* Russell)	1935	Christine Gooderson	1944
E. Dorothy Broadhurst	1921	D. Grayson	1939
K. G. Brooks	1929	C. C. Grew	1942
Marjorie Joyce Bunney		A. H. Griffin	1929
(*née* Monk)	1930	Estelle I. Hale (*née* Ballard)	1928
Marjorie A. Burmeister		Marguerita K. Hancox	1932
(*née* Briers)	1932	E. F. Harris	1922
Andrée Bushell (*née* Bailly)	—	Betty Hayes	1945
K. Chambers	1938	E. J. Hechinger	1939
C. S. Checkley	1940	R. W. Hickman	1932
Eileen M. Checkley (*née* Slater)	1941	Muriel Hildick	1921
Mary Cliffe	1925	G. H. Hind	1941
Patricia L. G. Codd	1945	G. J. Holdcroft	1922
Eileen Cole	1945	Emily H. Houlston (*née* Gough)	1924
Amy Coleman (*née* Gilbert)	1924	R. L. Howe	1939
B. Jean Daniel	1945	Joan Hubbard	1941
L. E. Ditchfield	1930	Iris L. Hunt	1941
G. Dudley	1925	Marjorie G. Jackson	1934
Pauline Dunn	1944	Dorothy Jessop	1942
T. L. Edwards	1931	Evelyn M. Jewkes (*née* Wilkins)	1939
Kathleen Elliott	1932	Evelyn Jones	1921
Constance M. Ellis	1936	Margaret E. Jones	1945
Florence V. Evans	1926	Sybil S. Jones	1930

A. J. King	1922	F. C. Roe	1915
Barbara Lloyd (*née* Collett)	1941	J. Betty D. Rogers (*née* Moore)	1940
Joan Lodge	1941	F. J. Rose	1931
C. G. Love	1935	Phyllis Ross	1927
J. D. McCann	1940	K. J. F. Rumming	1934
Margaret M. McShane	1938	Pamela May Rumming	
Phyllis M. Mann	1929	(*née* Woodward)	1934
E. Marsh	1932	Mary Scott (*née* Simkins)	1923
Isabel A. Mason (*née* Smith)	1932	F. B. Shaw	1922
Jessie A. Matthews	1928	Ruth Shaw (*née* Seed)	1943
J. May	1929	M. Joan Sheppard	1940
A. H. Mills	1937	Joan Shrives	1922
Muriel Mitchell (*née* Benton)	1923	K. Joyce Sibly (*née* Leonard)	1937
Beryl Mitton (*née* Beetlestone)	1936	Katharine Smailes	1933
M. Betty Morley	1944	Muriel Smallwood	1924
Dorothy M. Naylor		Constance M. Smith (*née* Miller)	1927
(*née* Chatburn)	1941	L. Pauline Snowdon	
Winifred Netté (*née* Grimshaw)	1931	(*née* Burden)	1936
Barbara M. Nicholls	1942	K. Spalding	1937
A. E. Joan Partridge		Rowena F. Stockwin	1935
(*née* Strangwood)	1938	Elsie M. Taylor	1925
Doris M. Peacock	1942	Marjorie Thomas (*née* Price)	1925
Elsie M. M. Perrins		N. S. Thompson	1936
(*née* Houlston)	1922	Phyllis Townsend	
Elfrieda T. Pichler	1943	(*née* Richards)	1925
Jessie Pickering (*née* Gray)	1938	Hilda Twiss	1941
Mary L. Pierce	1936	Sheila M. Wales	1945
L. E. Porter	1929	A. Lorna Walker	
Lilian Maud Powell		(*née* Chesworth)	1927
(*née* Cotterell)	1928	Gladys I. Wanklin	1926
Constance E. Pugh	1942	E. Marjorie Webb	1941
Monica Quaife (*née* Warriner)	1928	Doris E. Wegg	1934
A. Beatrice Raybould	1925	Eunice M. Wells	1928
Myra Rayman	1941	A. W. R. Wise	1934
Suzette Rickman	1935	Maureen E. Worthington	1945
Claire A. Roe (*née* Frebault)	1926	Isabel Yonge	1939

Also First and Third Year Students of the
Honour School of French, 1945–1946

For EU product safety concerns, contact us at Calle de José Abascal, 56–1°,
28003 Madrid, Spain or eugpsr@cambridge.org.

www.ingramcontent.com/pod-product-compliance
Ingram Content Group UK Ltd.
Pitfield, Milton Keynes, MK11 3LW, UK
UKHW010344140625
459647UK00010B/812